British
Defence Policy in the 1990s

A GUIDE TO THE DEFENCE DEBATE

Brassey's titles of related interest

COKER
A Nation in Retreat? Britain's Defence Commitment

WILKINSON & CHICHESTER
British Defence: A Blueprint for Reform

RUSI
RUSI Brassey's Defence Yearbook 1987

RANFT
Ironclad to Trident: 100 Years of Defence
Commentary BRASSEY'S 1886–1986

EDMONDS
The Defence Equation

RAMSBOTHAM
Choices: Nuclear and Non-nuclear Defence Options

British
Defence Policy in the 1990s

A GUIDE TO THE DEFENCE DEBATE

by

CHRISTOPHER COKER

BRASSEY'S DEFENCE PUBLISHERS
(a member of the Pergamon Group)

LONDON · OXFORD · WASHINGTON · NEW YORK
BEIJING · FRANKFURT · SÃO PAULO · SYDNEY · TOKYO · TORONTO

U.K. (Editorial)	Brassey's Defence Publishers, 24 Gray's Inn Road, London WC1X 8HR
(Orders)	Brassey's Defence Publishers, Headington Hill Hall, Oxford OX3 0BW, England
U.S.A. (Editorial)	Pergamon-Brassey's International Defense Publishers, 8000 Westpark Drive, Fourth Floor, McLean, Virginia 22102, U.S.A.
(Orders)	Pergamon Press, Maxwell House, Fairview Park, Elmsford, New York 10523, U.S.A.
PEOPLE'S REPUBLIC OF CHINA	Pergamon Press, Room 4037, Qianmen Hotel, Beijing, People's Republic of China
FEDERAL REPUBLIC OF GERMANY	Pergamon Press, Hammerweg 6, D-6242 Kronberg, Federal Republic of Germany
BRAZIL	Pergamon Editora, Rua Eça de Queiros, 346, CEP 04011, Paraiso, São Paulo, Brazil
AUSTRALIA	Pergamon-Brassey's Defence Publishers, P.O. Box 544, Potts Point, N.S.W. 2011, Australia
JAPAN	Pergamon Press, 8th Floor, Matsuoka Central Building, 1–7–1 Nishishinjuku, Shinjuku-ku, Tokyo 160, Japan
CANADA	Pergamon Press Canada, Suite No, 271, 253 College Street, Toronto, Ontario, Canada M5T 1R5

First edition 1987

British Library Cataloguing in Publication Data
Coker, Christopher
British defence policy in the 1990s:
a guide to the defence debate.
1. Great Britain—Military policy
I. Title
355'.0335'41   UA647
ISBN 0-08-035811-X

Printed in Great Britain by Richard Clay Ltd., Bungay, Suffolk

"What does it matter if you do not believe me?
The future will surely come.
Just a little while
And you will see for yourself."

(Cassandra, in Aeschylus Oresteia)

Acknowledgements

In this exercise in futurology I have been helped by a number of people, in the public and military services alike who would prefer not to be mentioned by name. It is because of this that it may be more necessary than usual to add that none of them are responsible for any errors of fact or lapses in judgement which the reader may discover for himself. Unfortunately, these are mine alone.

I owe, of course, a particular debt of gratitude to Tony Trythall and Jenny Shaw of Brassey's who provided me with the opportunity to write this book, who gave me every encouragement from start to finish, and who worked closely with me at every step. Such a relationship is untypical between an author and a publisher; without it this study would never have been written.

Contents

Foreword

RT HON SIR FRANK COOPER,
GCB, CMG, PC

One of the major difficulties of defence is the difficulty of bringing about change, in both a domestic and an international context. Many will, of course, argue that there is no need for change; they favour maintaining the "balance", cynically defined as the *status quo*. On the whole this seems to go against the lessons of history.

It is one of the paradoxes of the rapid growth of science, technology and engineering that changing the defence programme has become not only more difficult but excessively expensive. Vast sums of money are required to invest in a new and different weapons system. Whereas, say thirty years ago, it was expected that a weapons system would last no more than a decade, it is becoming increasingly obvious that from conception to obsolescence weapons systems are moving inevitably and inexorably towards the half century mark. It is almost unbelievable that less than forty years ago, Britain was able to afford the simultaneous development of three V-bombers, then one of the most advanced weapons systems of the day. Weapons have come increasingly to dominate policy because alternatives and changes cannot be afforded.

In the past few years more and more attention has been paid to seeking value for money when procuring equipment. In Britain there are a large number of programmes, costing hundreds of millions of pounds each. The cry is competition and efficiency. But there are massive industrial, economic and social problems if anyone tries to tackle these issues seriously. Furthermore, internationally in this area anti-Americanism quickly raises its head and for Europe closer collaboration tends to produce more industrial, social and economic problems than are politically soluble.

There is the continuing problem of research and development investment. It really is quite ridiculous that in Britain for every pound spent on Research and Development (R & D) only two to three pounds worth of equipment is bought. The only way of dealing with this is probably to set a new target ratio of R & D to Production to be achieved within a period of time. This is a brutal approach but it is in fact only resource pressures that force significant changes in defence policy other than there being a massive change in the world situation. Apart from France, the rest of Europe mostly does little in R

& D. The United States is increasingly protectionist. Which way do we look?

Policy in the broadest sense has also become more difficult to change. For Britain, there is the North Atlantic Treaty Organisation and the lasting constraints of the Brussels Treaty of the 1950s, with its commitment to a continuing major and specified presence on the "Mainland of Europe". Paradoxically, these legal arrangements were entered into at a time when we were still under the delusion that we were a rich country and the dominant power in Europe, possessing also the ability to exercise military authority on a near worldwide scale.

It is right that against this kind of backcloth the real problems of defence should be discussed. It is no use trying to be theoretical about them; there is a domestic and international reality which cannot be ignored. Will a British government be skilful enough to deal with the consequences in terms of relations with other countries, particularly the United States and our major European allies? Is the British population willing to admit that, in terms of industrialised countries, Britain is in the middle rank in terms of both economics and the military strength that can be afforded? Who has the political will?

Historically, Conservative governments have tried hard to maintain the "balanced approach". It is not part of their ethos to try and tackle the fundamental problems. It sets off powerful service and industrial lobbies. It rocks the boat. It upsets their supporters. Indeed, Conservatives have tended to become prisoners of over-enthusiastic support for defence, which they cannot fund. Historically, Labour governments have been ambivalent about defence; sustained in the post-World War II world by the experiences and attitudes of their older leaders. More recently they have not understood the domestic, international and practical difficulties of change.

For any Government, unilateral changes in defence policy and capabilities will react not only on defence but even more on economic, commercial and industrial relationships. This is true for Britain and the United States and for Britain and our European allies. The United States has eighteen Memoranda of Understanding: Europe has the European Community.

Britain is historically split-minded between the United States (the English-speaking world) and Europe. Britain has found this situation impossible to resolve. In consequence we have little that can be claimed now as being a genuine defence policy or defence strategy other than broad sounding statements, which can mean almost anything, or almost nothing.

There are real defence issues urgently needing discussion. It is not necessary to agree or disagree with the way Christopher Coker has exposed them. Everyone who cares and knows about defence should be grateful that they have been exposed. This book is about facing up to the real world – that is why it is so valuable.

Introduction

Specialisation tends to be the hallmark of academic research. Political scientists usually eliminate from their field of vision everything but their immediate area of expertise. In the field of strategic studies there are fewer neophyte writers than there are in many others. The reason for this is simple enough. We live in a dangerous age, even if we are not quite as pessimistic as Cassandra whose words begin this book. The Greeks lived in even unhappier times than ourselves. Their wisdom was summed up acerbically enough by Nietzsche in *The Birth of Tragedy; "The best is not to have been born at all; the next best is to die as quickly as possible."*

The strategists who have written about defence issues since 1945 have done so under the ever present threat of nuclear war, the ultimate catastrophe. In the early 1960s, when Britain's nuclear arsenal was one-fifth of that of the United States (not one-fiftieth as it is today), British writers tended to spend as much time writing about the Superpowers' defence policies as they did their own. Today we have become more inclined to consider our own future. Strategists even now, however, are acutely aware of their obligations, their membership of what Michael Howard has called that community of *"grey, inconspicuous ranks of specialist writers and officials who in all our countries gradually and incrementally are working towards minimising the danger facing mankind, even if they cannot eliminate it altogether"*.[1]*

In such a context specialisation is not very rewarding. We need to constantly bear in mind (even if we do not address them directly) problems of ideology, defence economics, arms control, questions which arise from the higher reaches of politics, because if we ignore them we reduce our own capacity to explain the past and probable future. For my own part, I have tackled each of these questions as the context within which British defence policy will be made in the 1990s. My views are based on a good deal of secondary reading, on the ideas of others, perhaps unconsciously assimilated over time. I can claim no "expertise" in any area except that of party interests and political beliefs.

My attitude to political parties, of course, has grown out of a system of

---

* Superscript figures refer to Notes at end of book.

values and beliefs that have, in turn, derived from my own prejudices, and passions. It is the duty of historians to execute their obligation to their readers by treating source material as honestly as possible. Although by the end of this book it will be clear where my own sympathies lie, I hope not to have misled those unsympathetic to my own opinions. I have tried to represent future outcomes as dispassionately as possible. The morality of history writing, according to one historian, "*is exclusively methodological*".[2] Fortunately, neither the political scientist nor the historian are required to divest themselves of values, only to admit to them, if possible comprehend them, and divorce them from the text.

One final word by way of disclaimer. Political scientists, by the nature of the work in which they are engaged, are always seeking to unlock the future, to bring us closer to the likely pattern of events by finding explanations, causes and effects of particular actions, usually with a prescriptive intent. This book is entirely about the future, where we go to from here rather than how we have reached the position we have. If the reader is interested in the past, and how it has shaped present party attitudes, perhaps I may refer him to an earlier work, *A Nation in Retreat*, to which this study is really a sequel. My first book was not intended to provide answers to the future, or predict the likely current of events, only to provide a record of our times, and hopes.

It offered no prescriptions. Nor does this. It is a futile exercise for academics to suggest what politicians should do; most who try have remarkably little understanding of political reality. This particular study merely offers the reader a suggestion of what lies ahead. It is impossible to predict whether some of the dead ends I have outlined will turn out to be new beginnings, whether the disasters and crises which lie ahead will prompt us to think again, whether desperate needs will create unforeseeable remedies. One of the reasons why I have no prescriptions to offer is that I believe there are no answers to the dilemmas of British defence policy, and that it is not the political scientist's job to provide them. Those dilemmas are so complex that they are most unlikely to yield to any simple or single solutions, a fact our politicians will soon enough discover for themselves.

1

The Acceptance World (1945–87): The Present Impasse

"What have we awaited these 40 years? Lack of time or experience?" (Elias Canetti, THE HUMAN PROVINCE, Andre Deutsch, 1985, p. 202

Past as Prologue

During the twenty-five years that followed the surrender of German forces at Luneberg Heath, Britain continued to play the role of a world power, tracing a path that had seemed questionable even at the turn of the century and which probably did reach an essential finality in the Suez debacle (1956). Even in the years that followed, however, most British politicians refused to recognise reality for what it was. Inevitably, historians have been prompted to ask whether it might have been better to have accepted the inevitable, to have reduced defence spending, to have accepted the necessity of choice. In fact, when we look at the period closely we will see that the option was not historically possible. In practice, events took their predetermined course from a script in which the places had been assigned in advance and the parts already written.

If we compare the post-1945 world with that of the early 1920s we will better appreciate why the United Kingdom acted as it did. In the 1920s Britain had rapidly demobilised. Expenditure on the Army was cut by half every year between 1919–23. By 1922 social spending equalled twenty-six per cent of all government expenditure. Where large numbers of troops were deployed they were deployed in Britain itself, forty-three infantry battalions to cope with the railway strike of 1919; fifty-six infantry battalions and six cavalry regiments to deal with the national coal strike two years later, almost the number of troops that the British believed were necessary to keep down India.

These trends threw up new opportunities in British politics, as well as new challenges. The regional basis of unemployment and unrest turned the Labour Party from a clique into the official opposition, and propelled it into government for the first time in 1924. The decision to enfranchise not just women but a third of all adult males who had not enjoyed the vote ten years earlier, created a political climate of great uncertainty. At the end of the war seventy-nine per cent of those entitled to vote had never voted before.

If the Conservative Party was to survive and remain the natural party of government it had to take those realities into account. Defence had to come second; the new voters had to be bought off with social programmes, not imperial promises, a choice which dictated a drastic rundown in defence forces. The results were all too apparent when the National Government decided to rearm in the 1930s. It almost left it too late.

Chamberlain found the Army in a lamentable state, most of its equipment of pre-1918 vintage, inadequate stockpiles of munitions, no heavy tanks at all, only a few lighter versions. The RAF's principal fighter was the Gloster-Gauntlet biplane; the country's major plane manufacturer, Westland, had only survived at all by making stainless steel beer barrels. Even the Navy, which was meant to be Britain's first line of defence, had fallen well below the tonnage in cruisers and destroyers allowed by the 1930 Naval Arms Limitation Treaty. When naval rearmament began, the Senior Service had to rely on the two most depressed industries of all: steel and shipbuilding.

Britain's exertions in the Second World War turned a third-rate military power into the third most important in the world. For those who had lived through the demoralising inter-war years, the metamorphosis seemed nothing less than spectacular. Reviewing the entry of British troops into Tunis in 1943, Harold Macmillan recorded in his memoirs: "*These men seemed on that day masters of the world and heirs of the future.*"[1]

Despite the traditional picture of a nation that had emerged from the war exhausted and dispirited, unwilling, or unable to shoulder the burden of world responsibilities, the British people were a very different people from 1919. The voters *had* voted before; and although they voted Churchill out, they expected Britain to remain a Great Power. They were not disappointed. Attlee expected and received national support for stricter coal rationing at home so that the Government could divert coal stocks to the British sector in Germany in the winter of 1946 and thus defeat the Soviet embargo. The British people who had only been required to pay for Imperial Defence in 1938 (with the modernisation of the Indian Army) accepted conscription in peacetime until 1962, as campaigns were fought from one part of the world to the next in the protracted process of imperial withdrawal.

They even accepted a larger rearmament programme, more extensive than Chamberlain's, in 1950, even though the Government had to fund it by abandoning the last stage of the National Health programme. Unlike the 1920s, social spending did not take priority. By 1951, Britain's defence budget (proportionate to its GDP) was larger than that of any other country. Attlee's rearmament programme raised defence expenditure from six per cent to ten per cent of GNP, or by two years' real growth. Opinion was not only unfavourable on the left. Even *The Times* deplored the "*starvation of industry*", the suspension of allowances on new plant and equipment previously promised, at a time when Germany and Japan were just embarking on their economic miracles.[2]

Twenty years earlier, *The Times* had also questioned whether Britain could rearm against Germany without threatening its own economic recovery. Writing in 1935, *The Economist* had suggested that public spending might be kept under control by disbanding the RAF.

In the 1950s any decision to have retrenched on a significant scale would have won little public support. The lessons of appeasement had brought home the need for high defence spending. Any decision to have cut defence substantially might have been psychologically traumatic. Adjusting to decline and the contraction of Britain's role had to be a gradual process if the British people were not to lose confidence in the political system, as the French lost confidence in the 4th Republic as the 1950s drew to a close.

Indeed, any decision to have reduced commitments prematurely, and adopted a little England stance would have been seen as an abdication of the country's international responsibilities. That those responsibilities were taken very seriously by the political élite and the public at large became clear from Britain's role in the Berlin airlift, the defence of South Korea and the formation of the Atlantic Alliance, in which Britain under Ernest Bevin took the leading role. The movement towards European unity was seen by comparison as parochial in content, and unpromising in scope. As Bevin complained in 1950, "*Europe is not enough; it is not big enough.*"[3] The British still saw themselves as one of the Big Three. Fittingly, the last British politician to play that part was Harold Macmillan, who twenty years exactly after his service in Tunis joined the Soviet Union and the United States in signing the Nuclear Test Ban Treaty, an achievement he always believed marked the acme of his political career.

Secondly, Britain did not face a challenge to its world position in the immediate post-war period at all comparable either to the threats it faced in 1919–22, or in the early 1930s with the rise of Japanese militarism. In the first period Muslim revolts in Egypt, which forced Britain to suspend its protectorate in 1924, the local uprising in Iraq in April 1920, the beginning of the Arab/Jewish massacres in Palestine in 1921, the onset of the non-co-operation campaign in India, which almost forced the British to concede responsible government in the provinces thirteen years before they were to do so in 1935, proved sufficiently debilitating to knock the Empire askew. When the Japanese threat to Britain's world position was first made manifest, the United Kingdom had fewer than seven battalions in China, only the promise of a base in Singapore, an inadequate naval presence in the Pacific, indeed a fleet which could only operate in war with the support of the United States Navy.

By comparison, Britain's position as a world power never came under threat after 1945, during the period of its imperial retreat. As late as 1966 the British still deployed a force of over 60,000 men in South-East Asia, a naval task force of eighty ships and part of its Vulcan nuclear bomber force in Hong Kong. As late as 1968 very large numbers of British soldiers were

serving in the Middle East, mostly in Aden. Until the mid-1960s the British
were not only able to discharge a world role; they expected they would
remain a world power well into the 1980s.[4]

Up to the very end, they maintained military superiority. Their only
defeat was more of a diplomatic reverse than a military setback. At Suez,
they lost not to Abdul Nasser but John Foster Dulles. If the Arabs began to
be armed with Soviet aircraft after 1955, it was not until the Aqaba crisis of
1967, when the Egyptians blockaded the Straits of Tiran, that Britain finally
concluded that it could no longer mount a military operation in the Middle
East without the support of the United States.

The only people to call Britain's bluff were the white Rhodesians who had
a better understanding of the limits of Britain's power, perhaps, more to the
point, the limits of its political will, than had the black African states of the
Commonwealth, who were staggered that Britain did not use force to end Ian
Smith's unilateral declaration of independence.

If the pressures from indigenous states were few, or easily contained, there
was no external threat at all to Britain's position. Of its two pre-war rivals
east of Suez, Japan had been defeated, the United States co-opted. After
1950, if not before, the United States, far from opposing Britain's presence,
actually sustained it. Throughout the period, America's capabilities, immense though they were, were clearly inadequate to match Britain's role. It
was not until 1973 that a United States carrier task force visited the Persian
Gulf for the first time since the Second World War; and not until 1976 that
the Americans established a base in Jufair (Bahrein) which had just been
vacated by the British. The greatest rift in Anglo-American relations after
Suez was brought about by Wilson's decision to withdraw from East of Suez,
a decision which threatened to leave a vacuum that the Americans felt
unable to fill.

As for the Soviet Union, it figured hardly at all in British thinking. It took
almost no role in any of the challenges which faced Britain in the Middle
East, and none in South-East Asia. The British "moment" in the Middle
East, as Elizabeth Monroe calls it, was brought to an end not by Moscow but
by Nasser and the Baa'thist party in Iraq. The two powers with whom
Britain almost went to war were not great powers at all, but Iraq (1961) and
Indonesia (1963-6). All this was very different from the strategic headaches
that the British had had to face before the Second World War.

So even if the British clung to a status which had lost any meaning, even if
British power was in decline, even if the pull-out represented what Lawrence
Martin has called "*a long recessional*", at least it was not a headlong retreat.
Indeed, because it was orderly, it did not provoke a hasty and ill-advised last
stand.

The third point of comparison between the 1950s and 1920s (and the one
which has endured to this day) was that, instead of being ignored, the
Services retained much of the influence they had secured in the war. In the

1920s they had had to contend with the Ten Year Rule (the belief that, for the foreseeable future, Britain faced no enemy or combination of powers which could possibly threaten its security). After 1947 the Service Chiefs were allowed to plan for a war which might break out at any moment. Deterrence rather than defence gave them a powerful voice, even if it was not always heard, much less heeded. The Services were allowed to dictate their optimal requirements, even if British industry couldn't always supply them with what they required.

The results, as it happened, were not very encouraging. Weapons costs escalated, lead times were extended beyond the time the weapons would have been of optimum use. Many fell far short of the Services' operational requirements – such as the de Havilland Vampire, Vickers Valiant, and Gloster Meteor.[5] Yet the Services could not accuse the governments of the post-war years of neglecting defence. Defence was not squeezed as it had been between the wars; far from it. Between 1952–65 twenty per cent of all Research and Development in aerospace was devoted to defence projects. Often, where the politicians cut programmes to save money, the Services got them reinstated: such as the new carrier programme (CVAOI), the re-introduction of the supersonic strike aircraft the TSR2, and a replacement for the interceptor Lightning which Duncan Sandys had intended to be the country's last manned fighter.

Many of these programmes were cancelled anyway, but if Britain's forces grew smaller, they also grew more formidable as well. By the end of the 1970s, thirty years after the war, Britain had its most effective peacetime force (if not the best equipped) in its entire history, although the country was poorer compared with its major trading competitors than at any time in the previous 200 years.

Future Conditional

Thirty years after the war, Britain was still committed to executing all but one of the roles it had chosen after 1945: to maintain an independent nuclear deterrent, to defend the United Kingdom, to maintain an army on the continent, and naval forces capable of providing convoy support and conducting anti-submarine warfare in the Eastern Atlantic. Only its vast East of Suez complex of bases and depots had been abandoned in 1968 (not without a rearguard struggle within the Cabinet by diehards, including the Prime Minister himself, who had fondly believed three years before that Britain's frontiers lay, not on the Rhine, but the Himalayas).

Clearly, the main crisis looming over the Services is that, for the first time in its postwar history, Britain is soon going to have to choose, as it did in the 1920s, between a military role and peacetime recovery, even between the roles themselves. As the White Paper on Defence admitted in 1981, the year of the last defence review, the seventh since the war, "*even the increased resources we plan to allocate cannot adequately fund all the force structures and all the plans for their improvement we now have". "Attempting too much and achieving too little"*, it added, Britain could not go on as it had.[6] As the Cabinet Office resolved the following year, one of the roles would have to go by 1986; one of the four priorities outlined in the 1975 defence review would have to be abandoned.[7]

Britain's failure to define its own role within the Alliance, to establish the terms of its role in postwar history, was perhaps to be expected of a country which has preferred to live from day to day rather than plan ahead. As George Urban recently remarked, forward planning probably runs against the grain of the British character, regrettably so since *"tactics do not make sense unless they serve a clear strategy"*.[8] The attempt by the First Lord of the Admiralty A. V. Alexander in the late 1940s to suggest that strategic priorities rather than the allocation of resources should determine defence policies, failed to impress his political masters.[9] Somewhat ironically, thirty years later, John Nott, who had attempted to cut the Navy more savagely than any one since Lord Geddes in 1922, echoed the same refrain: *"Strategy must come first and the programmes of the RN, RAF and Army must be tailored to fit that strategy, not vice versa."*[10]

It now seems clear that the next defence review (1988?) will reflect strategic planning for the first time in two generations. The present Government's attempts to hold the line as before, to avoid another review so close to the last, have failed disastrously. Michael Heseltine tried to eke out the resources he had by introducing cosmetic changes in defence procurement, including competitive tendering and fixed price contracts which, although useful, were not enough. Elsewhere, he tried to save money by cutting back projects, and spinning out others, measures which proved false economies, and in the long run increased unit costs. Under Heseltine, slippage became a rule of thumb – putting in orders today, paying the bills later, despite the knowledge that the Treasury would not come up with more funds.

His carefully staged-managed, not to say melodramatic, resignation over the Westland affair enabled him to leave with his reputation for integrity intact, although his tenure at the MOD had been marked by political dishonesty on an almost grandiloquent scale. In 1985, in an appearance before the House Defence Committee, he blandly asserted that rumours of forthcoming seven per cent cuts in the defence budget were not only untrue but would constitute an *"unthinkable denial of resources"*.[11] The very next year, his successor George Younger, revealed to the Committee that defence cuts of up to seven per cent could *not* be ruled out. As Hugo Young acerbically remarked, what Heseltine had done by deception, his successor had done by a feat of prestidigitation – by declining to admit that a budget of seventeen billion pounds, though large for a country of Britain's resources, was simply not large enough to maintain every role:

"*... in a budget of £17bn the candle ends are the most expensive known in the wax industry. These in the form of frigate orders deleted and refurbishments postponed are not to be derided.*"[12]

The 1986 Defence White Paper continued to deceive the public by claiming that there was no strategic case for drastic changes in Britain's defence roles, or even the need for a radical approach, given that each of the Forces' roles were "*more closely inter-related than at any time in our history*".[13] Like past defence papers, it had nothing particular to say and said it competently enough, with its emphasis on "*continuity, stability and consistency*" in defence spending.

Unfortunately, eight years since Mrs Thatcher's arrival in No. 10, the cosmetic exercises are beginning to lose their appeal, and now look far less compelling. It is, perhaps, telling that the first two defence ministers, Francis Pym and John Nott, should conclude, on the Conservative side, that present defence policy is bankrupt. It is perhaps significant too that there is, apparently, broad acceptance among all sections of the Party that change is necessary, that choices will have to be made, that it is not sufficient to abandon the old priorities only to recast them in a different form.

At the same time, there has been a signal change in the Labour's Party attitude towards defence, and, in particular, Britain's nuclear commitments. For years we have deluded ourselves that the defence debate was non-political when it was merely non-partisan. Thirty years on, the bipartisan approach which suited an age of certainty has faltered in an age of anxiety. If Attlee and Churchill, the architects of Britain's postwar defence policy, were to return to the political scene they would find many of its contours unfamiliar. The landscape is rapidly changing; its features, once so familar, are disappearing, possibly for good.

If the debate about "alternative defence policies" means anything, it is in the disavowal of the old conventions and historical realities which governed our lives. This is precisely the moment for the radicals in the Tory and Labour parties to come into their own, to assert the right, as well as the opportunity, for Britain to choose new defence options better suited to its economic circumstances, to proclaim the comforting message that Britain can create a world of its own making, a world which may be unreal for its allies, but real enough for the British themselves.

Service Dilemmas

The Royal Navy

"*There are two cries against the Admiralty which go on side by side: one says "we have not ships enough, no 'relief' ships, no Navy to tell the truth"; the other says "we have all the wrong ships, all the wrong guns and nothing but the wrong...*.*"* (Walter Bagehot, 1866)

The Royal Navy (RN), true to its name – the Silent Service – has done little to broadcast its claims, to cultivate a lobby in the country, or even a constituency in Fleet Street. As Admiral of the Fleet Lord Hill-Norton once remarked "*the idea of seapower has seldom been taken very seriously, even in a maritime nation such as Britain*".[14] At the height of British seapower, however, the admirals *were* able to rely on the Navy League, on panics about arms races, on jingoistic demands that battleships be built now, rather than promised tomorrow. As public support for a strong Navy has (perhaps inevitably) waned in an age in which control of the seas is seen to offer no protection against nuclear weapons, the Navy has been inclined to engage rather too much in the subtle play of politics to win the big points, and to pay too little attention to the public debate on which its future ultimately relies.

The Navy had a familiarity with politics from the very beginning of the postwar period, a gift for softening changes and disguising them, taking the sting out of the defence reviews when they came. In any other context, we might describe this facility as a genius for euphemism. After the construction of *HMS Vanguard* no one would pay for battleships, so the names were changed: cruisers were called *Daring* class destroyers; destroyers were called frigates.

Once it became clear that the government of the day would never agree to replace the 43,000 ton carrier *Ark Royal* with a class of similar shape or design, the Navy chose the designation "through deck cruisers" with great care in order to disguise its real intention to build smaller carriers on the sly. Once the funds had been voted, the title was switched again to "anti-submarine" carriers which accurately described their role. They owed their existence of course to the Navy's obsession with big ships. In the past, the main measure of naval power had been battleships and cruisers. Carriers like *Illustrious* and *Invincible* were all that was left to a former great power that was unable to match spending with its traditions.

As John Nott confirmed, when he addressed Parliament in 1981, had it ever known that the admirals were still wedded to the fading dream of once again patrolling the waters East of Suez, no government would have ordered them.

The Navy's ability to pull the wool over the politicians' eyes may have been impressive; as an answer to its own problems it was not particularly helpful. As a record of the times and the way politics were played in the MOD, it will probably only be of interest in the future to the policy makers themselves, those like John Nott who, once in office, came to have an instinctive distrust of Navy planners.

For what the admirals bought was time, not good ships. As the ASW carriers showed in the South Atlantic (1982), they were no replacements for the *HMS Eagle* or *HMS Ark Royal* which would both have been able to provide the Falklands Task Force with early warning, and much more impressive area defence, not to mention bombers which could have taken out Port Stanley airfield more effectively than Vulcans flown all the way from the United Kingdom. Perhaps, more to the point, carriers like *Hermes*, which could not operate Phantom fighters, could, and did, operate airborne early warning aircraft before they had their arrester wires removed, once their fixed wing aircraft were replaced with vertical take off Sea Harriers.

The same limitations were apparent with the Type 42 Destroyer, a destroyer by designation, a cruiser in all but name, since it was the major unit in the air defence of the carrier task force.[15] The Type 42 was too expensive to serve the needs of the Navy in the modern age, which is why so few were built. And those that were, were woefully underarmed in relation to their size, so that costs could be kept to a minimum. In the Falklands War two were lost, largely because they were unable to defend themselves against sustained air attack. Their highly expensive computer controlled defence systems often proved unreliable. Their 30-mm and 20-mm guns were little more than updated versions of Second World War weapons.

In short, the Navy's obsession with tradition, with maintaining carriers and cruisers under another name, did not serve it well in the first major engagement of the post-war period, where the Fleet relied as much as on the tactical ability of its commanders, and the outstanding seamanship of its men (not to mention a good deal of luck), to see the war through to a successful conclusion.

Its obsession with maintaining a maximum number of major surface vessels has also reduced the politicians' confidence in its judgement, and was a major factor in Nott's 1981 review. Stated very simply, the Navy has never been able to sustain the number of ships it has in port or at sea. Its pretensions and resources are ridiculously at variance.

In April 1980, two County Class missile destroyers the *Devonshire* and *Kent* had to be withdrawn from active service because the MOD could find neither the missiles nor the men for them. In recent years, they had never carried more than four missiles on board, even though they had a magazine capacity for many more. In the late 1960s when they were modernised, they remained in dry dock for four years, a refit which took so long that the Admiralty terminated the modernisation of another ship of the Devonshire class, and scrapped it in 1976, after only ten years of service (or half its active life).

It would be quite wrong, of course, to suggest that the fault was entirely the Navy's. The more we look at some of the failures of the past twenty-five years, the more one is struck by the fact that neither the Civil-Service nor British industry proved capable of providing the fleet the Navy wanted, and, for the most part, was promised (perhaps, too readily by the politicians). The reason why *Devonshire* and *Kent* were ridiculously unarmed was that they had been designed to carry the Seaslug I anti-aircraft missile. Shortly after they were completed the Ministry in its wisdom, decided to give them the Seaslug 2, a more up-to-date model which could also be used against surface units. Under the 1966 cuts, the plan had to be dropped, by which time the Seaslug I production line had been closed down.

British industry made its own contribution. The Navy has always searched for the greatest number of ships without asking itself whether supply can meet demand. In 1978 it had to shelve plans to build four new Broadsword class missile frigates because of already long delays in British shipyards, the result of all the familiar causes, shortages of skilled labour, the late delivery of steel, the failure of subcontractors to meet their delivery dates. Possibly, it would have been more sensible for all parties involved to have recognised in the 1950s that a navy can only be as strong as the society it serves. The admirals needed a broader view than that which they could see from their privileged and secluded vantage point, the narrow lancet through which they peered.

These problems were all uppermost in John Nott's mind when he embarked on his 1981 review. Its forerunner, Mason's review of 1975, had ordered a *"progressive reduction of one seventh of the planned numbers of destroyers, frigates, and MCM vessels"*, an increased number of nuclear powered submarines (SSNs) and a reduced number of conventional ones. Indeed, not content with these cuts, the Labour Government imposed an additional seventy per cent cut between 1975–7; for every £100 million saved in the 1975 review, there was an additional saving of £70 million as well.

Nott's review may have been sweeping, therefore, but it should hardly have caught the Navy off guard. Already, in 1980, in one year alone, the Government had taken out of service a helicopter cruiser, seven frigates and two inshore minesweepers. Although the Govrnment was able to cite an impressive list of ships under construction, including two aircraft carriers, six missile destroyers and four frigates, all but one of the frigates and two submarines had been ordered before the May 1979 election.

Nott's review, controversial though it was, with its announcement that the Navy's force of frigates and destroyers was to be reduced from fifty-nine to fifty by 1985, was therefore quite in keeping with all-party opinion since the mid-1970s, that the Navy was too large. Nott also perceived the Potemkin aspects of the Fleet since the late 1950s, such as large numbers and inadequate armaments, and dwelt more heavily than any of his predecessors on the failings he found himself once he arrived at the MOD. Despite his sweeping solution, its breadth did not show a disregard for detail. The detail which he had brought to his attention made his approach more radical than he would have wished by inclination, or political choice.

What did he find in 1981? Of the eight Amazon class frigates completed between 1974–8, only one was operational in 1979. Other units of the Fleet were suffering from crippling shortages of spare parts. In some cases equipment earmarked for ships undergoing long refits had been appropriated to keep ships at commission at sea. The shortages ranged from sonar buoys to electrical generators, which, when combined, added a twenty per cent increase to the time ships spent for refit. In many cases, captains, rather than risk further delays waiting for spare parts from civilian contractors, preferred to take their ships out to sea in the knowledge they were not fully functional.

The Government Nott served, of course, was not entirely without blame for this state of affairs. The previous year it had reduced fuel allocations for the Fleet by nearly forty per cent. When ships lie idle, morale inevitably tends to slump. After the comparatively modest fuel cuts of 1975, there was a sharp rise in the number of skilled men leaving the Service. Declining levels of seamanship were already a cause for concern in 1979 when the Conservatives came to power. Chief Petty Officers spent much of their time training ratings who should have been trained before they joined their ships. Sometimes as many as a third of the crew of any one vessel had never before been to sea.

The decline in standards was fully revealed several years later in the enquiry into the collision involving *HMS Southampton*, one of the Navy's guided missile destroyers. The accident, the report concluded, highlighted "*the current lack of bridge experience not only in the Southampton but in the rest of the surface fleet*",[16] a conclusion borne out by the fact that many frigates have only half the number of officers on the watch in the operations room (the nerve centre of a ship) that would be required in time of war.

Looked at in this light, Nott had only one question to ask in 1981: why deploy a force of fifty-nine frigates and destroyers which were spending three times as much time at sea as they had in the 1930s, indeed more time than they had in the Second World War, because so few were operational. If the Government did not intend to redress the deficiencies in equipment, fuel and training, if it was already strapped for cash, the situation was clearly untenable. In the first four months of 1981, some ships that were operational spent only one week at sea. Rather than gain the maximum support within the Navy by leaving as many doors open as possible, Nott chose to formulate a detailed policy of his own.

It was summed up very simply in the Defence Review *The Way Forward*: the Government intended to alter "*the balance of our investment between platforms and weapons . . . so as to maximise our real combat capability*".[17] In essence, this meant reducing the size of the Fleet substantially; for many in the Navy it constituted a "*major con-trick*" as Sir Henry Leach, the Chief of the Naval Staff described it; an initiative which involved "*a catalogue of half truths*".[18]

In fact, both men were right. Nott was right in appreciating the need to cut the Navy (if other commitments could not be cut instead – a matter which does not concern us at the moment); Leach was perfectly correct in arguing that unless the Navy received more resources, the Government would not even be able to maintain over fifty frigates and destroyers, as it claimed.

Unless the Government dramatically improved its rate of ordering, the Navy would face the prospect of operating an increasingly ageing fleet of destroyers and frigates, with rising maintenance costs and diminishing effectiveness. What did the fifty ship commitment amount to? A third of the ships Nott intended to retain were already old and would be obsolete by 1992. The desirable age of a ship is twenty-two years; the average age before it is decommissioned twenty-five. At the end of the 1980s a quarter of the Navy's newest frigates and destroyers would have passed twenty years in service.

Leach's strictures were not made any the less potent by the Falklands War, which appeared to reverse the 1981 review by allowing the Navy to retain its third ASW carrier, its complete Type 22 frigate programme and to reactivate some of the ships Nott intended to mothball or retire from service.

To maintain fifty frigates and destroyers would require orders for three ships to be placed annually for the next five years, that is three times the average level of orders since 1979. The other option, of getting the maximum life out of fewer hulls by extending the life of each ship to twenty-five years or longer, though mid-life refits, has already come under fire on grounds of cost. At eighty million pounds a time, it is impossible to imagine any government going for this option in the future.

From the rate of construction, it is clear that the Navy will fall short of fifty ships quite soon. If the replacements for ships lost in the Falklands are excluded, the average rate of ordering since 1979 has been under one a year. As the Commons Defence Committee argued in 1985, "... *a decision to invite tenders does not constitute an order; on the basis of the number of ships building and the age profile of the present destroyer/frigate fleet, further progress will have to be made* ... " (original emphasis).

For many members of the committee who were previously sympathetic to Nott's plans, and his reasons for going ahead with them, the Government's inability to implement them was a disappointment all the more acute in view of the optimism that the 1981 review had raised. In July Younger admitted for the first time the Government's target was "about fifty" frigates and destroyers, an enigmatic remark which concealed the fact that the figure was more likely to be forty-eight if the Type 22 programme is substantially delayed.[19]

The Royal Navy is not only threatened by the continued reduction in the size of its surface fleet. It also faces questions about its mission in wartime, some misgivings on the part of politicians of all parties which were most forcefully expressed perhaps in the Sandys Review of 1957, which stated blithely that "*the role of naval forces in a total war is somewhat uncertain*". Whether correct or not, it is an analysis which has enabled successive governments to advance the inevitability of an early nuclear escalation in Europe as ruling out the possibility of an extended war at sea. They have been reinforced in their scepticism by the other Services, most notably the

Army, which has often argued that it would take far too long for an anti-submarine campaign to take effect to allow the reinforcement of the Central Front. Ultimately, the war will be determined within the first few days.[20]

Nott planned for a short, sharp engagement in the Atlantic, as the only realistic option for a medium power, and the only reasonable scenario of a war in Europe. He was impatient of the debate within the Navy to decide whether convoys should rely on integrated air support which only a carrier group could provide, or whether they could be screened by frigates with helicopters on board, or cheaper ships with smaller hulls towing submarine detection sonar equipment.

He was the first to recognise that if the number of escorts fell from fifty-nine to fifty, even existing plans to escort convoys from west of Madeira to the Channel ports would be rendered questionable. Indeed, SACLANT was quick to raise the point at the time of his review, arguing that he would rather have obsolescent British ships than none at all, including the nineteen which the Government intended to sell or decommission.

The Government's answer was not to take the war to the enemy, nor to engage in the defence of sealanes which, SACLANT expects, will see over three thousand trans-Atlantic crossings in the first six months of a war. Indeed, Nott tended to question whether ships could be defended from modern range weapons, especially Soviet SSN-3 cruise missiles with ranges up to 300 kilometres and beyond, or Backfire bombers which some experts predicted could destroy forty ships a day (as opposed to the four at the height of the German U-boat campaign in 1943). His interest was in a more active ASW campaign at the outset of the war which would eliminate the threat in the Eastern Atlantic and deter the Soviet Union from reinforcing its forces by sending more SSNs through the Greenland-Iceland-United Kingdom (GIUK) Gap.

In this offensive, he questioned whether surface ships would have much of a role to play. He believed (not that he would have quoted Marx) that "*tradition weighs like a nightmare on the minds of the living*". He was convinced that the admirals had chosen to keep large numbers of surface ships at sea which might be pleasant to command but were not always the most effective systems for ASW missions. As he remarked just before his retirement from politics, the Navy had consistently declined to choose whether it wanted to meet the Soviet Union in the North Atlantic or to engage in convoy duty further south.[21] Clearly, he did not believe it could ever again afford both missions.

Like many Navy experts, he doubted whether surface units could operate 400 miles ahead of the main carrier battle group and bear the brunt of Soviet air attacks. He doubted whether the air defences which ships carried were sufficient without close air support. In the event of war, he suspected it would not be long before the Type 42 destroyers would be recalled to home waters where they would, at least, be protected by the RAF.

Nott's main interest was to carry the ASW war under water by relying on a large number of SSNs and providing them with better weapons. He clearly believed they would have a greater chance surviving in the hostile environment of the northern seas than carriers such as *Invincible* or even flat-topped warships. He would doubtless have opposed the decision taken after he had retired to reduce the phased number of nuclear powered submarines from twenty to seventeen.[22] Like Henry Stanhope, he believed that *"he who rules the waves in the North Atlantic could be he who rules beneath them"*.[23]

More recently the Navy has taken Nott's priorities a stage further, ironically it might seem, in an attempt to define a role unique to the United Kingdom and, by extension, the Navy itself. Drawing encouragement from the 1985 White Paper, which described the defence of the Northern Flank as being as important as the defence of central Europe, some naval authorities once again began to look very seriously at the "maritime strategy" outlined as early as 1981 by the United States Navy Secretary John Lehman.

In brief, the Americans have argued that NATO does not have enough ships available to protect convoys, or troop carriers as the Allies did in the Second World War. Given the likely rates of attrition in an extended anti-submarine campaign, it has become more important than ever to fight the battle of the Atlantic in the Norwegian sea, to recognise that sea control like sea denial is no longer defensive, but offensive in nature. As the Chief of Naval Operations of the United States Navy recently remarked, the prompt destruction of the opposing naval forces is by far the most economical and effective means of asserting control of the sea.[24]

Given the immense strength of the Soviet Northern Fleet, this may mean taking the offensive in the opening hours rather than days of a war by striking directly at the SSN bases in the Kola Peninsula, and the airbases as well. Forcing the enemy to defend his own airspace and sea-routes, his first line of defence, not his last, is certainly a plausible concept on paper. It requires of course *"going north of the GIUK Gap with sufficient power to defeat the threat"*.[25]

For a country anxious to return to the sea, to redefine its role in the world, it is clear enough why many Americans find the "maritime strategy" so compelling. What is not clear is whether a medium power like Britain, could deploy more than two carrier task forces north of the Gap; whether both task forces would not be faced with annihilation almost as soon as they had sailed beyond it.

So far, such patrols as there have been in northern waters appear to have been very few, and restricted mostly to the Barents Sea. In 1981 *HMS Glasgow* made a lengthy patrol in the area, followed by *HMS Liverpool* (another guided missile destroyer) in 1984. Because of the sensitivity of such exercises, few are made public. When the Minister of State for the Armed Forces was questioned earlier in the year about the presence of *HMS*

Splendid in the same theatre, he insisted on his right not to reveal information about the deployment of submarines.[26]

The problem is that the differences between the Royal Navy and the Northern Fleet have become more pronounced rather than less every year. If the Navy were ever to engage the Russians in an open conflict, it would find itself facing the most formidable opponent in its history, a fleet which has twice the number of submarines as the whole of NATO, and one and a half times the number of aircraft. Every five weeks a new SSN slides off the slipways. In addition to its Backfire bombers, each armed with anti-ship missiles, it has a substantial airfleet of 100 Badger and Blinder bombers, as well as several hundred other aircraft. In the face of such a force, it is not at all sure whether a carrier group could long survive in so restricted an "open sea" environment even if the agreed area of deployment was not the 750 miles of water between Greenland, Iceland and the UK, but the waters between the United Kingdom and Norway.[27]

A Labour Government would clearly never countenance such a strategy, given its preference for non-provocative defence. Without doubt it would be seen as provocative by the Soviet Union since most of its SSNs may be deployed to defend its nuclear missile fleet, not to break out of the Gap and disrupt the allied sealanes.[28] More to the point, given the extraordinary disadvantages under which the Royal Navy would have to labour, it might not be able to survive for long unless it was prepared to carry out a pre-emptive strike against the Backfire base at Olenogorsk, using sea-launched cruise missiles. Even then there would be questions whether the attack would succeed in removing the threat, or merely blunting it.

Against a cruise missile attack, a task force itself would probably be quite defenceless. As David Hobbs reminds us, technology is neutral; it favours neither the offence nor defence; the only thing that one can say for certain is that it makes war more complex, and therefore its outcome more unpredictable.[29]

Nor is there really much chance of persuading a Conservative Government of the merits of the strategy. In a nutshell, it would be far too expensive. There are two serious problems with the strategy as it stands which would have to be addressed:

The first is that forward defence would require much greater airpower at sea than NATO at present enjoys, or has enjoyed since the Royal Navy's ships were recalled to the North-east Atlantic in 1966, where the Government was persuaded the RAF could provide adequate air cover. Even if the Navy keeps its present three CVS, only the two that are in service at any one time have air groups allocated to them. Neither air group can in principle, therefore, be stood down for periodic breaks from duty. If the Fleet *is* to deploy way beyond the range of the RAF it will have to increase its Sea Harrier squadrons from five to eight, and possibly more.[30]

The problem could be solved if the United Kingdom went back to building larger carriers like the French, which can fly a whole range of conventional aircraft, from fighter-bombers like the Super Etendard to interceptors as well as rotary winged aircraft. Compared with the *Foch*, carriers like *Illustrious*, which worked closely with it in the Ocean Safari exercises of 1983, are strictly in the second league. Even with new fuel tanks to give them longer range, the Sea Harriers are still only capable of intercepting intruding aircraft at 150 mile range, compared with 1000 miles for the US Tomcats.

There are many advocates in Britain of larger carriers, including the former junior minister of the Navy Keith Speed, who resigned from the Government in 1981 in protest at the Nott cuts. Although he recognises the expense of constructing a vessel similar in size to the nuclear powered *Richlieu*, which is due to be operational by 1992, Speed makes no secret of his opinion that carriers of the *Invincible* class are quite inadequate to take Britain into the 21st century, or to engage in any future conflicts similar to that in the South Atlantic.[31]

All this may be true, but in practice the cost of three large carriers, each with their escorts and accompanying crews, could be as high as eight billion pounds. It is doubtful whether any British Government would be prepared to find the funds for such a force, even at the expense of Trident.

The second problem is that if the Navy is to engage the Soviet air force in direct combat by itself it will need a much more "layered" defence system than it has at the moment. It will need to upgrade the Sea Harrier FRS2, and develop a new generation STOVL aircraft configured for supersonic flight to enable more rapid interception. The next layer down is the Type 42 destroyer with its Sea Dart missile system. So far neither has been promised a successor. The research and development costs of developing such a layered defence are likely to dissuade any government from giving the matter much thought.

Ultimately, the Navy could only hope to convince the politicians that the expense would be justified by convincing them that an engagement in the Norwegian sea would to quote Conrad, *"revolutionise not the strategy and tactics of sea warfare, but the very conception of victory itself."* It is doubtful in the present climate that they would succeed, in part, one suspects, because it is not an opinion that everyone in the Navy is ever likely to hold.

The British Army of the Rhine

> *"Because NATO has been so successful as a deterrent, people are inclined to say that its forces are never required to fight; that they have no useful job to do and that there is not going to be a war* (Lord Carrington, 'Britain's Defence Policy', *RUSI Journal*, December 1970, p. 5)

It has been the constant complaint of some admirals (though not all) that but for the Rhine Army, many of the Navy's present problems would not have arisen. Stationing forces permanently on the Continent is not an idea that accords readily with British history or British traditions. Working with our European Allies, as opposed to our wartime partner the United States, seems more exceptional still. Why, asked the former Chief of the Defence Staff, Lord Lewin, not look after our own interests at sea when Europe "*cannot even get a satisfactory common agricultural policy, argues over the Community Budget and (cannot even get) . . . a common policy of foreign policy and defence . . . on the agenda*".[32] Here one hears, not for the first time, the authentic voice of nationalism with which for thirty years or more some military men have pleaded their grievances and their cause.

If they are attempting to escape from the modern world, on the face of it their qualms do have a specious attraction. The money saved from the closure of the Royal Dockyards, Sir Henry Leach reminded the Commons Defence Committee on two occasions in 1981, compared favourably with the £800 million lost in foreign exchange to pay for the 23,000 "non-effective" support services in Germany which kept the BAOR in being. The cutbacks in the recruitment of naval ratings in the past five years as part of the general reduction of 10,000 men ordered by the 1981 review (an order which was never cancelled despite a later decision to retain eight more frigates and destroyers) will inevitably mean that sailors will have to spend more time at sea, up to fourteen years of their career, which will impose intolerable strains on married life. Fortunately for the Army, the wives of soldiers serving in Germany are billeted in special married quarters with their husbands.

If the Navy sees itself as the principal victim of the commitment to the defence of Germany, that commitment is still absolute, as *The Way Forward* observed:

> "*Despite all the financial pressures on our defence effort, the Government has decided that the contribution represented by the large proportion of our land and air-forces we maintain permanently in the Federal Republic is so important to the Alliance's military posture and its political cohesion that it must be maintained.*"

The commitment is not one that the United Kingdom could renegotiate without the agreement of its Allies. Protocol 2 of the Brussels Treaty, as modified in 1954, laid down specific force strengths for the BAOR, which Article 6 defined as a minimum. At the time the figure included 77,000 men. Later it was revised down in two stages to 55,000 between 1957–9 in the wake of the Sandys Review, and the decision to abandon military conscription.

For the Rhine Army's critics, the present force levels are not the result of military logic, or even political calculation, but the consolidation, historically achieved over time, of a division of labour which has lost much of its meaning. The fact that the agreement is not open to review until the Brussels Treaty expires is itself a bone of contention. Britain agreed to station troops on the Continent at a time when it had a large conscript army, and was

Europe's largest economic power. Today it has one of the smallest armies in the Alliance and one of the lowest per capita GNPs.

The first challenge the Rhine Army faces, therefore, is one of cost. It is incredibly expensive to run. Over forty per cent of the budget is spent on maintaining it in being, despite the fact that the British provide less than ten per cent of NATO's front line strength. Local expenditure in Germany three years ago was nearly three times that of Polaris. Even in the peak years of the programme, Trident is not expected to exceed a quarter of what it costs the British taxpayer to maintain the Rhine Army at its current strength.

The Army is expensive to run because it is highly trained, perhaps the best trained force among any of the NATO armies, if not necessarily the best equipped. Its soldiers fire more tank shells in training than their German counterparts, even though they have far fewer tanks. In 1979, in an attempt to maintain a high state of readiness, the Army carried out no less than 282 exercises along possible invasion routes. Because it is so small, it cannot afford to be caught unprepared; because it trains so frequently, it is very expensive.

The immediate result of this is that the Rhine Army is prone to frequent cuts that are extremely debilitating. It has always had difficulty in keeping skilled men, a difficulty accentuated by the Government's decision to cut its allowances by up to sixty-five per cent in the hope of saving seventeen million pounds a year. Skilled manpower may begin to drain away as it has done in the past. Indeed, Michael Heseltine had to admit that the number of requests for premature voluntary retirement had risen to levels which had not been seen since the mid-1970s.[33]

In November 1986, a briefing document drawn up by the General Staff pointed out that the most recent round of cuts which the Government had demanded would inevitably *"result in a smaller, less well-equipped and less well-trained Army"*.[34] Not only are plans to produce a new Anglo-German battle tank (the MBT 2000) now threatened, it is also to lose the terminally guided anti-tank rocket it was promised. In addition, plans to acquire a battlefield electronic warfare system may be cut, if not dropped altogether. The Army now has to find savings of £150 million a year. Since no further reductions in manpower are possible, new weapons systems are likely to be sacrificed instead.

If the official view of the Army seems at times somewhat ambivalent, a product more of historical conditioning than rational calculation, others have a more exact vision of Britain's future in which the continental commitment hardly figures at all. If the costs are too high, there may well be a case for reducing the BAOR to a tactical reserve, a role which would fit in well with a growing insularity of temperament which is perhaps a sign of the age.

Such a proposal, opined *The Times* four years ago, would have two singular advantages: (1) it would dissolve the "tactical rigidities" imposed by forward defence (2) it would enable the United Kingdom to make substantial savings in the cost of its standing contribution to the Land Forces in Central Europe without effecting the day-to-day Order of Battle. If a smaller Rhine Army meant foregoing the British command of Army Group North, so be it. Since there would be no further need for a communications link between Headquarters BAOR and the Ist British Corps there would be additional saving in headquarter costs of ten million pounds per 1000 men.[35]

The Army has always been wary of such opinions which tend to appeal to the blue water school of politicians in particular. There is every reason to suspect, however, that they will come to the forefront of the public debate about defence as a decision will have to be taken quite soon whether Britain can ever afford to re-equip the Rhine Army on the scale of the early 1980s (which may well be seen in retrospect as its happiest decade).

In the 1960s the BAOR was the best trained but worst equipped force on the continent. Years of neglect inevitably left their mark on its sense of purpose, if not its morale (which, all things considered, remained remarkably high). Its only effective air defence system was Rapier, which could not be easily transported from one combat area to the next and which offered no effective protection to its missile crews. When Britain tried to sell the system in the Middle East, it was only bought on the understanding that it would be augmented with American-built armoured tracked carriers, a luxury British soldiers had to do without.

The Army's M72 66mm anti-tank rocket was hopelessly out of date, and frequently failed to detonate on impact. The Milan system did not reach the Rhine Army until the mid-1980s as a long overdue replacement for the ageing and largely ineffective Wombat recoilless gun, a fact which left British troops without a credible anti-tank capability of up to seven years.

Its armoured personnel carrier the FV432 had been designed in the 1960s, and required ever increasing maintenance. At least one in five battalions that should have been mechanised had to travel in unprotected trucks. The Army's tanks were no better. The Chieftain's engines were so unreliable that during one exercise in 1978 the Army congratulated itself that it had suffered only a 7/12 failure rate. Its soldiers laboured under even greater constraints with regard to transport. By the mid-1970s some British Army drivers were younger than the trucks they had to drive, many of which were of Second World War vintage. The new trucks which were introduced, instead of keeping up with the mechanised forces across country, were unable to move off the roads; others which could cross the countryside were unable to keep up with the tanks they were meant to supply.

Most of these deficiencies have now been redressed. Although delays in the introduction of the SP 70 155-mm howitzer have left many battalions still reliant on their Abbot self-propelled guns, guns which bear witness to the parlous state in which the BAOR fell ten years ago, other developments illustrate how much progress has actually been made. The Rhine Army now has a Tracked Rapier system (four batteries in each of its two regiments) which should not only help to destroy enemy aircraft but also dissuade the opposition from pushing home its attacks.

The new Challenger tanks have several advantages over the Chieftain; much improved armour and greater manoeuvrability, thanks to a much more powerful engine and improved suspension. Unlike its predecessor, Challenger's breakdown rate is quite favourable. During the Lionheart exercise (1984) the first tank to suffer engine failure was retired only on the tenth day. In addition to five Challenger regiments, the seven which will still deploy Chieftains have had their tanks upgraded, gaining in the process the same thermal image sight as Challenger, an improved fire control system and an up-to-date engine. Standing back from the many improvements that have been made in recent years, and contemplating the deficiencies that existed in the past, it is tempting to assume the Rhine Army has an assured future. The new technology has certainly helped the transition to a new era of high technology warfare in which defence is likely to have a significant advantage. The new weapons acquisitions have included television surveillance linked to a computerised system of communications which will make it easier to identify breakthrough points and seal them off as soon as possible. RAF support from its new Tornado squadrons, carrying terminally guided munitions, will provide much closer air-to-ground support than the Rhine Army has been able to count upon hitherto. New long-range artillery, when linked to Phoenix remotely controlled reconnaissance vehicles, which can send back pictures of the enemy force as they pass overhead, will enable the Army to engage Soviet armoured forces at much greater distances than in the past.

The changes, however, are misleading. Having completed the largest re-equipment programme in its history, the Rhine Army is already involved in the project definition phase of a totally new series of weapon systems for which a future government will be hard pressed to find the money.

In the field of light armoured vehicles the Army requires a replacement for its present generation of tracked reconnaissance vehicles.[36] Traditionally it has been able to cut costs by going for speed to provide protection. Now the generals believe the new model will have to have adequate firepower, preferably the expensive 105-mm Low Recoil Force Gun, which is capable of piercing armour.

In the field of support vehicles, the Army has already defined its requirements, requirements which have met with a muted response from a government already strapped for cash. The Government does not share the Army's belief that every vehicle should be armoured, even landrovers, if they are to be deployed on the Forward Edge of Battle (FEBA). It would probably prefer the Army to go for the cheap option of refitting the FV 432s now made surplus to requirement by the introduction of Warrior Infantry

Combat Vehicles. No doubt exaggerating the problems of tomorrow's battlefield, the generals would prefer any new system to be more than a patched-up version of the old. The more interest they show in new technology the more antiquated their forces seem to be. That is why they seem to have set their sights on a new truck of one point seven or two tonnes which will be much more expensive than any similar vehicle they have ever used.

The Rhine Army already has a sophisticated communications system in Ptarmigan. Inevitably its introduction has not diminished enthusiasm for the automated battlefield of the future; it has merely given it new life. A consortium is at present studying a vehicle mounted Air Defence Command Information Service (ADCIS) in the hope that the Army will be able to react more rapidly to airborne threats. The military planners are also investigating an integrated command and control battlefield management system for the Army's main battle tank similar to the LECLERC system the French intend installing in the near future.

Aware of the political pressures to keep spending within bounds, the generals are anxious to avoid complaints that ever greater funds are being squandered on unnecessarily expensive equipment, equipment which the nation can no longer afford for so small a return. In 1982 the Chief of the Defence Staff Field Marshal Sir Edwin Bramall maintained that the Army did not need the full spectrum of weapons, particularly if this meant paying fifty per cent more for a mere ten per cent improvement in performance. The Army recognised, he insisted, that there must be a limit to the amount of capital investment in the most expensive system of all – the tank, which would seldom be in a position to engage enemy armoured vehicles at further than 1500 metres, or continue fighting in closely contested engagements for more than a day.[37]

Such bold statements are not, alas, ones with which every general finds himself in accord. They are already engaged in an acrimonious dispute about the next generation tank to replace Challenger, which is planned to enter service before 2010. True to tradition, the planners would like the new tank (designated MBT 2000) to retain the priorities of firepower, protection and mobility, while recognising that in the past the first two requirements have led to a steady increase in weight which has negated the third, and increased costs significantly. If it is to afford a new tank at all, the Army will have to build one substantially lighter than the Challenger (fifty tonnes or less, not sixty-two) probably by reducing the size of its crew. By using a data-based system for computing and communications, each crew member could carry out the other's tasks from his own console.

The main debate so far as been over the MBT 2000's gun. The planners seem to be interested in a 140-mm gun with an automatic loader, a choice which, if agreed by Whitehall, would make it difficult to collaborate with the Germans who are known to want a more sophisticated weapon, one which can preferably be built in collaboration with the Americans. In addition to the problems which sole manufacture would cause for Vickers (which has taken over tank building from the Royal Ordnance) there is also considerable scepticism whether Britain needs a new heavy tank at all.

Many experts are convinced that the tank, if not already obsolete, may be reverting to its previous role as an infantry support vehicle. A totally mechanised infantry force, moving at 3 mph from one position to the other, supported perhaps by light armoured infantry on the *PanzerGrenadier* model, may increasingly win the support of governments ever conscious of costs, ever concerned to temper the enthusiasm of the General Staff with crude cost-benefit analyses, and more pessimistic assessments of the future of armoured warfare.

As a military investment, the re-equipment of the Rhine Army may prove to have been a qualified success, qualified, because it may well cut against the grain of the new doctrine of conventional deterrence which a Labour Government would wish to execute. If this were the case, there would certainly be no question of funding a new tank programme. Instead the Army would be offered double the number of anti-tank missiles which it already deploys.

The greatest challenge the Rhine Army may yet face may come not from a cost cutting Conservative Government, or from nationalist Tory MPs who would prefer to save the blue water Navy whatever the cost, but from a Labour Government committed to the continental commitment, but whose notion of the BAOR's purpose might differ radically from that of its commanders.

Would they ever be reconciled to the Labour Party's version of conventional deterrence? Perhaps, it is a difficult, possibly unfair question to pose until the situation actually arises. As Michael Elliot-Bateman has rightly observed:

> "*Many books have been written to explain (the) victories of the weak over the strong but in essence the victors succeeded because they were able to impose circumstances upon their adversaries for which their adversaries were not prepared, organised, or trained.*"[38]

The whole concept of conventional deterrence is based on this premise; that the West if attacked could impose its own conditions by channelling an attack along routes of its choosing, delaying the enemy armoured columns, and defeating the first echelon long before it had a chance to be reinforced by the second. Using precision guided missiles and submunitions, the Rhine Army would not have to defend the area in which it would be deployed but merely inflict an unacceptable loss rate (forty per cent) on the advancing enemy force.

As it happens, the Army might not find such a strategy entirely unconvincing, whatever the Labour Party's critics may maintain. It has recently adopted a strategy which places a great deal of emphasis on a high degree of manoeuvrability to reduce the time it would be expected to hold the German border east of Hanover so that it would have time to select the best defensive ground from which to launch a counter-attack. It is a strategy which is derived to a large extent from the lessons learned from *Exercise Crusader* in 1980 (the largest exercise since 1954); in part from the substantial re-equipment programmes of the last few years.

In the past, the Army planned to hold the initial attack with one armoured division, with three other armoured divisions held in reserve to contain a breakthrough, rather than shore up a crumbling defence. Today the 1st and 4th Armoured Divisions are based on the border behind a screen of armoured vehicles whose task it will be to identify potential breakthrough points. The 3rd Division, in the rear, will wait for the 2nd Division and 1st Brigade to be airlifted to the battlefield before the Russians have had a chance to break out.

Labour would find much of this reassuring, given its interest in "non provocative" defence. It is less "provocative", one supposes, to rely on air mobility, on units deployed by helicopter, equipped with nearly twice as many anti-tank weapons as normal, to reinforce a sector where a break-through appears imminent, or is at least feared. It would be less happy with the second task of such a force, namely to release tanks from their role as they see them, as dug in artillery, for a more free ranging role, including counter attacks against an exposed salient.

Reinforcement, however, is the weakest link in the BAOR chain, the least convincing part of the British commitment. *Lionheart* proved the old adage that it is better to travel in hope than to arrive. The embarkation and landing of British troops went comparatively well, but the journey to the front was chaotic. On several occasions the reinforcing troops arrived at the wrong place. Worse still, the exercise revealed that the total number of British tanks was ridiculous, even though they have been stretched from 469 to 590 since 1979, a number which in relative terms is actually too high given that there are insufficient crews to keep them fully operational. One supposes that if Labour promised to make good the deficiencies in the reserve element, its case against the tank would be much harder to counter.

Paradoxically, *more* money might have to be invested in the BAOR, not less, even if its numbers of men were pegged at their present level, if its divisions are no longer to rely on battlefield nuclear weapons.

It is clear, however, that the Rhine Army has already spanned a changing era in the history of Britain's commitment to the defence of Germany, and that the time of transition may well be drawing to a close. The greatest challenge of all may be not dealing with future cuts or criticisms from the backbenches, or the occasional editorial in *The Times*, but in coming to terms with a new generation of Labour politicians who, whatever their motives, share a growing conviction that the Army must stay on, not to defend the Germans, but reassure the Russians that the Western Alliance is non-provocative in intent.

The Royal Air Force (RAF)

In the 1960s the RAF was very much the Cinderella service. The Sandys Review of 1957 proved to be as devastating as the Nott review might in other circumstances have been for the Royal Navy with its emphasis on missiles not manned aircraft, on nuclear not conventional deterrence, even on surface to air missiles rather than manned aircraft.

Shortly afterwards it lost responsibility for the nuclear deterrent itself when the government decided to phase out the Vulcan bomber force in favour of Polaris. The need for cost-cutting deprived the Air Force of some of its most cherished programmes, including the all weather supersonic jet the TSR2 and the Anglo-French variable geometry plane (AFVG) which promised to take the RAF into the next generation more favourably placed than it had emerged from the last.

The planes it did get were considered quite inadequate for the tasks they had to fulfil. The Phantoms, although good, did not provide a long range strike capability. For that the RAF had to rely on the Jaguar, a plane the air staff had never wanted but which the politicians forced through in order to promote yet another Anglo-French collaborative venture.

In short, the Air Force which emerged in 1979 had too many roles, too few aircraft, of too many types, none able to perform any single mission with the versatility which modern warfare demanded. It even lost its East of Suez capability when the order for the FIII was unexpectedly cancelled. The Air Force may have kept its long range transport planes, its Hercules and VC10s, but it lost all its Andovers, Britannias and Belfasts, or almost half its entire fleet. In 1975 the V bombers were withdrawn from Cyprus when CENTO was disbanded; the ASW Nimrods in Malta also came home. The RAF followed in the wake of the departing legions, underpowered, undermanned, with indifferent morale only too aware of the fact that it could not even guarantee the defence of the United Kingdom.

Like the Army, the Air Force has been fortunate in the Thatcher years. It has undergone the most extensive modernisation for a generation, costing fourteen billion pounds over the past decade. The integration of the new Tornados and Harrier G3s has had a massive knock-on effect with aircraft changing roles and bases to a degree not seen since the introduction of the Vulcan bomber in the early 1950s. This year it will get sixty Harrier GR5s, the latest model. The re-equipment programme will make the RAF one of the best-equipped forces in Europe by the end of the 1980s, although not one of the largest, or necessarily one of the most versatile. In terms of all weather operations, for example, its Harriers and Jaguars are no better than the F-16.

Like the Army, the Air Force will also face a major challenge in the mid-1990s when its present planes will need to be re-equipped or redesigned to take account of new technology. Of all the Services, the RAF is the most vulnerable in this respect; of the three, it is flying in the slipstream of modern technology. The next ten years is likely to see a technological revolution based on microprocessors which will make many aircraft obsolete by the time their production cycle is complete.

Not all is gloom and doom of course. Computer assisted aircraft design could improve engine efficiency, and produce a thirty per cent improvement in aircraft performance (although at markedly higher cost). The present Harrier fleet could survive for as long as the Canberras (thirty years) if improvements in micro-electronics allow them to fly in all weathers, at longer distances, making them less dependent on ground control especially in aerial combat. As Air Vice Marshal Mason predicts:

> "...for the first time since the writings of Lanchester, Mitchell and Douhet, the potential of conventional airpower will soon be limited by imagination rather than by technology".[39]

The problem is whether the Government will be able to afford any of the items on the technical menu, or perhaps more to the point, whether it will be able to afford even a new agile fighter by the mid-1990s. It was meant to be in service next year; the intended target date is now 1995. As yet, however, the MOD has not placed any orders for the European Fighter Aircraft despite the fact that it is nearing the end of its project definition phase.

In short the RAF could soon find itself in the same position as the late 1970s when the Air Staff recognised that it had not enough air crews to enable a simultaneous phasing in of new aircraft (principally the Tornado) and phasing out of older combat squadrons. What it did not appreciate was that financial constraints would prompt the government of the day to phase out older systems much earlier than planned while slowing down the production of their replacements. Increasing metal fatigue required the Buccaneers to be withdrawn earlier than budgeted; the cost of keeping the Canberra bombers in service proved too high as well. At the same time the Tornado programme proved so expensive that the rate of deliveries was held at 44 a year, instead of increasing to 65 in 1985–6. By the end of 1982, Britain found itself with 100 fewer front line aircraft than the planners had intended – a drop of about one-sixth.

This time the situation is likely to be more criticial still because of the doctrinal clash between those who argue that the manned aircraft is obsolete, or will soon become so, and those who are convinced that it would be as foolish to rely on an all-missile force altogether. For the public at large the arguments on both sides are likely to remain obscure. The real meaning of the debate, its underlying rationale, may well go unremarked, leaving the politicians and services to fight the battle in a political no-mans land of their own making.

There has always been a strong lobby in the MOD for relying on missiles rather than aircraft to strike armoured formations, or penetrate Soviet air defence at much higher speeds than a Tornado. There has always been rather less support for defending airspace entirely with surface to air missiles. Certainly missile technology has improved out of all recognition in recent years. The self-initiating anti-aircraft missile (SIAM) can pursue a target from the time of launch, and thus follow it beyond its "line of sight". Laser technology is likely to make it possible to engage in range-finding in excess of fifteen miles although, because of the diffusion of lasered light by the atmosphere, it may actually be easier to intercept the booster phase of an intercontinental ballistic missile (ICBM) than a low flying aircraft.

The arguments against relying entirely on missile defence however seem far more compelling. In defending fixed assets, including airfields, aircraft are able to intercept targets at much greater ranges than missiles, 1500 kilometres in the case of the F15 compared with only 120 kilometres in the case of most surface-to-air missiles. In an age in which the effectiveness of missile systems is improving all the time, however, the use of manned aircraft must increasingly be confined to those roles which demand the skills of a highly trained pilot and for which there is as yet no satisfactory unmanned substitute.

As for offensive operations, Neville Brown is probably correct in arguing that the vulnerability of aircraft in flight does not seem to have increased as much as tanks in close order, or frigates in narrow stretches of water.[40] There is still further scope for improving the agility of aircraft by introducing aero-dynamic improvements before centrifugal stress imposes an impossible strain on pilots. The fact that we have not yet reached the frontiers of technology with regard to missiles or manned aircraft and that the advantage has not yet tipped decisively in favour of the former, would suggest that Britain still needs a complete weapons system, not an airframe adapted to the exigencies or fashions of the moment. To quote Mason again *"this particular road to Damascus is long and dark, but happily with no blinding glimpses of the obvious being mistaken for anything more inspirational"*.[41]

In the more immediate term the RAF's most serious challenge will be its allocation of missions. Technology may broaden or narrow the horizons of aerial warfare but spending will probably continue to be dictated by political realities, especially with regard to the RAF's most important mission after the defence of the UK, its support of the Rhine Army.

It is generally accepted that NATO air forces in Germany are outnumbered by about 3:1 in tactical aircraft. If the Rhine Army were ever reduced significantly, it seems likely that Britain's allies would look for a compensating increase in its tactical air contribution. At present RAF (Germany) has three bases near the Dutch border, at Bruggen, Laarbruch and Wildenrath with a single runway and two taxiways (the standard 1950s pattern). The only RAF combat base east of the Rhine is at Gutersloh, near Bielefeld.

For several years, the RAF had tried to make out a case for the construction of a fifth base which would add to the number of targets the Soviet Union would have to take out, as well as provide for an expanded helicopter fleet. A case can also be made out of course that if the airfields cannot be adequately defended it might be better to pull back the Tornado squadrons to the United Kingdom, and disperse the vertical take off Harriers to hidden sites. Some concern has been expressed in the MOD about the siting of RAF airfields in relation to their potential wartime role. The close proximity of those near the Dutch border is bound to render them *collectively* more vulnerable to air attack. When asked ten years ago whether a fifth airfield would help the Commander-in-Chief of RAF (Germany) pointed out the running costs were likely to be unacceptably high.[42]

At the moment, the RAF spends more than any other airforce in NATO in defending its airfields, providing concrete shelters for its aircraft, and housing many squadron command centres in blast resistant shelters. It is doubtful in the extreme whether any government would be able to find the money for a Rapier point defence system as well, or whether point defence would be very effective anyway against smart stand-off weapons.

As it is the costs of RAF (Germany) have begun to spiral out of control. It desperately needs more stand-off weapons of its own. The introduction of laser-guided bombs for the Jaguars and Buccaneers may look like a step in the right direction but it is questionable whether a Labour Government would find them suitable for a purely 'defensive' role.

Even in terms of pilot training the Air Force is threatened with declining standards in the near future. Fuel cuts hit the RAF very badly in 1985. Although RAF (G) escaped relatively lightly, training flights were seriously affected. As the Commons Defence Committee had discovered three years earlier, fuel cuts had reduced flying time so significantly that experienced pilots had chosen to surrender some of their own flying hours to allow their younger colleagues to spend more time in the air.[43]

Plagued with such problems, future governments may have little time to concern themselves with the defence of Germany when the defence of the United Kingdom itself could be greatly improved. Throughout the 1970s it was generally conceded that the MOD had taken insufficient note of the need to defend airfields at home. By 1979, the RAF had less than 100 fighters available for home defence, a role that was performed by twenty year old Phantoms. The Air Force, in fact, was so stretched that warships were given the task of defending naval bases at Lossiemouth and Kinross with their own Sea Dart missiles.

The likelihood of a major Soviet air strike against the United Kingdom is still a matter of dispute. Within the Air Force itself, however, three facts that are not open to question seem to have carried the day: (1) that Soviet reconnaissance planes regularly probe the UK's radar cover to test the response of RAF interceptors (2) that in the event of war about forty per cent of NATO's combat aircraft strength would probably be assembled in bases in Eastern England (3) that Soviet doctrine seems to assume that a European war can initially be confined to a conventional, non-nuclear confrontation. Soviet exercises appear designed to deprive NATO of time, time to make tactical re-deployments, time to reinforce frontline troops, time to agree on the release of theatre or medium range nuclear weapons.

The resources the Soviet Union might deploy against Britain from the start of a war might amount to five times the peak German bombing effort during the Second World War. Exercise Priory in May 1985 revealed just how exposed Britain was to air attack, how radar facilities were not able to match Soviet tactics, or electronic counter measures, how reliant the RAF would be on arming jet trainers like the Hawk with Sidewinder missiles to augment its present front line strength of 120 planes.

At present, 200 man hours of maintenance are needed for each hour of flying time. It might take ten men working night and day to keep a plane airborne for just one patrol. Such statistics have already convinced the Labour party that first priority must be given to air defence at home, not to the support of the Rhine Army. Indeed, if a majority of MPs, irrespective of party, ever came to believe that the next Battle of Britain would determine the battle for Central Europe, the arguments for reducing the front line forces on the continent, both in terms of aircraft and men, might become compelling.

The Nuclear Deterrent

Britain has had a nuclear deterrent since 1952; a submarine based system since the late 1960s. Its military rationale has not always been clear. When the Attlee government decided to press ahead with the nuclear programme in 1947 it did so purely to justify Britain's status as a Great Power; the Soviet Union hardly figured in its deliberations. As Lord Carver, the former Chief of the Defence Staff (1973–6) has argued, the military arguments for the deterrent have followed the political arguments, and have evolved to rationalise political decisions already taken.[44] Such an interpretation is debatable, but as Britain's great power pretensions have become no more than a memory, as the British find it more and more difficult to remember the actors they once were, the deterrent has become something of an anomaly, a strange consolation for the descent from power.

The debate about Trident and its future (if it has one) is more than a debate about defence priorities and costs. It is a debate about Britain's image of itself. Not many defence experts share the Government's obsession with Trident, not many of its allies either, but the Conservatives have come to believe in it fervently and expect their leaders to propogate the case for it with zeal, not bland detachment. The government's critics are equally convinced that Trident represents yet another attempt to escape the logic of history; that Mrs Thatcher's commitment to the programme masks real anxieties about the country's future influence, as the old certainties begin to disintegrate, leaving a new generation to evolve an identity of its own.

Why did the Conservatives choose Trident in 1980? The age of Polaris meant that it could not be continued indefinitely, not beyond 2005 and probably well before then. Even if it had been possible to replace its guidance, fire control and launcher systems, and rebuild the submarine hulls, the cost would have been prohibitive. More attractive would have been the purchase of the Poseidon (C3) from the USN which plans to retire them from service between 1993–9. A MIRVed system, with a range of 550 kilometres greater than Polaris, Poseidon would have been cheaper than Trident on paper, but it would have left the British Government to bear all the support costs alone as well as carrying the cost of building completely new warheads.

At a very early stage, the Government did consider the cruise missile option which David Owen originally favoured when Foreign Secretary, and has ever since, although he has found himself preaching to a largely unresponsive audience. Although it would have taken a great deal of R&D in British industry to develop the technology, the unit production costs would have been low, the weapons would have been extremely accurate. What told against it in the end was the limited range of the most obvious missile Tomahawk (2500 km). In order to fire their missiles, the submarines would have had to come perilously close to Soviet shores. In addition, they would have needed up to 400 missiles at sea to achieve the same effectiveness as a submarine-launched ballistic missile force. Unless a vertical launch system was developed at considerable cost, the missiles would have had to have been launched from torpedo tubes – a long and laborious process.

As Lord Lewin, former Chief of the Defence Staff wrote five years after the government opted for Trident:

> "*All this means that, for a given weight of striking power, cruise is in fact much more expensive than a ballistic equivalent. For example, a force of 11 boats each capable of carrying 80 cruise missiles would have much less assured deterrent capability than 4 boats each equipped with 16 Trident missiles; such a force would cost at least twice as much to acquire, and more important, about twice as much to run.*"[45]

Trident was purchased because it was thought to be the cheapest system available. Even when the United Kingdom found it had to buy the more expensive Trident 2 system the cost still seemed reasonable, three per cent of the defence budget over twenty years, six per cent of the equipment budget overall. The MOD Procurement Executive is still standing by its previous claim that in the periods 1985–90 and 1990–5 the cost will amount to no more than three point nine per cent and four point five per cent of the defence budget, and eight point five per cent and nine point six per cent of the equipment budget. If these figures are accurate, they would compare very favourably with the cost of the Tornado programme which, in its thirteenth year (1983–4), absorbed eighteen per cent of the equipment budget, or fifty per cent of the RAF's entire budget the following year.

If the country cannot afford the system, can it afford the new European Fighter Aircraft which may prove to be more expensive still? In 1982 Nott argued that for the same price the BAOR could deploy 300 tanks (but not the crews). Three years later, Lord Lewin argued that spreading the costs of Trident across the three Services might allow the Navy to run twelve extra frigates, the Army fifty five more tanks per brigade and the RAF fifty more Tornados. "*These marginal increases in NATO's conventional capability might cause the Soviet planners to recalculate how many days a conventional war might last. For the same cost Trident can convince them that war is not worth starting.*"[46] Trident has so many critics that it is difficult to summarise all the arguments they have put forward. Lewin's point about conventional savings seems not only compelling, but also unanswerable since even if Trident were scrapped, most expert opinion is firmly convinced that the savings would not be substantial, and that the twelve extra frigates, or 300 tanks would not be built.[47]

Similarly, the argument that Trident will present the Soviet Union with an unacceptable escalation in warheads at the very time that it is seeking a major across the board reduction also tends to miss the point. Trident will not be as massive an escalation in Britain's nuclear capability as is often claimed. Last December George Younger reiterated that though "theoretically" the United Kingdom could increase its number of warheads by a factor of eight, in principle it intended to merely double the number of warheads carried by Polaris.[48] Only 128 would actually be deployed.

As Trident's critics know quite well, only two boats can be deployed at sea at any one time (due to long and short refits). In the highly unlikely event of all the missiles at sea being targeted on Soviet missile silos in a counterforce strike, at least two warheads would have to be directed against each hardened silo to have a reasonable chance of destroying it. Given that the Soviet Union has 1,398 silos, Britain would be in no position to present the Russians with a serious counterforce threat; at most it could only destroy nine per cent or less of the Soviet landbased force.

The main threat to the government's plans would probably arise if the Anti-Ballistic Missile Treaty broke down, and the Russians upgraded their ballistic missile defences. One reason why the cabinet went for a gold plated system like Trident in 1980 was to avoid the need for expensive mid-life refits such as Chevaline. The Chevaline story could well be repeated this time at a cost no British Government could afford if the Navy had to change the existing ratio of warheads to penetration aids. Some of the missiles' propellant might have to be sacrificed to accommodate more warheads or decoys which would mean greater reliance than ever on United States technology. Britain might even have to consider building more missiles, or more submarines at a cost which can only be guessed at.

By the time Britain would have to decide whether to replace Trident with another system (2010), the cost of continuing an independent deterrent may prove too high. It is more than likely that Trident, if it is deployed on schedule, will be the last system ever supplied by the United States, and possibly the last deterrent Britain will ever deploy.[49]

Even now it is questionable, whether all things considered, Britain should be in the nuclear business at all. At the heart of the Trident issue lies the suspicion that Britain is still play acting, in the hope not of deterring the Soviet Union, but bluffing the world that it is still a power of importance, playing its hand well, indeed with confidence, but not quite convincing itself.

Defence Industry

The problems of the defence industry crystallise the dilemma of being a medium power with a strong technological base but not the capacity to realise its potential. Only public ignorance, or indifference, has allowed the Civil Service, and the governments which it has advised to tax the citizen more highly than any other country in Western Europe for the privilege of keeping up with Germany and France. The British people are paying more for the privilege than they may imagine; certainly more than they can conceive.

If the defence budget is already too large, consuming too much of the nation's resources, the defence industry is now so widely spread over 270 Parliamentary constituencies that relatively few MPs are immune to its pressures. The MOD is now the largest single employer in the country. The scale of its operations is now so vast that orders for equipment under fifty million pounds do not even go to Ministers for approval. As Martin Ince concluded in a recent study:

> "... The UK, the USA and France are in a class by themselves when it comes to the fraction of their military budgets spent on R&D. In the years 1981-4 the UK spent almost thirteen per cent of its military budgets on R&D, ahead of the other two, and way in front of the next in the league, Sweden. This stems from the fact that the UK has adopted a semi-superpower military role, requiring expenditure – and research and development – across a wide range of military objectives.".[50]

Very little of this has been in the public interest. British companies have failed to become market leaders in most fields over the past thirty years, with one major exception: defence electronics. Unfortunately, the money spent on defence rarely has any direct (or even indirect) civilian application. Most military R&D is product innovation. By comparison, most of the innovation on which civil industry depends is in the improvement of the manufacturing process, not new product development. It is through process innovation that companies compete for markets by selling goods more cheaply or improving their quality.

Perhaps, even this would just about be acceptable if the defence industry was especially efficient. Instead, it is often incredibly wasteful, and unable to meet Service demand. Because it has been allowed to function without Parliamentary scrutiny, it has frequently underperformed. Indeed Parliament has been singularly remiss in reviewing whether the taxpayer has got value for his money. Unlike the United States Congress, the Commons has never insisted on financing all major procurement projects individually, and demanding progress reports. The first time MPs ever asked for such powers of scrutiny was in 1982 when the Select Committee of Public Accounts suggested it should be given confidential summaries of the costs of major defence projects.

The demand arose over the scandal of Chevaline costs which had risen in a matter of years from £300 million to £1 billion. Of course, it is not at all clear how much Parliament would have been told, considering that Joel Barnett, the Chief Secretary to the Treasury (1974–9) knew nothing of the Chevaline project during his entire period in office.[51]

Chevaline has been far from the only disastrous procurement decision in terms of cost. In an attempt to make sense out of a complex situation, let us focus our attention on four very different projects which have cost the taxpayer an inordinate amount of money for very little return:

(1) Type 23 Frigate

Since 1969 the production costs of naval frigates per ton has increased with relentless regularity, at an average rate per annum of eighteen per cent. This rate of increase has far exceeded the inflation rate during the period. Extrapolating from current trends the price of a Type 23 frigate would be as high as £1 billion by 1996, £3 billion by 2003. Such exercises are, of course highly misleading.[52] They do confirm, however, that the price of major systems is rising by six per cent a year in real terms, and as high as ten per cent or more for aircraft and ships. Lord Trenchard, Nott's Minister for Procurement, was right to maintain that "*the best we could hope for was that the economy as a whole would be growing at the same rate* [as the rise in the defence budget—two point five per cent p/a] *so that the defence budget would not take any greater share of GDP*".[53]

The Navy found itself at a crossroads in 1969. It could have opted for cheap ships like the offshore patrol vessels of the Castle class (1,250 tons). It went instead for the Type 23, arguably the worst possible choice, not only because it turned out to be more expensive than planned (£100 million not £60 million) which made it impossible to purchase as many as required; but because the Navy was also forced to build a much cheaper off-shore patrol vessel (OPU3) than it originally wanted.

Typical of the high technology ship of the present era, the Type 23 has an EH-101 helicopter, Stingray torpedoes, the Seawolf surface to surface missile system and a medium calibre gun. But, like many modern weapon systems, it is also poorly designed. It was described some years ago in Naval Staff Requirement 7069 as a slow, poorly armed vessel, a vulnerable, inefficient fighting ship with a speed five knots slower than most other RN ships, and a hull life that was expected to last only ten years. As the paper noted, with traditional British understatement, the Seawolf *"should provide at least fifty per cent survivability"*,[54] a rate which proved totally inadequate in the South Atlantic against the thirty-year-old aircraft of a Third World state.

(2) Tornado

The Tornado cost the United Kingdom £250 million more than the British aerospace industry received in work from the programme. It was only fitted into the budget at all because although forty per cent higher than the present estimated costs of Trident, most of the expenditure took place during a period (1974–84) in which the total defence budget rose by twenty-eight per cent in real terms and spending on equipment by a remarkable eight-seven per cent. As Malcolm Chalmers notes, had the Government attempted to fund the programme during a period of zero growth, the consequences for other equipment programmes would have been very severe.[55]

This would not have mattered if Tornado had fulfilled its promise. Unfortunately, like many collaborative ventures which perform several different operations, it is not especially proficient performing any one. At Laarbruch the planes have had to be modified on a regular basis to ensure that the avionics continue to function when the plane's twin cannon are fired. Although the design fault allowed the initial production cost of the aircraft to be kept artificially low, it resulted in about one quarter of the aircraft being grounded.[56]

Another problem with collaborative programmes is that they have to perform so many missions that they become highly complex to handle and highly labour intensive. It took British ground crew in Germany three years to achieve the proficiency level they had on Buccaneers. In addition, although the number of ground crew per squadron increased from 100 to 150, Tornado proved exceptionally difficult to keep in service once it had taken to the air. In 1984 sixty per cent of Tornado sorties ended with the aircraft becoming unservicable; often every plane in a squadron was inoperative by the end of a flying day.[57]

(3) Tigerfish torpedo

Since the war the United Kingdom has embarked on twenty-five torpedo projects of which only three have been successful; and sixteen have been cancelled. The sorry story of the Tigerfish torpedo (the most expensive of all) reveals the price Britain still continues to pay for the privilege of building its own, rather than buying "off the shelf". Like many such projects it illustrated that the MOD never had any clear purpose in mind, and insufficient will to control the enthusiasm of the scientists. No one manager was responsible for the overall programme; no single contractor had total overview of the process.

The Tigerfish was meant to enter service in 1967; it was eventually deployed in 1979. By then it had cost the country a staggering £1 billion. Unfortunately, even then the torpedo proved so unreliable that the crews were reluctant to fire it for fear of buckling the vanes on their nuclear powered submarines. The captain of the submarine that sank the Belgrano decided to play safe by using a torpedo of Second World War design instead (admittedly against a Second World war ship).

With hindsight, it seems clear that Britain would have been better advised either to have entered either into joint venture collaboration, or bought off the shelf rather than embark singlehandedly on so ambitious a programme. The country can no longer afford to build its own torpedoes; it may not even have the technical skill. The financial and technical resources it does dispose of would probably be better employed in winning commercial markets overseas.

(4) Nimrod Reconnaissance aircraft

Perhaps, the most sorry story of all was the Nimrod aircraft which the Government decided to build in 1977 in preference to participating in the NATO funded AWACS (early warning and control system). Had the decision gone the other way Britain would have had to find at most £500 million. In the event, the MOD spent well over £1 billion for the GEC Nimrod, before being forced to cancel the programme for lack of progress earlier this year. The contrast between the clear preference of the RAF for AWACS and the dogged determination of the politicians not to face up to reality could not have been greater.

The present Government, in particular, combined solemn warnings that intervention on GEC's behalf could not be relied upon with hardly less earnest intimations that considerations of "national interest" would make such intervention inescapable when the moment came. In the end, George Younger summoned up the courage to challenge his own party in its belief that buying British meant buying the best.

It was particularly surprising that the Labour Party chose to make a political issue out of the decision, since it had preached for years that resources spent on defence could be spent to greater effect in the civilian sector. R&D plus the procurement of equipment now accounts for forty-six per cent of the defence budget compared with thirty-two per cent when Fred Mulley took the decision to purchase Nimrod nine years ago.

GEC is an especially good example of a company that, in a highly competitive age, continues to lag behind its Japanese and German counterparts because of the energy which it expends in building expensive weapons systems for which there is no market outside North America and the Middle East. Thirty-two per cent of those employed in the company's military production branch compared with only two per cent in its consumer products division are qualified scientists and engineers. The Maddock Report (1983) on the electronics industry arrived at the inevitable conclusion that it was precisely because the industry was so deeply involved in defence that it was so demonstrably lacking in entrepreneurial skills. In another report drafted on the Cabinet's behalf, Geoffrey Chandler was equally outspoken in his conclusions:

> "The absorption of a large number of qualified scientists and engineers by the defence industry requires higher overall numbers of such personnel rather than lower numbers in civil innovation. If our defence commitments cannot be reconciled with these requirements then in time they will themselves become unsustainable as a result of continuing relative economic decline."[58]

In deciding to press ahead with Nimrod, the Callaghan Government failed to grasp the point that Britain could no longer expect to pursue every technological option in the defence of "the national interest", a concept which is often so nebulous as to be meaningless. There is no particular need, indeed, to buy British when the equipment which results is likely to be below standard, late in delivery and of questionable operational value. One of the most sensible decisions the Wilson Government ever took was the cancellation of the TSR2 which would have cost plane for plane 135 per cent more than the American FIIIs the Government chose to purchase instead.[59]

If one takes such factors into account, then we can see how defining national security in the narrow terms of buying British presents the country with a highly dubious trade-off between self-sufficiency and a reduced level of defence provision. In the case of Nimrod, there was no justification for buying an aircraft that no other nation would ever have wished to buy in the light of the considerable technological risks inseparable from the development of such a sophisticated project.

Such, then are some of the problems of Britain's defence. It has a Navy whose instincts are still those of a former era, an Army which is efficient but depressingly small, an Air Force better equipped than at any time in the past twenty years, but whose ability to defend the country's own airspace is still sadly deficient. The defence industry, still rich in human resources, does not serve Britain as well as it might; or, perhaps, in some respects, serves it too well.

Clearly, there is room for radical reform, for the exercise of political choice. Some moments in history are probably more open to change than others. We seem to be moving rapidly towards such an opening. Only when we have passed through it will we know whether the options chosen were sensible or not. In the following chapters I shall try to sketch the context within which the options will be taken, as well as those which are most likely to be pursued. In the meantime, politicians with a deep personal commitment to a particular vision of the future are likely to struggle toward their goal, however remote and improbable the outcome may seem.

In life, as in any game whose outcome depends on luck, the only response to unfavourable odds is to try harder, not to throw in one's hand while the game is still in play.

2

Farewell to Arms? The Political Context of Decision Making (1988–95)

A generation is a difficult entity to describe. Not all groups of contemporaries have thought of themselves as a generation, a group apart from their predecessors, aware of its own particular collective identity. Mrs Thatcher's generation will come of age in the 1990's. Whatever her success, or failure, her policies, and personality have already stamped themselves on the British people as those of few other Prime Ministers have. That is the uniqueness of the Thatcher phenomenon.

What makes a generation aware of itself is a consciousness of having shared a unique historical experience, and that this experience distinguishes those who have shared it from those who have not. Those who lived through the early Thatcher years (1979–82) shared two significant experiences: one of the worst recessions in British history, with unemployment reaching new levels, yet a Government firmly convinced that it had reversed, not merely arrested, the nation's economic decline. The second experience was the Falklands war, in retrospect a minor event, an historical footnote, but a significant one for all that. The Falklands Factor may have won Mrs Thatcher a second term in office, but this was less important than the echo of past history it evoked. In rallying almost unanimously to the flag, the British people showed just how profound were their historical memories.

If a Labour Government comes to power it will attempt no doubt to portray the war as a tragic mistake, a painful diversion from the realities of everyday life. As for the economic experiment, try though it might, the left has not concealed its fatal ambivalence to the whole affair; a mixture of revulsion at the human cost in terms of unemployment, guilt of having acted so foolishly in 1983 that it had never any chance of gaining power, and envy, perhaps the more potent for being unconscious, that it is still possible for a Government with principles to propagate them so forcefully.

For thirty years the electorate had become weary of empty promises. In the 1960s and 1970s it lived through a period of stop-go economics, an overheated economy under Heath, an IMF rescue package under Callaghan. Those who lived through this period saw it even at the time as undignified, tawdry, entirely empty of meaning. It was a period which also carried none of the fears which obsess us today, the social issues, the politics, the anxiety of nuclear catastrophe. It was a comfortable world, but a rather dull one, in which the national decline seemed so endemic that it was taken for granted.

Mrs Thatcher's generation has a sense of awareness, even a sense of the moment through which it has passed as a point of history. A change of consciousness has meant that we all see our situation as different from the past; old orthodoxies have been challenged, new fears generated, a window has been opened on a future which is still tantalisingly difficult to predict. If our economic circumstances change for the worse, as seems likely, if the past which Mrs Thatcher has conjured up comes to seem anachronistic, if not a little unreal, if the public is drawn into closer contact with some of the abrasive realities which we have so far been able to escape, then the public mood itself may have to be taken into account in the defence debate in a way that we have not seen before.

The Context of Decline

The British people have lived with the challenge of economic decline for so long that they have come to take it for granted. Unfortunately our perception of it is likely to be sharpened by the events of the next five years far more than by the events of the last seven. Despite high unemployment, living standards have risen for those in work; the poor have become poorer but the rich have done much better than many of them can recall. Manufacturing industry may have suffered but invisible exports and oil have kept the economy afloat allowing the Government to increase defence spending in real terms by twenty-five per cent.

For much of the period, of course, we have been living through an artificial boom that no Government can hope to sustain. Manufacturing decline presents a serious threat to economic recovery. Contrary to the Labour party's claims, it is not entirely a phenomenon of the Thatcher years, even if the Government's policies may have speeded up the process. In the United Kingdom, output per worker far from growing as it did everywhere else in the West actually fell by three per cent between 1970–80.

Indeed, no one could claim that the Conservatives have penalised industry. The level of investment subsidies and tax allowances to industrial corporations was so high that net taxes on corporate profits were exceedingly low during Mrs Thatcher's first term in office.

Unfortunately they were not low enough to halt the so-called "deindustrialisation" of the early 1980s, the "wasting of the economy" in Sidney Pollard's graphic phrase. Industry is important because it still generates higher revenue than any other form of economic endeavour. Unless Britain wins back its competitive edge in manufacturing it is difficult to imagine any

Government being able to contain defence spending at its present level. The City may still be the world's largest financial centre but the fact that invisible earnings have become the mainspring of the country's balance of payments is cause not for congratulation, but some concern. A ten per cent fall in manufacturing exports would have to be balanced by a twenty per cent increase in service exports, a rate of increase which the United Kingdom has never achieved. Indeed increased productivity and managerial efficiency have just about helped Britain to keep the same share of service exports that it had in 1970, a remarkable achievement to be sure, but not one likely to be repeated in the future.

The defence sector has also been cushioned from economic reality by major oil exports which are already beginning to decline. Between 1975-85, oil revenues, in terms of additional exports and imports saved, amounted to a quarter of all export earnings. More important for the Ministry of Defence they provided an extra six per cent of Government revenues. What makes the balance of payments problem so worrying is that, if oil had not been available during this period, the deficit on current account would have been as high as £2.7 billion in 1983, and as high as £5 billion the following year. Without oil, cuts in public spending would have been much harsher, something akin to the Labour Government's four per cent cut in real terms in the two years 1976-8. We should also remember that if the Callaghan Government had not borrowed from the International Monetary Fund, cuts in spending would probably have been harsher still.

The failure to cut public spending, as the Conservatives promised in 1979, is yet another indication of the British condition, another sign that the Thatcher experiment has been more psychological than real. Despite seven years of Thatcherism, state spending is still out of control – at present seven per cent higher in real terms than it was ten years ago. The defence budget has expanded too quickly, as the Left always claimed. That is why defence cuts, even under the present Government, are likely to rise steeply after the election campaign. High spending has made it impossible for two successive Chancellors to cut taxes sufficiently to help the lowest paid escape the poverty trap, or lighten the load on the small business sector on which the British economy still relies for sustained growth. After several years of badly missed targets, Nigel Lawson was able to claim a PSBR undershoot for 1985-6. In spite of the fact that the figure was distorted by the revenue raised by once and for all privatisation (£5 billion) the Government still has to cling to its PSBR target. It is, after all, the only remaining plank in the medium term financial strategy as originally framed, the only evidence that the Government is still on course.

The future of the economy, in other words, is fairly bleak. Falling oil revenues, and rising public expenditure, coupled with the first balance of payments crisis since 1973 may knock Sterling completely askew. Another Sterling crisis on the scale of 1967 would lead to another punishing defence review. A Labour Government would probably repeat its policies in the 1960's, pushing up GDP to create greater job opportunities at the cost of higher inflation. Renationalisation at the same time of British Telecom, British Airways and British Gas would depress investor confidence. Higher public spending would demand higher taxes which would discourage foreign investment.

If the present Government's management of the economy is any guide, the Conservative party's approach would probably not be much better. A third Thatcher administration would probably keep the PSBR low enough to hold down inflation, in the hope of avoiding deflationary measures altogether. Low taxes and deregulation, if pursued simultaneously, would of course further reduce Government revenue. In order to keep social spending as high as possible, in a climate far more austere than the country has seen for a generation, something would have to give, probably defence.

Faced with the familiar balance of payments crises of old, both parties would probably follow the same stop-go measures. Both would probably restrict credit, Labour more than the Conservatives, a move which would further undermine the competitive edge of British industry. Neither has probably learned the lessons of the past, that industrial recovery should be put first, and everything else second, including inflation and unemployment. For twenty years successive Governments, Labour and Tory alike, have chosen to squeeze medium term credit, adopting a variety of short term fiscal programmes on a purely *ad hoc* basis to deal with crises as they arise.

A Labour Government, while increasing taxation, might also be tempted to introduce a measure of protectionism which would free interest rates from the burden of supporting Sterling. But unless taxes and interest rates were cut at the same time (which would require a major reduction in public spending) then the experiment, while novel, would be as unrewarding as the experiments of the 1960s. Unfortunately, the party is committed to increasing public expenditure in the belief that it will be able to increase demand and thereby employment. If the budget deficit is not to grow out of control, if the Government is to keep borrowing to a minimum to avoid another IMF loan (with the fiscal restraint the Fund would insist on) some items of Government expenditure will have to be savagely cut back: with the two most likely candidates being industrial subsidies and defence.

The services would be foolish therefore, to expect any relief from a Conservative Government. Its main obsession after 1988 will probably be the payments deficit not inflation; its remedy to go for export led growth. But with less than seven per cent of the world's manufacturing output, the United Kingdom is now totally reliant on the United States to promote free trade. If the United States Congress adopts protectionist measures of its own, or the United States and the European Community find themselves involved in a trade war, which was only just averted at the eleventh hour earlier in the year, the international economy will simply not grow fast enough to narrow the gap between exports and imports. Indeed, if the Government remains true to its abolition of exchange controls (1979), it can expect a massive outflow of capital, not inflow of export revenue, an outcome which will distort the terms of trade even further.

It may be useful at this point to look at two very different forecasts, representative of two different schools of thought in an attempt to predict more accurately the shape of the economy in the period 1987–95. Neither are likely to be entirely accurate, but they do at least offer one version of history which has yet to be made, or unmade, depending on one's point of view.

In 1986 the Cambridge Faculty of Economics (which has long been associated with the Left) produced a model from which no Government could draw much comfort. The authors chose the most optimistic set of assumptions they could, including the growth of world trade by seven per cent a year, and the sustained competitiveness of British exports helped by a fifteen per cent fall in the rate of exchange between 1983–6, which they assumed would hold for another ten years. They then factored in another index: the growth of non-oil output by two and a half per cent per annum, a rate which would ensure that oil revenues would not become completely exhausted for at least ten years.

TABLE 1 Exports and Imports of Manufactures as a Percentage
of Domestic Spending on Manufactures

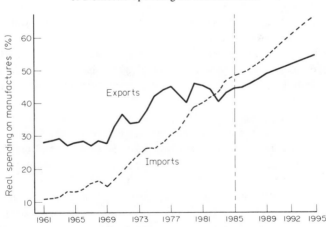

Were this to happen, the deficit in trade in manufactured goods would rise from £3 billion (1985) to £23 billion (measured at 1985 prices) by 1995 (See Table I). Even if invisible exports were to rise substantially, together with capital gains from overseas income, the deficit on the capital account by 1995 could be as high as five per cent of GDP. A figure this high could only be sustained by heavy borrowing, which would render the United Kingdom a net debtor nation, facing a rapidly growing burden of debt interest.[1]

Depressing as this scenario may seem, an analysis by the National Institute makes equally depressing reading. The prospects as well as the performance of the economy were not rated very highly. Far from it; the Institute's medium term projections for the period 1987–91 would suggest that we have not even begun to pay the price for living beyond our means, one of the Prime Minister's favourite phrases during the recession of 1979–81.

The Institute's assumptions were far less optimistic than those of the Cambridge school; possibly because it had less to prove as regards the "impartiality" of its predictions. Far from growing by seven per cent a year, world trade, it suggested, would grow by four and a half per cent, well down on trends before 1973 but consistent with trends since the 1973 recession. A decline in North Sea oil by four and a half per cent a year would reduce annual GDP by twenty-five per cent. The price competitiveness of British exports would only remain constant if the Sterling exchange rate remained constant, a highly doubtful assumption. (See Table 2)

If the Government were returned in the election and went for tax cuts, the average growth of GDP would be marginally lower than the projected growth rate in productivity. Without tax cuts the economy would still grow but painfully slowly. If cuts were to be made until 1991, the faster pace in domestic demand would fuel import demand and increase the country's trade deficit. If taxes were cut in the first two years only, followed by a real devaluation in Sterling in 1989, the current account after deteriorating sharply, might eventually level off.[2]

Clearly, these forecasts are open to challenge, but coming from an Institute sympathetic to the Government, they suggest that in the critical years 1987–9 the politicians will have little room for manoeuvre. The 1988 Defence Review is likely to be far more savage than John Nott's review in 1981. On the Cambridge estimates, a further review in 1991/2 (before the end of a five year term) would probably be forced on the Government by economic circumstances. A reduction in defence spending to four point nine per cent of GDP rather than its present five point five per cent would seem more than likely before the Tories again went to the polls.

The Cambridge school did not suggest what might happen under a different administration; the National Institute did, providing a model which did not attempt to take into account all the Labour Party's manifesto promises, only the main elements of its programme: higher social security benefits, higher public spending on goods and services, higher taxes, lower national insurance contributions by employers, as well as the introduction of a minimum wage (the most controversial of all its promises and the one that it can probably least afford).

The authors concluded that none of these initiatives would probably

TABLE 2: Medium Term Projections on alternative policy assumptions

	1987	1988	1989	1990	1991
Case A: No tax cuts					
GDP: total (% change)	2.1	1.5	1.6	1.1	1.0
non-oil (% change)	2.6	1.7	2.0	1.4	1.2
Manufacturing Output	3.1	2.2	2.7	1.7	0.9
Current balance					
£billion	−4.9	−5.2	−5.0	−4.1	−3.6
Public sector deficit					
as % of GDP	4.7	4.0	3.7	3.3	2.7
Case B: Tax Cuts 1987/91					
GDP: total (% change)	2.4	1.9	2.1	1.5	1.3
non-oil (% change)	2.9	2.2	2.4	1.8	1.5
Manufacturing Output					
% change	3.5	2.5	3.0	2.0	1.1
Current balance					
£billion	−5.5	−6.9	−7.9	−8.2	−8.8
Public sector deficit					
as % of GDP	5.1	5.1	5.0	4.8	4.4
Case C: Tax Cuts 1987/8					
+10% real devaluation (1989)					
GDP: total (% change)	2.4	2.1	2.7	2.2	1.4
non-oil (% change)	2.9	2.4	3.1	2.5	1.7
Manufacturing Output					
% change	3.6	2.8	4.3	3.8	2.3
Current balance					
£billion	−5.6	−7.2	−12.4	−11.7	−8.2
Public sector deficit					
as % GDP	5.1	5.0	4.5	3.3	2.4

(National Institute Economic Review November 1986 p 32 abbreviated)

reduce employment by more than 350,000 over three years; that the introduction of a minimum wage would make little difference to inflation, and that with the real exchange rate unchanged, the current balance would deteriorate by about £4.5 billion in two years. Over a five year period, unemployment might be cut by one million before rising again, the rate of inflation might be pegged at nine per cent, the balance of payments would remain in permanent deficit.

What all this means in terms of defence spending can be seen from Table 3 – a comparison of two different forecasts by the Institute, which I have adjusted so that we can compare Labour spending plans (as just described) and the Government's expenditure targets for 1988/9 (outlined in its 1986 White paper).

TABLE 3: Public expenditure projections 1994/5 under a
Conservative/Labour Governments

(£billion, 1985/6 cost terms)	Conservative Government	Labour
Defence	17.0	16.0
Employment	3.6	5.0
Transport and Housing	6.9	9.9
Education and Health	40.5	42.5
Social Security	45.0	50.5
Trade, Industry & Energy	0.6	3.1

(National Institute Economic Review November 1986 pp 34, 81)

The significance of these figures is daunting for the Services when one recalls that defence expenditure is already £17 billion. In 1985 before the decision was taken to cut defence spending by one per cent the Government estimated that it would be spending £19.9 billion by 1989, a figure David Greenwood believed would have to be eventually readjusted to £24.6 billion.[3] Clearly, the defence sector may be in for the largest single structural change since the Sandys review of 1957, which cut the 2nd Tactical Airforce in Germany by half, and began a substantial phasing out of the Rhine Army which was only halted by the Berlin crisis of 1961.

What the politicians of both parties have deliberately concealed from the public is the endemic nature of Britain's decline. In such circumstances it may be politically attractive but quite irresponsible to promise to hold defence spending at its present level (as a percentage of GDP). The Conservatives seem to believe that the decline has been reversed, although the United Kingdom has fallen to eighteenth place in terms of per capita GNP. The Labour Party still seems to believe that the only mistake it made in the 1970s was not borrowing more and allowing itself to become preoccupied by the rate of inflation. Most of its members seem to have forgotten that Callaghan's Government, not Mrs Thatcher's, saw the first major break in post war growth.

The real situation is rather different. As Sidney Pollard writes, the United Kingdom can no longer be counted amongst the world's most advanced nations, despite pockets of expertise (such as commerce) and isolated examples of technical excellence which are marketed, if at all, rarely successfully. It would be unreasonable therefore to expect that Britain can maintain a major military establishment for very much longer. " ... *the world has passed Britain by – as if, in a convoy travelling together, all the other ships are sailing serenely on while Britain has gone aground helplessly watching the rest of the convoy disappearing over the horizon".*[4] Unfortunately the military metaphor seems all too apt.

The tide of public opinion:

> *"Not until I was fifteen did... I begin to doubt the venerable character of history. I refused to believe any longer that the men and nations of earlier times were different from those of today, that their lives had consisted not of everyday events but of scenes from Grand Opera. I knew it was our teachers' duty to crush us as much as possible... the history they set before us was a hoax devised by grown ups in order to belittle us and keep us in our place."* Hermann Hesse. *If the war goes on: reflections on war and politics* Panther: 1985 p 57)

Since the war, British Governments have always been able to take public opinion for granted when drawing up policies on defence. Disgusted with appeasement, in which they had connived with the politicians, the British people made no demands for a drastic reduction in defence spending. By the end of the 1940s Britain was spending more than ten per cent of its GNP on defence. The anticipated reversion to the manpower levels between the wars did not take place. Nor has it. If defence spending has fallen, it has not fallen to its pre-1938 level, a quite remarkable outcome given the country's descent from power.

Obviously the British still do not consider themselves overtaxed when it comes to defence spending. According to a Gallup poll conducted for the Institute for European Defence two years ago only thirteen per cent of those polled knew that Britain spent less than ten per cent of its GNP on defence.[5] Considering that throughout the 1970s up to ten per cent of those canvassed believed that the country should spend more[6] the cost of belonging to the Atlantic Alliance seems to be considered a cheap investment in the future.

Secondly, the prestige of the Armed Forces has never been higher in the nation's history. Twenty-five military conflicts since the war, most recently the Falklands, have won unqualified public respect for the professionalism of the Services, who have shown a certain *élan* sadly missing in British society at large. Even if the contours of that society are changing faster than we know, the Armed Forces, unlike the police, seem to have maintained public esteem.

As David Widgery of the Socialist Workers Party claims *"it's the political content not the national expiry date stamp that counts"*, an argument he produced in defence not of the *"upper class England of warm gin and tonics in the Members Enclosure"* but *"those people who carry those sensible, unconventional values... whether punk rockers, or pickets, or peace dancers or dreads."*[7] Excepting the peace dancers, who are in a category of their own, the men who were to line the miners' picket lines in 1984, like the punk rockers who voted for Mrs Thatcher the year before, were almost unanimous in their support of the Falklands war.

Indeed the peace movement, now rapidly diminishing in numbers, drew very little popular support, compared with the advance it made in Germany and the Netherlands, where it may have changed the political landscape permanently. The apocalyptic vision of approaching destruction formed part of a middle class, not popular, imagination. Until 1983, its members really did think of themselves as members of a new movement, representatives of a new age, part of a great collective experience with its own fixed idioms and shared obsessions. Like many self-appointed trend setters, alas, they were merely people who took themselves too seriously, in part because the Nation did not take them seriously enough.

In the end they found themselves travelling a different road from the general public. They may have captured the Labour Party and even convinced the electorate that it was the true party of disarmament, but a larger percentage believed that the Conservatives were the party of defence, and it was defence not disarmament which carried the day for the Government in 1983.[8] Far from being popular, CND's policies were too radical, and too intensely nervous. The women of Greenham Common lost public respect, not only because of scurrilous treatment by the press but because they surrendered too easily to humanity's worst fears. Whether they loved or hated mankind, they seemed quite unable to look it straight in the face.

Finally, British governments have been able to rely implicitly on one of the legacies of the war, the fact that the British remained an intensely international people. If Alan Taylor is right to claim that the Battle of Britain was the last great moment in British history,[9] the British people have lived off its memory ever since. After the war they clearly felt that they had made too many sacrifices to be reduced to "*a cold and unimportant little island where we should all have to work very hard and live mainly on herrings and potatoes*", as Orwell remarked of the Empire in The Road to Wigan Pier.[10] Even if this is a fate Britain cannot escape, the British have been willing to pay the price of protracting the decline as long as possible, a feat which their political leaders have accomplished with consummate skill.

Churchill continued to inspire a generation even after he had passed from the political scene. The sense of heroic destiny he painted for the public in the war survived him. Opposition to Britain's membership of the European Community was frequently couched in terms which suggested that the British were not ready to turn their back entirely on history, recognising perhaps, that membership would not lead to still greater triumphs to come. J. H. Plumb may be right in his observation that the "*pasteboard pageantry paraded by the political establishment did not signpost the future*", but he is far too sweeping in suggesting that once the war had come to an end, it influenced neither popular actions nor beliefs.[11]

During the Falklands War (1982), memories of the past were certainly rekindled, even if some of the old passions were clearly spent. Never again, though we probably don't know it, will we have such a stage, or such a military task to perform. It is doubtful whether we still have arms to perform it.

Yet, with the passing of every year, its glories look faded. The Falklands factor has not worn well. The public seems to look at it ironically, aware that it was an anachronism, a last imperial rally, not really a modern war at all. Pride in the sheer professionalism of the Armed Forces remains, but the struggle itself was too brief, too illusory perhaps, Mrs Thatcher's appeal to the national spirit a robust revival of a previous age. Five years on it would appear that the British people may finally have lost the will to fight their way back into history as the French did under de Gaulle.

A combination of circumstances may fast erode public support for high defence spending, if our anxiety about war diminishes, if our fears seem false, if arms talks once again yield results or are seen to, if the moral purpose behind the Alliance is lost, most importantly of all perhaps, if we ever come to believe (to quote Taylor again) that like Churchill in 1940 Margaret Thatcher in 1982 was the penalty we paid for reading history too avidly.

International security will be only one of a succession of problems to which British society will have to respond as the century draws to a close. Balance of payments crises, a declining infrastructure, an ageing population more inward looking than the young, a youth inspired by visceral concern for famine victims, for transient causes, many of them lost before they have even been taken up, may all contribute to narrow the nation's frame of reference. Our economic future as we have seen is likely to be more austere than at any time since the late 1940s with no war memories to sustain us. Our crisis of identity may be greater still, not as we lose an empire but as we are overtaken by powers like Italy and Spain, by the nations of Southern Europe, not our neighbours in the North.

As our self respect ebbs, our political life may become more polarised. Engaged in rescuing what we can, whether jobs or even our bearings as individuals in an increasingly alienating society, the British people may develop a certain dumb obstinacy towards the world at large, not least the arcane conflicts of the Superpowers. The public will not be totally indifferent to events around it but it is unlikely to be so continuously preoccupied by them as it has been hitherto. There will be matters of more immediate moment to spare too much time for socialist "internationalism", or appeals to the past. Loyalties are likely to be increasingly shaped not by governments or politicians, but by personal fears, and economic needs.

Even today the British appear to many foreign observers as essentially bewildered, if not yet despairing of the future, *"anxious and melancholy in the middle of an expanding universe."* (to quote De Gaulle). The next ten years are bound to become a crucible in which new ideas are born and take shape, anti-Americanism, neo-gaullism, Bennite nationalism. Political life will become a market place for the peddlers of each of these creeds and many more. With them may come greater confusion of mind than ever. Governments may never be able to take the public for granted again.

3

Journey Without Maps: The International Context (1988–95)

THE international context within which British Governments will have to manoeuvre over the next ten years is likely to present new challenges, rather than new opportunities. It is unlikely that the present constraints under which they labour will be removed, or even eased though the possibility cannot be ruled out. If anything, British defence policy is likely to be determined by a radically different political environment, the contours of which can be sketched but not delineated with any accuracy.

By the mid 1990s, if not before, the Americans will probably have begun to define themselves no longer as Europeans *manqués*, but part of a distinct political culture, formed by a distinctive experience. Compared with a moribund and provincial Europe, long past its economic prime, the world of the Pacific will present greater promise, and a greater challenge. The next generation of Americans may react either by attempting to withdraw from history altogether,[1] or enter with enthusiasm into the Pacific era which has beckoned since the turn of the century. "*You cannot help but feel*" opined President Reagan in 1984 "*that the great Pacific Basin with all its nations and all its potential for growth and development – that is the future.*"

The Soviet Union, as usual, will have its own interest in turning East. In a speech at Vladivostok last Summer, Gorbachev signalled rather plaintively that the Soviet Union too was a Pacific power, that it would of necessity play more than a secondary part in the new arena of Superpower politics. For a power which occupies a quarter of the Asian landmass, and a tenth of whose citizens are of Asian descent, exclusion from the Pacific age would be another indication that its power had peaked, that it was a society in an advanced, even terminal stage of decline.

For Europe however, the most immediate challenge will be its response to the changes which are likely to take place within the Soviet Union itself, and more unpredictably within Eastern Europe. There are opportunities here as well as threats, the promise of reform as well as the risk of instability. Upon Gorbachev's success in reducing defence spending and keeping the Warsaw Pact at peace may well depend a Labour Government's hopes of a closer understanding between the two powers, a Conservative Government's hopes of lower defence spending.

The onset of the Pacific era will probably pass Europe by. Its role will be less apparent in world affairs than it has been at any time since 1950; the proprietary instinct with which it once watched affairs unfold will probably give way to a sideline diffidence, the modesty of the onlooker.

As it withdraws more and more into itself, Europe will have to define its own identity if it is to play any role at all. As Zbigniew Brzezinski pointed out in an interview four years ago, the older generation in NATO could afford to be Atlanticist precisely because it was *"politically Americanised while culturally non-Americanised."* Today's generation *"tends to be culturally more Americanised than ever, but politically more de-Americanised than before."*[2]

Will this result in greater defence co-operation, or as Edward Thompson hopes *"a peaceful European opinion acting as a third negotiator between the Superpowers with the ultimate objective of reunifying European societies and culture."*[3] Whichever of the two alternatives appears most attractive will depend on where one stands. As Denis Healey warned the Labour Party before the 1983 election, if America's leadership of the Alliance faltered, Europe might seek refuge in nationalism, not neutralism, a prospect which he described in his usual dismissive style as *"chauvinism with an inferiority complex".*[4] At times one cannot help but feel that, like Werner Held, what Mr Healey most dislikes about chauvinism is *"not so much the aversion to other nations, as the love of one's own."*

Looking back on our own decade, we can see in it the shape of a tragic play, tragic because Europe is having to respond to events no longer of its own making. In that sense the Reykjavik summit of 1986 may be seen as the *peripeteia*, the point where the action turned; the year in which the United States served notice that it might one day leave the European scene, the time when Gorbachev established his power in the Kremlin, the moment when the bombing of Tripoli, though a minor affair in itself, revealed a gulf in understanding between European and American opinion which may never be bridged.

In a period of great change it is often advisable to take refuge in the past. Britain, however, is likely to be faced with a choice between extremes, between Thatcherism and Socialism, Atlanticism and Neutralism, nuclear and non-nuclear defence policies. Confronted by a multiplicity of choices, it is not at all clear which the British will opt for. It is always possible, of course, that they will discover as they did in the 1930s, to quote a bitterly disillusioned Orwell, that:

"Creeds, parties, programmes of every description have simply flopped, one after another. The only 'ism' that has justified itself is pessimism."

Perhaps, a text for our times?

United States and NATO

"The Atlantic era . . . must soon exhaust the resources at its command and the Pacific era destined to be the greatest of all, is just at its dawn." (Theodore Roosevelt 1898)

When President Reagan came to power, a number of deeply unfavourable trends were working against the capacity of the United States to sustain its role in the world. The cost of defending its worldwide security system was mounting. Years of deficit financing had given rise to massive indebtedness which was diverting capital from economically productive investment, progressively crippling its capacity for economic renewal.

In some respects, particularly his budget deficits, Reagan promoted these trends; yet in other respects, in particular the response to the Soviet challenge, the urgency of his vision was communicated to the American people, if not the European Allies, with great success. In Europe, Reagan's rearmament programme was frequently portrayed as provocative. Promised "a generation of peace" by Nixon at the height of détente, Europe had felt *"freed from its obsession with security."*[5] Now it was confronted with an administration on the offensive, one which eschewed arms control, even détente, in the interest of reversing America's "decline".

The very concept of decline carried with it the idea of renewal, of recreating a past that had been lost. In his policies and pronouncements, Reagan satisfied a wistful yearning in the public mind, a yearning for the lost years of certainty and fulfilment. Essentially he was a man of his time, place and opportunity. His time was the crisis in American foreign policy occasioned by one of the most indecisive Presidents in its postwar history, a time of disillusionment and uncertainty. As Philip Larkin observed in Next Please *"always too eager for the future we pick up bad habits of expectancy."* The United States expected too much of détente, and retired angry and frustrated, ready for the largest re-armament programme since the Korean war.

Reagan's place was the United States, a country that still believed in its own importance, but had become unsure of itself and its mission. It was looking for some compensation for the disappointments of the past; Reagan restored its self-confidence, if not its self-respect, by invading Grenada and bombing Tripoli in the struggle against state sponsored terrorism. Reagan acted and spoke as if the United States was not in decline but at the height of its power, an opinion few challenged, perhaps from force of hope rather than habit. *"Our days of weakness are over"* he proclaimed in a State of the Union address *"the United States is safer, stronger and more secure in 1984 than before."* He may have spoken in political hyperbole but he conveyed (perhaps for the last time?) the view that the Americans were a special people, with a special mission.

His opportunity was novel also. The United States was at a vital crossroads in its relations with Europe. Europe was at a crossroads too in its relations with the United States. America was no longer an expansionist power, but a *status quo* one, anxious to retain its position in the world. Its imperial urge was over; it was no longer interested in being the world's policeman, only a nightwatchman on limited contract. But it still believed in itself, and in the application of military power. It wished to play a more active role in areas of the world where its interests were under threat. It did not wish to be tied down in a continent (Europe) from which it was divided by power, and ideology, just as Europe was cut off from the United States by geography and prejudice. They were both allies of a kind, but allies who once having been much closer, had begun to turn their back on the great endeavour which had brought them together in 1949.

What the future will hold when Reagan passes from the scene is far from clear. It would seem that sooner rather than later, however, the Americans will wake up to the fact that, despite the most expensive military build up in the country's peacetime history, very little has changed from the Carter years except America's self-respect. How long that will last either is anyone's guess. If it falters, Europe is likely to be left in the cold.

Ever since Reagan came to power, his administration has been concerned at the extent to which the structure of the American Army, geared almost exclusively to fighting a European war, has detracted from its ability to fight in areas elsewhere, a fact which was tellingly driven home by its lamentable performance in Grenada. The problem of fighting on two fronts at once is no nearer solution than it was ten years ago. The United States can still only fight a one front war. The *Pressure Point 84* exercise three years ago showed that, even if the United States Army in Korea had called on all America's NATO reserves and reduced its stockpiles in Europe to fifteen days supply, the conflict would still have ended in defeat or stalemate; there would have been no question of actually prevailing on the ground.

Reagan entered office pledged to restore America's power in the world at large as well as to narrow the gap between NATO and Warsaw Pact forces. The Defence Guidance Report of 1982, which outlined military planning for the next five years ranked the Gulf second only to the defence of Western Europe. In the event, Europe was fortunate that Washington decided to commit the 24th Mechanised Division to the Rapid Deployment Force, reallocating a division from Pacific Command, rather than from NATO.

The Alliance cannot be happy, however, that of all the Services the one that has done least well out of Reagan's rearmament programme has been the Army; that it has continued to receive a smaller share of the budget than the other two (twenty four per cent), that it has not been given an additional 200,000 men, although the Navy has achieved its total of 600 ships, and the Air Force received the extra air wings it was promised. With only 781,000 men, and a large proportion of its funds swallowed up by the costs of hardware and personnel, the Army has to perform so many roles and missions that its commitment to NATO has inevitably come into question. What has actually happened is what Pierre Hassner in a different context has called "the relativisation of NATO" in American strategic planning, a trend which was already under way when Reagan came to power.[6]

The manpower problem is perhaps the clearest evidence of this phenomenon, a problem which must cast doubt on the administration's claim that the United States is a stronger European power than it was four years ago. As a Congressional report recently discovered, since the RDF might have to call on as many as 440,000 men in a war, and since the Armed Forces have not increased in number, the conventional balance between NATO and the Warsaw Pact might be weakened in the event of a two front conflict by as much as twelve per cent within the first two months. Its conclusion was that the balance could only be redressed by adding four more divisions to America's All Volunteer Force at a combined cost of $37.8 billion.[7] No administration is likely to find such funds in the future. The report also concluded that the existing situation is not much better. Even if the RDF remained at its present force strength and drew upon fewer reserves committed to Europe, the force levels at NATO's disposal would still be twenty per cent under strength.

The airlift problem must also raise doubts about the credibility of America's real commitment to the defence of Europe. A 1982 study found that its capacity to airlift forces to Europe was eighty per cent short of the optimal amount. Even a bare bones supply to the Middle East and European theatres simultaneously would still require fifty-eight per cent more lift than the United States could provide.[8]

In the light of these deficiencies, future United States administrations, especially, those with links to the military reform movement, will have no option but to make the best of a bad situation by adopting new tactical doctrines, not entirely removed from the principle of conventional deterrence. Some observers will see this as a sensible and long overdue recognition of the realities of modern warfare; others as a shallow rationalisation of structural deficiencies which might have been corrected, a transparent political exercise intended to reaffirm a conventional commitment which is no longer very credible. It can also be argued, of course, that even if the new tactical doctrines are sound, the United States Army is unfortunately no better equipped than it was under Carter to execute them effectively.

Under the present administration, the Army has already begun to think of restructuring its European forces, not around the immensely costly MI tank which has fallen far short of its original specifications[9] but around armoured attack helicopters such as the AH 64 Cobra. Is it wiser for the United States to continue supporting its NATO allies with forces that it can neither reinforce nor sustain, or to design a more modern force that can get where it is needed as soon as possible?

The trouble is that the very flexibility of the new forces means that they might at any time be reassigned to a (secondary) theatre, where they might also become the mainstay of American operations. The MI tank would be useless in the Middle East, and even Korea. The two new light infantry divisions which the United States is planning to bring into service in Europe would be more useful in a different terrain altogether where they would better be able to perform the role for which light infantry forces are designed: for short, pre-emptive surgical operations such as the invasion of Grenada, not participation in a heavy armoured war of attrition. They may well be capable of being airlifted to Europe in a third of the time it would take to lift a heavy armoured division, but speed is hardly the only criterion for restructuring one's forces.

With its Airland Battle doctrine, the Army has, at last, redefined its operational concepts to take account of its weakness in numbers. Even without the manpower crisis, of course, the realisation during the Vietnam war that the United States had become too dependent on firepower and attrition would probably have turned the minds of the Army chiefs to manoeuvre oriented doctrines eventually. The Airland Battle 2000 paper published in August 1982 argued that, by exploiting the enemy's vulnerabilities – particularly its predictable echelonment of forces and rigid command and control system, the United States could win not only the first battle but also the last.

At the moment, however, the practical application of the concept is many years off, while the means to execute it remain as elusive today as they did when President Reagan came to power. A recent Congressional study found grave deficiencies in the communications equipment of the Seventh Army upon which it would rely to identify breakthrough points. It found even graver deficiencies in its wartime intelligence units (CEWI) on which it would have to rely to determine movements behind enemy lines by the second echelon forces.[10]

Intelligence deficiencies apart, the United States does not have enough reserves to execute an Airland Battle campaign. At present, American commanders in the field would rightly be reluctant to embark on dangerous envelopment manoeuvres and counter-attacks with the existing force strengths at their disposal. In an attempt to overcome this problem, the Defence Department tried to re-shape the Army's divisional structure by providing one support battalion for each brigade. But the Army would find it difficult to shift brigades from one divisional area to another without losing combat support, a danger which first became apparent in the "Reforger" exercises of 1982.

If the realisation of Airland Battle is still some years off, the Europeans are intensely sceptical of this practical (if not necessarily pragmatic) approach to the problem of conventional deterrence. The vision of changing dramatically NATO's ability to defend Europe by enhancing technologies, which are for the most part already in use, may have a superficial attraction. NATO does, after all, have a lead (though not a commanding one) in the micro-miniaturisation of highly sophisticated sensor and guidance systems on which Airland Battle, would rely to neutralise or destroy enemy forces before they have arrived on the battlefield. But the Europeans, while drifting towards conventional deterrence, are also drifting towards non-provocative defence as well.

When Reagan passes from the scene, the military reform programme will probably push ahead with the programme, oblivious to Dean Inge's observation that there are two kinds of fallacy: the fallacy of believing that because things are old they must be good; and the fallacy of believing because they are new they must be better. For however much money the United States may invest between now and 1995 in modern conventional weapons, to gain the confidence to dispense with battlefield nuclear weapons entirely, it will run up against the paradox that an effective denial strategy might actually lower the nuclear threshold for the Soviet Union and force it to reconsider *its own* policy of "no-first use".

While there seems little doubt that the Soviet Union would prefer to prevail without resorting to nuclear weapons, prevail it must. Until recently it was able to rest assured that its tank force was not threatened by air, that only five per cent might be destroyed by aircraft, ten per cent at most, a strikingly small number given the experience of the last war.[11] Now the Americans believe that NATO has it within its grasp to reduce the tank to its old role as an infantry support vehicle; to offset the Soviet Union's advantage in tanks; if not turn back a blitzkrieg attack, certainly blunt it, to make it difficult for the enemy to meet the trade-off between armour and mobility without which present Soviet strategy is unlikely to be very convincing. The report of the European Security Study in 1983 believed that the Alliance could destroy sixty per cent of a Soviet armoured division, the Soviet criterion of "annihilation", by conventional means using the latest submunitions. At the moment, it could only achieve such a target by launching 2200 sorties by conventional aircraft with 250 kilogramme unguided bombs, or twenty-five sorties using ten kilotonne nuclear weapons.[12]

The problem is that faced with such cost the Russians might well feel constrained to revert to an earlier doctrine of carrying out pre-emptive nuclear strikes against militarily-significant targets in the belief that a nuclear response from NATO could be contained and the subsequent defence of Western Europe rendered impossible.

As a concept there is much to be said in favour of attempting to reduce an attacking force by delaying the movement of reserves to the battlefield as the Allies successfully did in Normandy. But the two questions NATO will have to resolve are whether it should give a high priority to this mission, and whether the technology is worth the expense.

If NATO cannot hold the first echelon attack, the rest ceases to have much relevance. The BAOR is not convinced of the wisdom of the American argument. As the former Minister for Defence Procurement Geoffrey Pattie remarked in 1984 there is *"little merit in annihilating the Soviet second echelon at the risk of bringing NATO's early defeat by the first."*[13]

Fearful of being overwhelmed by an initial Western defence, the Soviet military seem to have significantly downgraded the strategic importance of their reserves, focussing their energies instead on the creation of Operational Manoeuvre Groups (OMG), twenty or thirty in all, powerful enough to punch a gap in NATO's defences. Blitzkrieg of the past may already have been reassessed; but its psychological impact still seems to be highly valued by a military establishment that is convinced that it need only prevail in the opening days to paralyse NATO altogether, or certainly render it incapable of a nuclear response.

Should NATO further strengthen its direct defences to hold out against a reinforced attack, or should it try to prevent the second echelon from ever reaching the front? In an attempt to save money on the first, the Americans are almost certain to place their faith in new technologies that still have to be tried and tested. Seven years ago, long before Airland Battle was conceived, Dan Smith talked of NATO's eternal quest for *"technological submission"*, its perpetual hope of using technological advances to reduce the requirements for manpower.[14] Such a quest may prove the Alliance's undoing if it decides to invest more in indirect defences than improved mobilisation and sustainability in conflict.

Unfortunately, however compelling the arguments against the new technologies may be (and they are compelling only at the moment) the Americans are unlikely to be convinced. To expect the Seventh Army to rely as it has for thirty-five years on a defensive strategy requiring sustained combat is probably to expect too much. Its inadequacies in this field have a long history. They first came to light in the Hollingsworth Report, then in the NATO flexibility studies which prompted the then Supreme Allied Commander Europe (SACEUR) Alexander Haig to devise a programme of short term measures to improve readiness, reinforcement and rationalisation, and finally, in the more widely publicised Nunn-Bartlett Report, whose findings had an impact well in advance of its publication.

Despite these studies and the present administration's efforts, the situation today is still pretty lamentable. Many units would still suffer significant shortages of equipment in combat operations while many more reinforcing units have been stripped of their equipment altogether. The Army National Guard units assigned to Europe have only eighty-nine per cent of their wartime equipment; the US Army Reserve less than forty per cent. Because of shortages in active army units and the slow growth of the Individual Ready Reserve (IRS) it has been estimated that full mobilisation would produce a shortfall of 120,000 trained men.

In Europe itself, spare part shortages are acute, not only for equipment which has long been in use, but also for new models such as the MI tank. The M60A3 tank has insufficient spare parts for its fire control system. Replacement units for the AH64 helicopter are not stocked at the direct maintenance level, with the ironical result that it could become, not a combat craft at all, but merely a very expensive observation helicopter.

While the Army has attained its personnel recruitment goals, most combat units are still critically short of manpower. Officer and NCO shortages have resulted in unmanned squads, neglected maintenance and indifferent performance – a liturgy of complaints familiar from the Carter years. In August 1982 the 82nd Airborne Division fell to its lowest operational strength since 1971. American combat units have only ninety per cent of their authorised NCO strength.

In short, despite a huge military build-up, there are twenty-five per cent fewer Army units ready for combat than there were in 1980. A similar problem afflicts the United States Air Force. The number of Air Force units considered "fully or substantially combat ready" has declined in the last seven years by more than fifteen per cent. Readiness has not increased because the Administration has invested too much in too many roles. A senior American NATO commander told a Congressional Committee in 1982 that flying hours were well below the level at which he could feel confident. Whenever flying hours have increased, the USAF has tended to use up expensive spare parts faster than they can be replaced.[15]

The Seventh Army, in short, seems no better prepared to fight or sustain a European war than it was in 1980; only appearances have changed. The political consequences of this development could well come to a head over the next five years. If NATO continues to lose its primary importance to the United States, relative to other commitments, if despite the Reagan defence programmes the United States Army cannot restore public confidence in its effectiveness, the Congress is likely to insist on much higher defence spending by America's allies.

In retrospect, it is remarkable that Reagan has kept the critics at bay so long. The criticism that the Europeans have not done enough to justify the continued deployment of the Seventh Army has run like a *leitmotif* through much of American reporting. In 1982, in *The Wall St Journal*, Paul Seabury suggested that the mere possibility of a US withdrawal would compel the Europeans to decide once and for all "*where they stand*". In *The Washington Post*, one of the architects of the military reform movement, Jeffrey Record, a one time staffer for Samuel Nunn, argued that it was "*impossible to justify the deployment of (US ground forces) on behalf of rich, indolent allies . . .*".[16] That veteran neoconservative, Irving Kristol, has suggested repeatedly that "*there is no active public opinion in favour of keeping the troops in Europe, only public passivity before a long standing commitment.*"[17]

The criticism comes not only from conservatives. Even liberal Democrats, including the former Presidential aspirant Eugene McCarthy, are of the opinion that the United States, in the strict sense of the word has "*few, if any, true allies*", only clients that it maintains at immense cost to itself.[18] The thoughts of many Americans are turning increasingly to unilateralism (not isolationism), with some seeking complete pull out of American forces, like Maxwell Taylor who thirty years ago opposed just such a policy when he was Chairman of the Joint Chiefs of Staff,[19] and others deriding the Europeans as "free riders" who have not only lost confidence in the United States but also in themselves,[20] a view that was endorsed by Sen Levin, who was responsible for initiating the annual Pentagon reports on the effectiveness of the European contribution to NATO.[21]

The anti-European voices in Congress are becoming louder every year. Many Congressmen have become convinced that the Europeans have seized upon nuclear deterrence as a marvellous excuse for not increasing conventional spending. In 1983, the very year that Cruise and Pershing missiles began to be deployed, Congress blocked funds for the modernisation of the 155mm nuclear shell – the first time it had ever refused to finance a NATO ammunition system. At the same time, the Senate insisted that the new Joint Tactical Missile for the United States should not be deployed in Europe in a nuclear role.

Unfortunately, any coincidence of interest which might arise in the future from Congress' reluctance to upgrade battlefield nuclear weapons and a Labour Government's unilateral decision to remove them is likely to be offset by an unseemly squabble over tactical doctrines. For the military reform movement's understanding of conventional deterrence differs markedly from that of the European Left. Any serious attempt to push ahead with Airland Battle 2000 (which would require nuclear or chemical attacks) or Airland Battle which would not, would be seen as provocative in intent, and destabilising in its results. Indeed, it might even be seized upon as evidence that the United States is actually planning for a war it no longer believes it can deter, but which it no longer intends fighting with nuclear weapons.

In Germany, the Peace Movement has already begun to focus attention on the new conventional doctrines now that the Cruise debate has been fought and lost. The disruption of military convoys and radio traffic by 10,000 protesters during NATO's *Lionheart* exercise, the largest in forty years, together with similar demonstrations against combined American-West German manoeuvres in the Fulda Gap, may be pointers to the future. If the Americans were to attempt to force the Alliance to adopt tactics which appeared to make it an offensive, rather than a defensive alliance, then much of the public support on which NATO was able to count on at the height of the Cruise debate might fast erode. The Labour Party has already condemned Airland Battle for its "blitzkrieg" tactics and come out forcefully against the emerging technologies up on which it relies.[22]

As E. P. Thompson in his role as President of the European Nuclear Disarmament Group wrote in *New Society* in 1984:

"The conventional weapons of the First and Second World Wars were hideous and their "modernised" successors will be hideous in the extreme. It is no longer sufficient to clamour for nuclear disarmament. If European nations should go to war the distinction between nuclear and conventional will soon be lost. We must enlarge our objectives: we must work to disallow any kind of recourse to war." [23]

If conventional defence too seems to have no future, the United States will find it increasingly difficult to justify tying down 320,000 American troops in Europe to fight a war that cannot be won, or to provide a nuclear tripwire that the Europeans no longer seem to find reassuring. In Europe, as elsewhere in the world, American power largely turns on the attitudes and assistance of its allies. Because nothing in the Reagan administration's increased defence spending has changed that central reality, the next few years may see the dawning of the Pacific age much faster than might otherwise have been the case.

People have been predicting the dawn of the Pacific age, of course, since the century began. As early as 1898 W. T. Stead wrote to Lord Morley that the centre of the English speaking world was shifting westwards. [24] In the 1920s and 1930s America's first priority was very much the Pacific; even during the war the Pacific First strategy, though strictly denied, was attested to by British military observers in Washington. If Britain had been capable of containing Soviet influence in Europe, the United States intended to focus its attentions almost exclusively on the Pacific. [25] Only the collapse of British power forced it to think again.

Marshall's Atlantic Union, Herter's Atlantic Community, Kennedy's Atlantic partnership, may be seen by historians of the future as a brief *entr'acte*, an interlude during which the stage was set for a different play, even if the same set of actors, the two Superpowers, may still play a leading part. If Roosevelt in 1944 was ahead of his times, Herter was certainly behind them. [26]

The most perspicacious of American geo-politicians Brooks Adams, though living at the same time as the most famous, Thayer Mahan, clearly foresaw that the centre of world politics would move to the Pacific, and that the United States could not escape its consequences. Adams wrote two books *The Law of Civilisation and Decay* and *America's Economic Supremacy*. The second ignored Japan; the first believed that the United States would only be threatened by economic competition. His predictions almost came true. Ironically, he thought that the United States would lose its Atlantic markets only to capture those of the Far East:

"Our geographical position, our wealth and our energy predominantly fit us to enter into the development of Eastern Asia and to reduce it to a part of our economic system..." [27]

If events have not quite come out as Adams expected, he accurately predicted the move of American trade from the Atlantic to the Pacific Basin. Since 1978 America's trade with the Pacific has been greater than its trade with Europe. In 1982 the difference amounted to $13 billion. Although America incurred an overall deficit, after Canada, Japan is nevertheless the second largest purchaser of American goods.

At this stage in the story it is difficult to see what this may mean for America's links with Europe, but there seems no doubt that they will gradually diminish. Addressing this theme a few years ago, the American Under Secretary of State, Lawrence Eagleberger, confirmed that the United States would have to begin establishing institutional links with the Pacific Basin countries quite soon. "*Those links will not be identical to those forged with our European friends, as they will reflect the differences in the relationship*",[28] an enigmatic aside which suggested that neither China nor Japan would probably wish to enter into the entangling military embrace which has characterised the post-war relationship between Europe and the United States.

Whether or not the Asians join forces with the United States, it is probable that America will feel the necessity to augment its military presence in the area to match that of the Soviet Union, as the latter power also turns east as well. Adams not only believed that East Asia would enter the American economic orbit, he also added "*that as these great struggles for supremacy sometimes involve an appeal to force, safety lies in being armed and organised against all emergencies.*"

As long as the United States continues to remain a Superpower, it will never be at peace. Conflict will remain part of its everyday experience, conflicts, of course, of a limited, preferably distant, kind. As Europe becomes increasingly preoccupied with its own interests, the Americans are unlikely to maintain a military presence until the end of the century if force reductions with the Soviet Union can be mutually agreed. The legions will be summoned home to fight other engagements, to defend interests perhaps of greater moment, or under more immediate threat. The exercise will be a necessary evil for those who believe the United States has no other option, a noble crusade for those who believe in the struggle against communism (if that too has much more of a future), tragic of course for those, American soldiers and enemies alike, who have not yet learned to ask the reason why.

Gorbachev, the Soviet Union and Eastern Europe

"*West Germany has nothing to gain by a having as a neighbour a bloodless East Germany on the verge of collapse because it is being sapped of its vital forces. On the contrary, what it ought to want is a prosperous state that bears it no grudges; with whom it is possible to negotiate and reach an understanding. It is entirely up to the East German leaders to make their country a paradise of freedom and well being where even the West Germans dream of going to live*... (Michel Tournier *Gemini* (London: Methuen 1981) p. 418)

When the West embarked upon détente in the early 1970s, it never spelled out what it expected of the Soviet Union, except in terms so general as to be largely meaningless. The same may come of Gorbachev's reform programme to which the Labour and Alliance parties attach so much importance. They may well be disappointed if they imagine the reforms will be substantial enough, or introduced fast enough, to make a decisive change in our perceptions of the Soviet state, and thus our need for perpetual vigilance.

The emergence of Gorbachev, though long predicted, has left many observers of the political scene in this country deeply divided. There are some who see him as a bold new statesman, a morally courageous *provocateur* posing questions which others have been afraid to ask, an embattled Cassandra trying to save his country from economic sclerosis and political decline. There are others who see the new regime as a revision, not a rejection of the old, still Marxist-Leninist to the core, even if it has eschewed some of the outworn rhetoric. It may have abandoned the trumpery of Marxism, but not its values. Finally, there are those who believe that, in attempting to achieve reform, the degree of efficiency to which he aspires, Gorbachev will run up against obstacles of every kind – party *apparatchiks*, defending entrenched privileges, the inertia and corruption of officials, the sullen reluctance of the Soviet people. If he attempts to impose discipline on a society which is deaf to his message he may symbolise in his person, the capricious and arbitrary power of the Soviet State.

As always, the truth probably lies somewhere in between. Gorbachev will remain a man of the system, always and unmistakably. For all his breadth of vision, he will be unable to escape his origins as a party *apparatchik* (albeit of a rather novel kind). What he has so far offered is a new tone, a new imagery and a new rhetoric, not new policies, or none that have fundamentally changed the Soviet system.

His tone is matter of fact, at times angry and bitter at wasted opportunities and tests that were never taken. He has been outspoken in his criticism of Brezhnev, and those around him (most of whom at the higher level of the regime have already been despatched into early retirement). His imagery is the true naming of what went wrong in the 1970s, work without productivity, foreign adventures which yielded nothing, military expenditure which increased to no particular purpose. His language is that of the KGB, stripped of the old Soviet neologisms reduced to the plainness of fact. The old stock phrases which served the Soviet Union for sixty years, "*party mindedness*", "*moral political unity*", and "*adherence to Marxism – Leninism*" have been replaced by such phrases as "*businesslike efficiency*", "*eradication of red tape*", "*openness (glasnost)*", and "*social dynamism*". The new vocabulary is a sign that the leadership wants to move away from the ideological stagnation of the 1960s into the twenty-first century as a modern, effective state.

It would be wishful thinking, however, to think that the system will substantially change. The leading role of the party, and the Central Committee, the nationalisation of industry, collectivised farming, the state planning system are likely to remain. Even if he wished otherwise, Gorbachev would be unable to introduce any fundamental changes. It will take a long time for the Gorbachev generation to come of age, and when it does it may be little different from its predecessors. Its members may be technocrats perhaps, not bureaucrats, with bold ideas, and novel methods but they will continue to work within a centrally planned economy, within a state administration which in the economic field alone employs no less than fifteen million public servants.

Gorbachev knows that if economic reform is to be pursued, he will have to reduce the bureaucracy, introduce greater initiatives for state-owned enterprises, and provide economic incentives for the rest. His main task will be to change the burdensome structure of state economic management in the face of relentless opposition from all but a small minority who have the confidence to do well in a decentralised system, without having to rely on the power and privileges which they are guaranteed as long as the present system remains unchanged.

No-one should minimise the task confronting the new leadership. It needs to reverse the economic decline by the end of the decade, restoring the pre-Brezhnev rate of growth to five point five per cent by 1990. If it fails, Soviet industry will face critical shortages at the very moment that it will need to re-tool for the next generation of weapons. Fortunately for Gorbachev, Brezhnev gave the defence sector such a high priority that "*almost all of the production capacity to support current defence procurement plans for the next six years is already in place*" according to the United States Defence Intelligence Agency.[29] So far the military can continue producing its MiG 23s, SU 27 fighters and T80 tanks at the same rate as before. The crunch will come in the early 1990s

If the growth rate does not pick up, Gorbachev will have more than a restive military to think about. General disillusionment would undermine his entire campaign to increase worker productivity without lessening central control. The failure to reform the system would dampen the expectations of a new generation that expect to be its chief beneficiaries. If Gorbachev himself came to be seen as a spent political force, a victim of the system from which he rose to prominence, resentment could express itself in student protests and regional riots which would immediately put in jeopardy the relationship with the KGB upon which the reform programme largely turns.

The KGB wanted the regime to be modernised. It was appalled at the extent of corruption within all reaches of Soviet society, embarrassed at international contempt for the gerontocracy which ran the Soviet state, angered by the apparently relentless growth of military influence in the Politburo and Central Committee. The military has been demoted. Its chief representative, Defence Minister Marshal Sokolov is a political cypher, the original No. 4 not No. 2 in the Armed Forces, a man who has been denied the Politburo seats held by his immediate, and more imposing predecessors Andrei Grechko and Dmitri Ustinov. Yet the alignment with the KGB is a febrile one, a tactical partnership motivated by coincidence of interest, not a common vision. The KGB wants to reform the system, not change it. If the result of Gorbachev's more radical proposals is political unrest and social instability, the reforms may come to an end. How great an impact a reversal of policies would have on the West is a matter for speculation.

It is in an attempt to reduce military spending in the future, and win West European (if not American) support that Gorbachev has embarked on a foreign policy of retrenchment – one which, while vigorously defending Soviet interests, expects fewer resources to be expended in their defence. *"We require a radical break with traditions of political thinking"* Gorbachev announced in a keynote speech in Vladivostok *"with problems of war and peace... and on international security."* He even went on to denounce *"the egotistical attempt to strengthen* [Soviet] *security at someone else's expense"*. Advocating mutual security, Gorbachev now argues that the Soviet Union can only be secure if its adversaries feel secure as well.

Fifteen years ago, Henry Kissinger defended détente on the understanding that since absolute security for any one nation meant total insecurity for the other, only through mutual insecurity could two countries ever hope to reach agreement. Gorbachev's updated form of détente – less a grand strategy than a pragmatic adjustment – does not seem to accept that premise. His objectives are somewhat different. His attempts at summitry, together with the endless series of arms control proposals he has put forward, seem designed to divide the Western Alliance by holding out the prospect of a security partnership with Western Europe, not the United States.

The Soviet Union, of course, has not entirely abandoned hope that deals can still be done with the United States, that an arms control agreement can still be reached, that under a different administration there may even be the possibility of an agreement to disagree on certain fundamentals, and to respect those differences of interest. But since 1982, commentators with a deep knowledge of the United States, such as Georgi Arbatov and Alexander Bovin have been arguing that greater stress be placed on Western Europe as the weak link in the chain. The new approach is a simple one" *We have one common European house with two entrances, but that should not be an obstacle.*" The attempts to find common accord between COMECON and the European Community, Mrs Thatcher's visit to Moscow, the increased emphasis on the reduction of conventional troops in which the Europeans themselves will be expected to play a role are all attempts to deal with Europe directly.

It is too early to say whether a British Government would take advantage of the situation, or not. Gorbachev's own standing in the West is likely to be tested quite soon by changes in Eastern Europe which, from a strictly

European standpoint, may weigh more heavily in London's mind than Washington's. What happens in Eastern Europe between now and the mid-1990s may largely determine whether there is likely to be much chance of a security partnership of the kind the Soviet leadership seems to be seeking.

Reforms in Eastern Europe are almost certainly likely to follow once Gorbachev has established his position. Yet the situation in Eastern Europe is very different from that in the USSR. Reforms will have to be "controlled". A disciplinarian at home, Gorbachev will demand discipline from the East Europeans as well. The East European leaders will have to ensure that liberalisation does not degenerate into insubordination, or that the Warsaw Pact fragments under the strain. Effective membership of the Pact and control by the Party will remain the essential *sine qua non* of Soviet policy.

Unfortunately for Moscow, a succession crisis could rapidly undermine the Soviet Union's position and with it Gorbachev's authority as well.

Gorbachev will have to move over the next five years to appoint his own people to the main European positions of control. Western political observers frequently label East European politicians as "Stalinists", "hardliners", "moderates" or "liberals". The description is valueless. Liberals return to conservative thinking when necessity dictates, conservatives become liberals. Everything depends on who is in power in Moscow. Gustav Husak in Czechoslovakia was once a nationalist before 1968 when he became a firm advocate of "democratic centralism", the accepted Soviet model. Stefan Olszowski was a reformist prior to becoming one of Poland's leading hardliners. Their messages merely change with the interests of their Soviet constituencies.

Soviet control today is much less intrusive than it used to be. Until Dubcek took over as First Secretary, it was common practise in Czechoslovakia for the Soviet Union to approve beforehand not only the candidacy of Central Committee members but also the leading Secretaries in Regional Party Committees as well[30]. Brezhnev exercised much less direct control than any of his predecessors; in a sense he was more easy going, certainly more cautious. Even so, during his long reign he replaced three out of the five East European leaders, coming to terms with Kadar (Hungary) and Zhikov (Bulgaria), not because they were Brezhnevites, but because they were indispensable. Ulbricht was the most notable casualty; he returned from an official visit to the Soviet Union to find he had been sacked *in absentia* because of his opposition to Ostpolitik and the MBFR talks in Vienna.

The changes in Eastern Europe are likely to be as dramatic, and as unexpected, as Tsedenbal's dismissal in August 1984, a man who had been the faithful General Secretary of the Mongolian Communist Party for forty years. Interestingly, each successive cycle has had a distinct political content. Both 1953-7 and 1965-70 were periods of economic reform; they were followed by periods of economic stagnation. Eastern Europe urgently needs to reform if it is to overcome latent economic decline which, at any moment, might trigger off the type of political disturbances which brought about Gierek's fall from power in Poland in August 1980, and with it the ever threatening prospect of Soviet intervention. Such an outcome might destroy, once and for all, Gorbachev's credibility in the West as a "liberal" reformist leader.

The Soviet Union may consider itself relatively disadvantaged economically; its Warsaw Pact allies are considerably worse off. Even though they may possess a much higher per capita income than most developing countries, the difference is actually not that substantial. If we omit the thirty least developed countries, per capita income differences amount to a ratio of four to one. These differences are certainly considerable but they are not as great as those between the countries of the Third World and the Western industrialised economies.

As the East Europeans have come to recognise the enduring nature of their own economic crisis, they have begun to realise that with the exception of the GDR and Hungary their economic problems are very similar to those of the Third World. Poland in particular now relies on subsidies from its Soviet bloc associates, particularly Hungary which in 1981 agreed to reschedule a twenty-five million transferable rouble debt and to treat extra deliveries after the imposition of martial law as "Aid". Czechoslovakia agreed to speed up the planned delivery of goods even if Warsaw defaulted on its contractual export obligations.

Several socialist countries suffer from debt problems almost as serious as those which afflict the more vulnerable economies of the Third World. In November 1981 the IMF stopped disbursing funds to Romania from a standby credit of almost $1.5 billion. By that time the country's net debt to the West was $9.6 billion, twelve per cent of an estimated net debt of $80 billion owed by the Socialist Bloc as a whole. For some years now, the East Europeans have only been able to service their existing debt by borrowing even more from Western capital markets. At the beginning of 1982 COMECON needed $25 billion to pay for supplies from Japan and Western Europe.[31]

Whichever way the East Europeans will turn to escape from a poverty trap of their own making they will run grave political risks. If they reform and go for greater incentives and worker differentials they might begin to *"broaden the base of the revolution"*, an acceptable compromise in a country like Afghanistan, quite unacceptable even in Hungary. Reforms may be necessary, but they carry a far greater political risk politically than they do in the Soviet Union, where the power of the State is much greater, and the population more apathetic, or trusting of its leaders.

The economic situation also has major implications for defence. Sixty per cent of the Warsaw Pact's ground forces are made up of East European troops, a significant number. Despite the economic recession, despite the

Pact's refusal to complement NATO's Long Term Modernisation Programme (1978) in any but defensive systems, despite its refusal to match NATO's three per cent real increase in 1977, defence spending as a percentage of GDP has remained constant since 1970. Despite a declining economy, the defence burden has increased in every country except Romania.

The Pact has only succeeded in carrying this additional burden by squeezing personnel costs, indeed halving them in the case of Hungary and Bulgaria between 1965–85. By comparison, expenditure on R & D has grown extraordinarily rapidly. It is difficult to see how the Pact can maintain this situation much longer. Conscripts pay could hardly be lower. Reducing officers' salaries might be politically dangerous, not only in Poland, where the regime relies on military support, but also in Bulgaria which almost experienced a military coup twenty years ago. On the other hand, any substantial reduction of defence expenditure would be unacceptable to Moscow at a time when it is trying to reduce its own military costs. The only solution seems to be Mutually Balanced Force Reductions along the lines which have been discussed to very little purpose in Vienna since 1968.

Substantial progress in the MBFR talks would solve two problems at once. It would ease the burden on the East European Allies, and lessen the likelihood of a major political crisis which would force the Soviet Union to intervene. In the past, such actions have resulted in increased force levels in Western Europe, Britain being a notable case in point. In 1961 the rundown in the BAOR was stopped by the Berlin crisis; the Army did not drop from 87,000 to 45,000 men as planned but was pegged at the number deployed today. In 1968, the Czech crisis did not stop the redeployment of one of the Army's six brigades and the loss of one of RAF(G) bases at Geilenkirchen, but it did lead to a major re-equipment of the 2nd Allied Tactical Airforce. Two years later, the 6th Infantry Brigade was sent back.

The new leadership in the Kremlin seems quite sincere in its wish to reduce force levels in Europe, by upto fifty per cent according to a proposal first made in September 1984. Whether it will prove successful in carrying the West is a different matter. Its own proposals in the light of past experience are themselves quite disingenuous. At times it is difficult to assess what is more astonishing; the scope of its present proposals or the uncritical acceptance of them by those who should know better. Plausible though they may seem, they are far too sweeping and in some instances seem quite false.

Very often, data is not available, or meaningless. Even if this were not the case, NATO's demand for cuts in manpower would be irrelevant if the Pact restructured its units, giving them greater firepower. At times, the two sides have been living in totally different worlds, cocooned from each other's reality. In 1975, in a rare breakthrough in the MBFR talks, the Soviet Union, having previously refused an American offer to reduce its battlefield nuclear weapons in return for the withdrawal of a Soviet tank army, offered instead to phase out tactical nuclear missiles of its own. It has never been clear since the Soviet Union agreed to withdraw 20,000 soldiers from the GDR providing NATO decided not to upgrade its theatre nuclear forces whether the Russians have ever considered mutual force reductions useful in themselves, or only as a bargaining counter in nuclear diplomacy.

No-one should underestimate the difficulty both sides will meet in accomplishing their ends. Verification is still likely to prove a stumbling block, even though both sides have at last agreed to an exchange of information on troop strengths, mutual inspection, and the identification of exit and entrance points for the movement of troops. Differences, however, still remain over how the new rules should be applied or enforced. The West wants a more stringent regime, the Soviet Union a very lax one.

On the other hand, the Russians seem to have come near to conceding the principle that, in the first instance, their own forces together with those of the Americans will have to be reduced, that it is unreasonable to expect reductions to apply across the board to the West Europeans as well, in particular the Germans. Although, as recently as February 1985, the Soviet Union amended its proposal, so that national European forces would be dealt with in a second stage, this principle too could lead to a good deal of misunderstanding.

Finally, there is still fundamental disagreement on whether to go for armaments reductions in the first phase and manpower cuts in the second. The experience of the Soviet Union's unilateral reduction in 1980 was that it would prefer to withdraw its units with their equipment intact. That too will be a matter for further discussion.[32]

Even if the talks were to succeed, a British Government, intent on reducing the manpower strength of the Rhine Army, is unlikely to derive very much from an agreement, even if one is negotiated within the next five years. One of the members of the United States team who has had most experience of the Vienna talks has suggested that even if the two sides were to accept a ceiling of 700,000 ground troops over a five year period, negotiated over three stages, the reductions of non-American troops would be quite minimal – eleven point five per cent, which for BAOR would mean a reduction from 56,000 to 49,330 (a number still higher than Macmillan envisaged before the Berlin crisis of 1961).[32]

Such a reduction, while useful in itself, and possibly even stabilising to the military balance, would not contribute significantly to stability within Eastern Europe on which any further reductions by the Soviet Union would depend. In that respect, the much ridiculed diplomatic ivory tower at Vienna or Stockholm (to which the MBFR talks may be moved) offers not a shelter from the world, but a quiet eminence from which the diplomats can better view their own world with its own preconceptions. When one surveys nearly twenty years of diplomatic negotiation, it is clear that the diplomats should be seen not so much as lofty observers as political Simon Stylites, each aloft on his own pillar above the continually changing security scene, able to make very little sense of the confusion below.

Events in Eastern Europe and Soviet perceptions of change will determine whether or not Britain can adjust its force strengths to a more "appropriate" level. In that respect, Britain will have to await the outcome of circumstances which are not only beyond its control, but which at times seem often to be beyond its understanding.

Arms Control and Deterrence

"War makes rattling good future history, but deterrence is poor reading." The Third World War August 1985 (Sidgwick & Jackson 1978)

Confidence in the nuclear deterrent has been the touchstone of Alliance stability since the days of massive retaliation. The deployment of Cruise and Pershing 2 missiles in 1983 despite sustained anti-nuclear protest on the part of the Peace Movements of Western Europe, and a concerted Soviet policy of disinformation, seemed to be not only part of the continuity of the past, but to have confirmed the European governments in their resolution. NATO never seemed to have been stronger. Nothing could have been further from the truth.

Unfortunately, the full meaning of the Cruise debate escaped most European politicians. The deployment may have provided a transient satisfaction that the Alliance was in good repair, but it was clear that NATO could never go through the same crisis again. Mrs Thatcher believed that it marked a great victory for common sense over emotion; but the victory was contrived, a defeat disguised. True, the British Government may have stayed the course from start to finish; it may have shown extraordinary political courage, but Cruise was an American system, its deployment an American decision.[34] It did not take long for the United States to conclude that, if Labour came to power, the missiles would be sent packing.

Even without the constant threat of removal, the despairing prospect of a battle fought for nothing, the Reagan administration believed that the fruits of the victory were hardly worth the struggle. Neither Cruise nor Pershing 2 actually matched the SS 20 threat. The Soviet missile's greater range, together with that of the Backfire bomber, which was rarely mentioned in the debate, afforded both systems relative immunity. In 1979 the Pentagon had considered building a medium range ballistic missile (MRBM) which could have reached the SS 20 sites, but pressure from Congress forced the USAF to drop the item from its budget.

The choice of 572 missiles as well, had no military rationale. It was what SACEUR called a measure of "*political expediency*", the most the Europeans were willing to deploy. To have matched a much larger number of

MIRVed SS 20s, the United States should really have sent over three times the number.

In addition, the introduction of Cruise did nothing to redress the operational inflexibility of NATO which would probably have rendered them unusable. SACEUR had no authority to release them. The decision making process was cumbersome, the chain of command unreliable. Since the Soviet Union never wavered in its insistence that it would retaliate against the country that had installed the new missiles, as well as the state from which they were launched, it might have been more sensible not to have offered the Europeans dual key control of the new systems (which the British Government declined on the grounds of cost) but complete control since the Americans were probably never likely to have launched them. The idea of a purely European intermediate force might have represented a significant advance.

As it was by 1984, the year of Reagan's re-election, the legacy of bitterness, disunity and defeatism left by the Peace Movement's actions looked quite likely to keep the Alliance on the defensive for many years to come. In Europe, many observers congratulated themselves that the missiles had been deployed, that the crisis had been weathered, that the debate had disabused the Peace Movement of any lingering hopes that it could paralyse Governments or intimidate them.

In the United States, the lessons of the episode appeared to be very different. Hopes that the Europeans would assume greater responsibility for nuclear decision making fast evaporated. Only successful pressure from the United States could do that, and at what price? The Europeans had nothing else to offer, no higher defence expenditure (the four per cent increase in real terms asked for by General Rogers) to raise the nuclear threshold, no real acceptance even now of the need to co-operate more closely. The scars of the 1979–83 debate seem to have encouraged the administration to lower its sights even further, to find in a radical new deal with the Soviet Union a way of eliminating intermediate nuclear weapons altogether, in the hope of concentrating Europe's mind on conventional defence.

As it happened, the Soviet Union had never been opposed in principle to such a suggestion, for reasons that were self-evident. In October 1979, Brezhnev had offered to withdraw SS 20s unilaterally if Cruise and Pershing were not deployed. Later he proposed that arms control negotiations should start without delay. A similar offer by Andropov in 1983 suggested that, for once the Soviet Union might be persuaded to bargain away its decisive advantage in theatre nuclear forces.[35] By 1986 the two negotiating teams in Geneva finally reached an agreement that both sides would limit their respective forces to 100 Cruise/Pershing and SS 20s apiece; and that these too would be withdrawn at the end of ten years. On the United States' part this was an implicit recognition that Schmidt's call in 1977 to restore the theatre nuclear balance had actually failed; that the balance could only be restored by each side voluntarily disarming, even if this left a conventional imbalance that the Europeans found inescapably worrying.

At the Reykjavik summit (1986) the deal that was expected to be signed was lost sight of in an acrimonious discussion about SDI. Yet within months of the summit, the two superpowers went further by agreeing to discuss the complete elimination of intermediate forces, a process which may even be extended to include medium nuclear systems as well. In accepting the zero-zero option (the offer not to deploy Cruise if the SS 20s were withdrawn) the British Government implicitly associated itself with measures which a few years before would have been dismissed as the stock in trade of an administration whose passion for grand designs – the elimination of nuclear weapons from Europe – seemed to bear little if any relation to reality.

It would seem that, on this front at least, the United States is moving in the Labour Party's direction, perhaps from a different set of premises, but moving nonetheless. Sometimes summit meetings serve not so much to break new ground, as to throw light on trends previously obscured. In some circles it has become fashionable to describe American policy as disillusioned. With the passage of time, it seems more accurate to characterise it as a policy which, beginning with no illusions, may soon degenerate into one of general indifference.

A Labour Government is also likely to find America's position on strategic arms talks far more to its liking than a Conservative administration. Here too the United States seems to have completely lost interest in the original set of propositions with which it started out in 1981.

The Reagan administration came to power, after all, convinced that arms control had left the United States a hostage to fortune. The case it brought against the SALT 2 Treaty was not entirely unconvincing. Arms control could never be an end in itself, or an alternative to modernising America's strategic arsenal. The real threat to arms control came not from Reagan, but from his predecessors like Richard Nixon who told Congress after the signing of SALT 1 that the treaty was "*linked organically to a broad understanding on international conduct*", or President Carter who in his inaugural address announced that the objective of arms control was the elimination of all nuclear weapons from the earth.

Expecting more of the process than it could deliver, both men had, in different ways, blurred the distinction between arms control and disarmament. Reagan inherited the failure of arms control and merely returned to the past to redefine it. He promised a SALT 3 that would be both realistic and effective, a treaty that would be actually ratified because it would take note of the aspirations and anxieties of each side. Ironically, within a few years of his inauguration, he too was promising to bring the nuclear era to an end by deploying SDI; and within a few years of that offering a fifty per cent reduction in nuclear warheads as the first stage to the elimination of all nuclear weapons, an objective so unrealistic that the Europeans, the great advocates of arms control, began to see it as the greatest challenge the Alliance now faced.

The process began almost immediately after the SDI programme was announced. Concerned, perhaps over much so, that the programme might be deployed by the end of the century, the Soviet Union made a series of offers to persuade Washington to drop it altogether. There was no other way to interpret its moratorium on anti-satellite and nuclear weapons tests, its offer to reduce its MIRVed ICBM warheads to 3,600, as well as to accept a freeze of United States intermediate forces at (1985) levels of deployment.

As the months passed, the Russians continued to offer even sharper cuts in nuclear forces in return for an undertaking by the United States to extend the Anti-Ballistic Missile Treaty of 1970 by a further fifteen years, a measure which would have prevented the deployment, if not testing, of SDI systems. In June 1985 they offered a limit on strategic warheads of just over 6000 – nearly forty per cent below existing levels.

At the end of the month, in a speech in Glassboro, Reagan spoke of a *"turning point"* in the arms control talks. In a letter to Gorbachev in the following month, he offered not to deploy a space-based missile system for seven years in return for deep cuts in the nuclear arsenals of the two Superpowers. At Reykjavik the two sides agreed in principle to a fifty per cent reduction in all nuclear warheads, as an interim step towards their eventual elimination.

While a Labour government would be happy enough with such an outcome, a Conservative Government would clearly find it far from reassuring. In February, Sir Geoffrey Howe poured scorn on the vision of eliminating all ballistic missiles (the American version), or all strategic offensive systems (the preference of the Soviet Union). Neither idea he argued was realistic; neither promise would be believed by either side.[35] Even the President's own advisers had warned him at Rekyjavik that the margin of error in verifying compliance of the agreement, 100 warheads for every thousand, while unimportant at existing levels, might become critical once the arsenals had been reduced by fifty per cent.

Such misgivings have continued to be voiced in the United States, where both Henry Kissinger and President Ford's former National Security Adviser Brent Scowcroft have insisted that nothing less than eighty per cent cuts would assure either side of *"mutual security"*. If Moscow and Washington are seriously talking of reducing the number of warheads, the only way of proceeding towards such a goal must be the outlawing of MIRVed systems. As Kissinger confessed in his memoirs, his worst mistake had been to go for an ABM Treaty instead of an agreement to disallow the Superpowers from putting more than one warhead on each missile. Inevitably, the number of targets had increased exponentially to fit the number of warheads that could be deployed. Before MIRVing, the United States had considered it necessary only to threaten twenty-five per cent of the Soviet population with annihilation; after 1969 the figure rose to thirty-four. This was not deterrence, but war fighting; it was not a confession that a country could not survive a nuclear exchange, but a determination to prevail if a war ever broke out.

Clearly the two sides have a long way to go before they would ever agree to disinvent an untested but accepted technology any more than the United States would abandon a programme like SDI which may only work by reinventing the laws of physics. Both sides are a long way from the heady days of the Vladivostok summit (1974) when they actually trusted each other to limit the number of warheads to three per missile. Clearly, the two powers are not even in hailing distance of such an age. The emphasis these days is on verification, on cast iron guarantees, the idiom of a more hardheaded, less impressionable era. Strategic nuclear weapons at present levels may survive the 1980s. Any agreement to reduce warheads by half may collapse at any moment through deliberate or accidental misunderstanding, however eager an American President may be to press ahead with such an agreement.

More to the point, America's enthusiasm may only last as long as its own belief in SDI, which may or may not survive the passing of the Reagan administration. It was the French sociologist Raymond Aron who argued in *The Century of Total War* that what made modern conflicts different from those of the past was the element of "technical surprise". America's European allies were as much taken by surprise by Reagan's intention to press ahead with SDI as were the Russians, perhaps more so since the latter had had a programme of their own for some time.

In a speech in March 1985, Geoffrey Howe asked whether the new system would "*permit adequate political control over both nuclear weapons and defensive systems, or might we find ourselves in a situation where the peace of the world rested solely upon computers and automatic decision making*"? The following year Neil Kinnock launched a ferocious attack on the SDI system, claiming that it was not only a "*destabilising fantasy*", but a new phase in the arms race to which the Soviet Union would feel compelled to respond. The Star Wars programme, he claimed, was one of the greatest menaces to peace in any generation.

In the event, Mrs Thatcher's government has accepted SDI. A Labour Government never would. And yet, ironically, what explains its own dislike of deterrence, its very irrationality, also explains the President's belief in the programme. Both parties would like to live as if human existence was ordered, ethical and rational, to escape the present world in which the only certainty is that of mutual assured destruction should nuclear weapons ever be used. The promise of the SDI programme projects the same unconscious desire to escape into original innocence, a desire all the more powerful for being unrecognised. Both seem to find solace not in the fundamental violence of man but in his scope for freedom of choice. Both see the division of Europe as artificial and unnecessary; both believe that the Western world need not be imprinted with the code of self-annihilation.

Despite forty years of peace, despite everything we have learned and everything we know, both parties insist on trying to behave "rationally" even though the only metaphysical reason for doing so is the fear of annihilation itself. Kinnock believes in conventional deterrence; Reagan seems to yearn for an age in which war will once again have "rules" (as he confessed in a whimsical moment to Gorbachev at Reykjavik).[37] Both parties seem to find something ethically distasteful in the thought that since 1945: *"the rules of the game have been changed in a very significant way. No matter how violently a limited conventional war is being conducted... the combatants will probably be spending at least as much time worrying about the violence held in reserve as they are with the battle in hand."*[38]

If the next administration presses ahead with SDI, if a Labour Government insists on relying entirely on the promise of conventional deterrence, the very premise on which NATO is based will be brought into question. What both would be trying to do is to create their own reality, to substitute their own fictional representation for the world that exists at the moment. Their representation, alas, is likely to prove quite false. As Max Weber remarked in his essay "Politics as a Vocation":

> *The world is governed by demons, and he who lets himself in for... power and force as means, contracts with diabolical powers, and for his action it is not true that good can follow only from good and evil only from evil, but that often the opposite is true. Anyone who fails to see this is indeed a political infant."*

The European Option

The history of European defence co-operation has been such a long succession of failures from the collapse of the European Defence Community (EDC) in 1954 that one might, perhaps, be forgiven for writing off the past as an epilogue rather than prologue to the future but for the fact that European security is, once again, on the political agenda.

It is somewhat ironical that in this sphere, if no other, the British have actually been in the forefront of European initiatives. If the collapse of the European Defence Community owed something to British, as well as French intransigence, the British have been much less lukewarm in their commitment to a European role in NATO, even if they have never favoured a distinct European "identity". Indeed they were responsible for two major European organisations, the Western European Union (WEU) and the Eurogroup, which Dennis Healey set up in 1969, and which could only have emerged as a European security caucus by forfeiting their status as organisations "contractually linked" to NATO, an outcome which might have promised great French participation but one in which the United Kingdom has shown little, if any, interest.

In the context of defence procurement, however, the United Kingdom has never been especially receptive to collaboration with its European partners, compared for example with West Germany, seventy per cent of whose spending on arms has involved at least another European partner. The British percentage is less than twenty per cent, surprisingly so when one recalls that the 1970 Defence White Paper concluded that:

"There is only one way in which the European Allies can bear a fairer share without increasing their defence expenditure to an extent which none of them would regard as politically realistic in present circumstances: that is by co-operating more closely with one another."

As always, Britain has been a victim of its past. Immediately after the war, while German industry was being dismantled, the American war machine demobilised and Soviet production struggling to recover from the ravages of war, Britain may, for a brief moment, have had the strongest defence industry of any of the powers. Certainly, for the first few years, it was the largest exporter of military equipment and aircraft in the world. Even as late as 1953, its output was greater than the whole of Western Europe.

Old habits die hard; traditional attitudes survive much longer. It was not until fifteen years after the 1970 review that the country's economic circumstances finally forced it to give serious consideration to European procurement. It had no choice considering that it was suffering acutely from the threat of "structural disarmament", a phrase coined by Thomas Callaghan to describe what happens when a nation's defence budget plus exports provides too small a market to bring armament development and production costs down to a politically affordable level.[39] As early as the Plowden Report in 1965, the Government of the day recognised that if the aircraft industry was to survive, it would need a market far larger than the national base. Following the report's publication Britain did pursue European co-operation of a kind, but only on a project by project basis rather than on a continental scale.

The reasons for limited co-operation have never been entirely spurious, though they may well have been less than compelling. As a power still possessing a significant technological base, Britain has never wished to become simply a sub-contracting production agency for weapons designed by other countries. Different British Governments have also tended to question whether the actual savings derived from collaborative projects are actually as great as often claimed. A point in case is surely Tornado, the most expensive single procurement programme ever entered into by a British Government, more expensive than the projected costs of Trident. It also came into service long after it was due. As the number of parties in a programme increases so do associated management problems and inevitable delivery delays. Too often political considerations which made the Anglo-French Jaguar programme popular with the Government have made the Services less than enthusiastic in their support.

These reservations, notwithstanding, it looks inevitable that the United Kingdom will push ahead with European collaboration. The present ratio of research and development costs to profit, at least two to one (excluding spares) cannot be sustained much longer without bankrupting ourselves. Britain cannot continue to spend more than half its publicly funded R & D on defence. The writing on the wall this time is not a forgery; it is very real.

The only way savings might be made without European cost-saving arrangements would be to increase exports to the United States. In 1972 an official of the Ministry of Defence pointed out that any discrimination against defence purchases from the United States might lead to counter-discrimination against Europe.[40] Since Britain's penetration of the American market is the highest in Europe, the Ministry has always been sensitive to this threat. But even if British sales in relation to purchases are probably nearer 2.2:1 rather than 3.1:1 as official figures would suggest, the United States is not a captive market. Indeed at a time of unprecedented R & D in the private sector, the United States may not remain a secure market for much longer.

London's unqualified support for the Independent European Programme Group (IEPG) clearly reflects the fear of structural disarmament. Their joint experience in recent years seems finally to have convinced its members that the advantages of joint procurement are many – including improvement in efficiency, and a reduction in waste. Not all these objectives will be achieved in every case, but a beginning has been made in some which may itself ease the way for the others.

The IEPG may never be made accountable to the European Commission as the Klepsch report urged back in 1978, thereby establishing in the process a distinct European presence in NATO. But Britain's positive role at the November 1984 meeting surprised many who expected her to be less than enthusiastic in her support. Somewhat to her own surprise, Britain has become the IEPG's leading exponent.

In the future, the acid test of European intentions is likely to lie less with the traditional defence industries, such as the next generation helicopter on which Europe's four main manufacturers have still failed to agree than with the range of emerging technologies which promise to transform tomorrow's battlefield. 200 such systems were identified by the IEPG in April 1984. With Britain in the chair, the Eurogroup was able to agree that the Group would be the best forum for discussing ET, the only chance of escaping from Europe's impending "*industrial helotry*" which a British Prime Minister predicted twenty years ago.[41]

The French, who were not represented, begged to differ. They have long argued the merits of working through a completely new forum Eureka which is intended to give the European defence industry a competitive edge, and to make Europe itself far less dependent on American technology.

As long as the Conservatives remain in power, we can expect the British to remain suspicious of the entire programme. They have long expressed their doubts about the wisdom of protectionism to which the European Community has been moving steadily, if slowly, since 1983 when the French put forward the proposal that Europe needed to protect its high technology industries for at least five years, if only to allow them to reach international standards of competitiveness.

London's opposition to Europrotectionism may reflect a more pragmatic understanding of the desperately weak position in which European high technology now finds itself. Europe has only five per cent of the world market in integrated circuits; less than three per cent in computers. Production of the 256K memory chip, which has been in production in the United States and Japan for at least five years, only began last year.

Europe's vulnerability has been further aggravated because of the changing terms on which high technology goods are traded. American technology is no longer as readily available as it was in the past. The time when countries such as Japan could develop a semi-conductor industry with United States assistance and then break into the American market with such devastating effect may have passed. Most American electronics companies are no longer prepared to sell licenses to non-American firms unless they can enter into technology exchange agreements. The problem is that, in a growing number of areas, Europe no longer has much technology of its own to exchange.[42]

Like everyone else, the British have found themselves increasingly at risk. Even American companies passing into British ownership have been debarred from further work on projects that have already been initiated. British businessmen have found themselves frequently denied visas to attend conferences on sensor technology. Even when British and American companies have teamed up, they have been prevented from gaining access to American technology. In some cases, companies in the United Kingdom have been sent components for assembly prior to transmission back to the United States.[43]

Partly in recognition of these disturbing developments, Britain was the first country to sign a Memorandum of Understanding with the United States (1985) to allow British firms to tender for work in 18 different areas of SDI research. Of all the European powers the British clearly believed they were in the best position not only to take the lead, but keep it. They already had entered into another, much older Memorandum of Understanding concerning Pentagon procurement which placed British manufacturers on an equal footing with their American counterparts by relieving them of tariff barriers – a privilege British companies don't even enjoy in the European Community.

Over the years the special relationship has also produced some return, particularly in one of SDI's main areas, charged particle beam research, in which British and American scientists have both co-operated at Malvern.

Mrs Thatcher's Government was apparently convinced that the SDI programme might rely on British technology in areas in which Britain was
still the acknowledged world leader, such as ultra high speed optical computing.

Is she correct in that assessment? Will the United States ever give the
British project leadership in any part of the SDI programme, or will they be
left with individual research commissions which will have little if any
impact on the standing of European high technology? The evidence at the
moment suggests the British Government may have deceived itself, or at
least been over sanguine.

These fears are more frequently voiced by British industry than they are
by the British Government. At present the country's deficit in information
technology (imports less exports) has grown by a factor of ten in the past five
years. Some forecasts even suggest that imports may snatch three quarters of
the expected income from the domestic demand for electrical goods by the
mid-1990s.[44] The electronics industry, in particular believes its future
would be more assured if it received more money from Eureka (the
European scientific research programme) than if it were paid on a sub-
contractual basis by the United States.

If Britain's need for Eureka subsidies is real, why has the British
Government been reluctant to fund the programme? At a meeting in
Hanover in November 1985, Geoffrey Pattie, the Minister for Technology,
talked of the programme providing a "*sharp focus*" to European collaborative projects.[45] Nevertheless, the size of its secretariat, the limited scope of
its operations, even its links with the European Commission, have still to be
decided – until which time its efforts are likely to remain out of focus for
some years. It is significant, perhaps, that the British chose to describe
Eureka as a "*searchlight*" capable of identifying promising areas of collaboration, not in the words of the former French foreign Minister Roland
Dumas "*an accelerator*" between the drawing board and the market
place.[46]

It is concern for the market place which largely explains Britain's position.
True to its economic beliefs, the present government has taken the view
from the very beginning that the European governments main contribution
to high technology should be the dismantling of internal trade barriers rather
than the provision of subsidies. Inevitably, this rigidly market oriented
approach has been taken by some as further evidence of lack of enthusiasm,
a typical holding operation by a country whose commitment to Europe has
never been strong, whose belief in European co-operation can be measured
in terms of its singularly small contribution to the European Space Programme.

Such attitudes, while understandable, are over cynical, and probably
misinformed. The difference between Paris and London are genuine disa-
greements of principle. The French hope that Eureka will stimulate new

technologies; the British wish merely to tackle the problem from the demand end, to identify the sectors in which co-ordinated research may pay off exceptionally well.

As always, as in so many other areas in which defence figures prominently, French support remains largely unfulfilled. Its less than enthusiastic support for an open market in the Community at the Luxembourg summit in December 1985 finally persuaded the British to take part in the SDI programme on the understanding that there was nothing incompatible with participating in both projects.

If a Labour Government is returned, it will immediately withdraw from SDI; its commitment to Eureka is likely to remain rhetorical rather than real. It is unlikely that more money will be found for any of the technologies now under discussion, that Labour will see in Europe an escape from its own NATO dilemmas. But then Europe itself may share the same belief, if never explicitly stated.

For the IEPG initiative of November 1984, launched by the British, has not been the only attempt to promote European defence collaboration. Since 1982 the French have once again re-discovered the WEU, and its own special agency, the Standing Armaments Committee (SAC).

When the French first proposed resuscitating the institution, the British were distinctly sceptical. In 1975 the Labour Government, concluding that the Eurogroup was "*the best available means for developing greater European co-operation*", had gone on to ask the WEU Assembly to give the Eurogroup its fullest support, despite the existence of the Assembly's own Standing Armaments Committee.[47]

At the WEU's thirtieth anniversary meeting in Rome in October 1984, Mrs Thatcher's Government reiterated its overriding commitment to the IEPG. Indeed in a widely quoted address shortly before he left for the summit, Michael Heseltine argued that it would be absurd for the WEU to duplicate work that was already being performed adequately by other NATO bodies.[48] At Rome, the British were scathing in their criticism of the WEU, suggesting that the SAC should be disbanded altogether on the grounds that it was merely encroaching on work undertaken by the IEPG, a proposal which won only Dutch support. Their second proposal, that the two WEU committees, the SAC and the Armaments Control Agency, should be merged and turned into a think tank, met with no support at all.

Once again it is possible to represent both suggestions as gestures to be expected from a country whose support for the WEU had never been especially marked in the past. But on this occasion, at least, London had every reason to be suspicious of French support. For although the French Government had reluctantly agreed two years earlier that the SAC should be allowed to carry out studies in parallel with the IEPG without seeking the WEU Council's formal approval, the SAC had only been allowed to proceed on a case-by-case basis. Somewhat grudgingly, it allowed the SAC Secretariat to help the Committee on Scientific Questions assist in the production of a major report on high technology co-operation, without allowing it to collect any data from public sources.[49]

In the end, Britain's approach did not revolve around the competing claims to be taken seriously by the SAC and the IEPG, important though the respective claims undoubtedly were. The British remained intensely sceptical about the desirability of a specific European defence organisation in NATO which might give the European pillar of the Alliance greater substance, if not necessarily a specific identity of its own.

The British only agreed to go along with the reforms agreed in 1984, the reorganisation of the SAC, the attempt to make the Council more accountable to the Assembly, the suggestion that Foreign Ministers should meet twice a year in the WEU itself, in the hope of restoring something of their European image which had been tarnished, if not permanently damaged, by years of acrimonious debate over Britain's budget rebates in the European Community. They probably intended to convey a signal that they had no intention of missing yet another European bus. The revival of the WEU seemed, at last, to have provided the first opportunity in years for a trilateral initiative by Europe's three leading military powers, a chance to move away from the bilateral links between Britain and the United States, and France and West Germany. Ironically, the different interests of the three countries were revealed almost immediately, a fact which merely underscored what Heseltine had implicitly suspected, that there was no foundation at the moment on which a trilateral initiative could be based.

The WEU's revival, which ended almost as soon as it began, revealed that Germany's links with Washington were almost as important as Britain's, if not as close. At a meeting in May 1984, Mrs Thatcher and Chancellor Kohl had agreed to a cautious approach to reviving the WEU, arguing that it was far too early to talk of creating a specifically "European voice" on defence issues. For her part, Mrs Thatcher only consented to the WEU initiative at Fontainbleau the following month because she was persuaded that something had to be done to convince the United States Congress that the Europeans were pulling their weight. Unless the view to the contrary was fast corrected, she claimed *"the temptation will grow for America . . . to look towards interests outside Europe"*.[50]

In normal circumstances, American support would have been immediately forthcoming. The Americans have never been opposed in principle to greater European co-operation. Dulles indeed was only won over to the WEU as an alternative to the EDC in the mistaken belief that the Council's right to take decisions by a simple majority rather than unanimously would eventually transform it into a supranational body.[51] Almost twenty years later, during the final session of the Defence Planning Committee in 1973, the United States Defence Secretary, James Schlessinger, threw his full support behind the French Foreign Minister's attempts to revive the organisation, despite the fact that Jobert and Kissinger had clashed earlier in the year over their mutually exclusive understanding of Atlantic partnership.

Unfortunately, the latest French attempt happened to come at the worst possible moment; when the United States was trying to win European support for the President's Strategic Defence Initiative. In a letter from Richard Burt, the Assistant Secretary for European Affairs, following the first ever meeting of Foreign Office officials from the WEU countries, the United States advised its members not to attempt to reach a common position on arms control matters outside the NATO framework.[52] Since the Europeans had been at pains, publicly and privately, not to represent the WEU initiative as an anti-American gesture, they were bound to take Burt's warning to heart. Within a few days of the letter's receipt, the German Government agreed that the WEU was not an independent body, but *"contractually linked"* to NATO.[53] In April it supported the British interpretation that it would be some time before the European states would be able to take an independent position on SDI *"We are at the very beginning of a dialogue with the United States"* Heseltine maintained *"Until you have completed the dialogue, you cannot determine the extent of co-ordination."*[54]

By then, however, it was clear that the French too had begun to question the wisdom of reviving the WEU. They certainly appeared to be in no hurry to define what the three agencies which the Ministers had decided to establish (covering disarmament, security and defence, and armaments development) were actually intended to accomplish. By then, they too were worried about America's reaction. In a paper written by a leading French official, Francois Heisbourg, Paris was warned that Europe would need the best possible relations with the United States to dissuade it from weakening its commitment to Europe.[55]

In fact, the whole exercise seems to have had no other objective but to keep West Germany in the Atlantic fold, in order not to drive a wedge between Europe and America. Once Germany began deploying Cruise missiles in 1984, once the Peace Movement had clearly failed in its immediate purpose, the initiative lost its *raison d'etre*, and with it its momentum. The French subsequently turned to the more far-reaching project of European Union to keep the Germans firmly aligned with the West, a project which promised to bring together everything that had evolved outside the scope of the Treaty of Rome in the past fifteen years from foreign policy co-operation, to the European Monetary System (EMS) and last, but not least, European security policy.

Ever since 1985, the WEU has failed to fulfil its promise. Its budget is still derisory; far from being increased, as the Rome summit proposed, it has actually been cut in real terms. Contact between the Council and the Assembly has continued to remain limited; indeed the President of the Assembly was moved to express deep dismay about its lack of progress.[56]

Not only have the French stifled political expression by its members, they have created a political environment in which participation can have no meaning for the participants, other than the role playing to which one of its founding fathers, Mendes France, feared that the organisation might be reduced.

The fate of the WEU initiative must also cast doubt on David Owen's hopes of Anglo-French nuclear co-operation, as the first step to an all European deterrent. When Owen and Steel visited Paris before the SDP Party Conference they sounded out their hosts on the possibility of buying the M4 missile or the new M5, which they believed could be fitted into the launch tubes of the two submarines under construction by Vickers. Shared patrolling and targeting with the French would not require two control centres. Political control would still lie with London and Paris. The effect of this Alliance suggestion, like nearly everything else it suggests, was to stir a controversy rather than resolve a doubt.

If the Alliance were to support a Conservative minority Government after the election, the matter would be entirely academic. But it would be extremely problematic. The warheads which are being designed to fit the Trident missile would be ready to go into production in 1989. They would have to be redesigned to fit the French M5. Flight testing would also be required, as would a programme of underground tests, presumably using French facilities in the Pacific. Although this would not be particularly popular with many Tory MPs, the Government has begun to give serious consideration to an Anglo-French deterrent in the absence of any other European nuclear system such as Pershing or Cruise. As Sir Geoffrey Howe told the Brussels Institute of International Relations earlier this year, both countries would still have "*more than enough nuclear weapons to maintain that element of uncertainty about our reactions which is crucial to deterrence.*" If joint patrols were mounted with the French, only three Trident submarines would have to be built which would enable the Government to cut costs by twenty-five per cent and bring the force down to Polaris levels of a minimum deterrent.

After the Reykjavik summit, the Europeans seem to have accepted that the United States will expect them to take a far larger share of responsibility for their own defence. Co-operation between the two countries in the nuclear field has actually increased in the last two years though in what areas remains still unclear. But even were it to increase, it would require a great effort of political faith to believe that French co-operation could ever be counted on for very long.

If Europe has lived with the threat of nuclear war for forty years, in the last analysis its Governments have never really believed the United States deterrent would be used. The French have managed to win public support for the *Force de Frappe* largely on the understanding that, since the country's departure from NATO's integrated military command, it has become to all intents and purposes non-aligned, still able to exercise the right to choose.

Several years ago, in an article in *Le Monde*, the former Secretary-General of Giscard d'Estaing's party, the UDF, acknowledged that in the event of a sudden Soviet attack, any forward French positions in Germany would be overrun in a matter of hours, or days, leaving France with a strategic deterrent aimed at the Soviet Union. "*In this situation*" he opined "*the French people would naturally prefer to negotiate or surrender as in 1871 and 1940 rather than annihilate millions of Russians, inviting the same fate in return.*"[57]

Although President Mitterand spoke rather blandly of extending the French deterrent to cover Germany during his visit to Bonn in 1982 it is doubtful whether the Germans took him seriously. The broadening of Franco-German strategic consultation that October came in the same year as a ten per cent cut in French conventional forces, which followed a much larger cut of twenty-five per cent the previous year. The resources spent on building a seventh atomic submarine and buying the Hades missile for the early 1990s are no substitute for conventional forces, since it is only at the conventional level that Franco-German co-operation has any meaning.

Over the next five years it seems most unlikely that French thinking will change significantly, unless the Government is prepared to court the possibility of outspoken public opposition to the deterrent on which it is coming increasingly to rely. As Michel Debré, Pompidou's Defence Minister, said in 1972 "*the decision to employ nuclear weapons can only be made by a single nation.*"[58] If a future British Government ever toys with the idea of pursuing the Anglo-French option it might do well to recall the remark of Gen Pierre Gallois, that "*It is hardly credible that (a nuclear power) would court the risk of total destruction merely to ensure the protection of another state.*"[59]

There has always been a tendency for the British to think the worst of themselves, to denigrate their own achievements and take the blame for the sins of others. Writing in *The Times* at the end of 1985, David Watt remarked on "*the tension between the ingrained internationalism of an old imperial power and the new defensive nationalism of a deflated nation*", trusting that out of that tension might one day emerge "*a genuine post-imperial synthesis.*"[60] In that sense, the British have always thought of themselves as antagonistic to the idea of European defence co-operation, as an ingenué, unheeding before the fact, unprepared after it, unable to learn from its own history, or its recent decline.

In reality, it is not the British who stand in the way, even if they once did which is questionable. Their espousal of an open market for the Community at the Luxembourg summit offers the best prospects for the Eureka programme. Their own ideas for European union put forward at the Milan summit suggest that, at last, the main European powers are moving along the same road, if not in the direction of the WEU, perhaps towards the inevitable conclusion that, one day, the European Community will have to widen its discussion of security matters, to encompass defence.

The central problem is not the lack of institutions, of which there are far too many, but the political will, in particular the problem of tackling the special relationship between the United Kingdom and the United States, symbolised by the Nassau agreement in 1962 and the exclusive Franco-German relationship predicated on the 1963 Treaty, which was originally intended to be open to other signatories as well.[61] The key lies in Paris, not London, though Britain must be taken into account. There may well be *geometrie variable* in Eureka (a typically Gallic phrase to describe countries moving at different tempos) but unless there is trilateral co-operation in the field of security, European defence is likely to offer not a vision of the future, but the memory of past opportunites lost, an inverted Proustian remembrance of things that might have been had history only taken a different course.

4

Between the Acts: Some Current Trends

"Fighting a war which might not have to be fought defending what no more existed to defend, following campaigns which did not take place, mourning for the living and looking for strength to the dead, strangely, sadly and rather foolishly the Thirties drew to a close."
(Malcolm Muggeridge *The Thirties* (London: Hamish Hamilton 1940) p 318

The proliferation of books on the Atlantic Alliance, all suggesting a range of alternative military strategies, has become the hallmark in recent years of NATO politics, sustained and encouraged by a significant industry of interests – political parties, think tanks, academics and pundits, whether involved in private debate or public discussion. On military matters, if nothing else, we seem to have kept an open mind.

Concern about the Alliance's future is hardly novel. If one looks at any book on the Atlantic Alliance written in the late 1950s, prognostications similar to those of today seem to abound. Writing thirty years ago, Klaus Knorr was only one among many to ask whether NATO could withstand a crisis of confidence, whether it could still defend Europe against Soviet aggression[1]. The questions raised at the end of the 1950s, in retrospect NATO's first and most successful decade, reveal that hardly a year has gone by when its future has not been questioned.

If our fears today tend to be expressed more forcefully, it is perhaps because NATO seems to be nearing a mid-life crisis. Its fundamental purpose has been found not to be a purpose at all but simply an instinct. With the imminent departure of an American President whom the European public has never found credible, and the prospect of an indefinite term in office of the most presentable Soviet leader the public can recall, an era seems to be ending, and another beginning, in which the Alliance may be left leaderless and adrift in a changing world.

Three developments over the next ten years may enable the Alliance to survive, but survive in a different form. Of necessity, it seems fated to evolve from a less cohesive value-based institution, into a more interest-based organisation, with the interests of its members more narrowly defined than ever.

For Britain, the most important of the values to disappear, will probably be the special relationship with the United States, which for better or ill, has been one of the major features of the post war political landscape. Doubts, of course, about the value of the connection have been voiced for more than twenty years. Since Suez (1956), Conservatives have questioned the wisdom of relying on a "fickle" friend, unpredictable in its policies, inconstant in its friendship. Since Vietnam, when Mr Kinnock's generation came of age, there has been a detectable element of disquiet about the United States on the Labour backbenches, hitherto an unease not often declared, not even perhaps realised but intuitive which has now gone far beyond the stage of intuition.

There are many political figures who think American policy foolish, moralists who think it immoral, radicals who think it "imperialistic", economists who have never believed that Europe should be too closely tied to the American economy. The deployment of Cruise missiles marked a political *caesura* between one age and the next, an issue which revealed dissensions of an altogether different scale. Mrs Thatcher's particular gloss on the special relationship has not eased those doubts, but reinforced them; her rhetoric has been unfortunate, too self-conscious, unnecessarily contrived. The only note it has struck has been a false one.

That is not to say that the Labour Party wants to abandon the American link completely, or the road that its leaders have taken in the past; but it clearly sees the journey in different terms. Mrs Thatcher understands Alliance cohesion as reliability and predictability in British actions, support for American measures against terrorism, muted silence on issues such as Central America on which, in private, many cabinet ministers have voiced grave misgivings, the belief that words such as friendship, trust and solidarity cannot be used too often.

As Labour travels down the unilateralist path, the Conservatives clearly see they have an *"historic duty"*, to use Mrs Thatcher's own words, to maintain the Atlantic link for as long as possible, on the clear understanding that if the Americans departed, leaving Britain *"exposed to the threat of nuclear blackmail there would be no option but to surrender"*.[2]

Yet all is not as it seems; indeed the links already seem more fragile than the Government cares to admit. The day before Mrs Thatcher rallied the party faithful at Brighton behind the American flag, Sir Geoffrey Howe had warned the same audience that the more seriously Gorbachev took the Labour Party's chances of gaining power, the less he would feel bound to negotiate a balanced arms control agreement.[3] Unfortunately, the arms accord which the President seemed ready to accept at Rekyjavik a few weeks later seemed so "unbalanced" in the Soviet Union's favour that Mrs Thatcher had to scurry across to Camp David to bring the Administration back into line. Between that visit and her earlier mission in December 1984, to discuss the principles of SDI, the British in general seem to have discovered something about the trans-Atlantic bargain and a good deal more about themselves.

Although acknowledging co-operation as a factor, the Labour Party disputes that the relationship can ever again be exclusive in an increasingly dangerous world. Britain, it believes, has an equal responsibility to reassure the Soviet Union, to recognise that in a nuclear age "*it is not a matter of security against an enemy, but security together with the enemy.*"[4] This concept of security partnership was first coined by Helmut Schmidt;[5] but, as we shall see, it is no longer exclusive to the Germans. Overconfident about detente, apprehensively looking for new allies within Western Europe who share its aspirations, the Labour leadership is looking to play a role that goes far beyond Churchill's and Macmillan's initiatives at détente (which at the time were both criticised by Eisenhower and de Gaulle), much further than Harold Wilson's limited role in the CSE process.

Whether the United States could ever accept a security partnership between the Soviet Union and the United Kingdom is another matter. For her part, Mrs Thatcher has claimed, perhaps, predictably, that "*it would take us along the road to a fearful and fellow travelling Britain*".[6] That certainly may be the view from Washington which may feel a sense of abandonment, even betrayal, not to say suspicion, of Labour's motives. Perhaps, the fatal error in Labour calculations would be to press ahead with a special understanding before relations between the Superpowers themselves have improved, for it is doubtful whether Britain could ever again play the intermediary role it did in the 1950s which led to the signing of the Test Ban Treaty in 1963.

The final development we must address is whether by turning its back on the United States, demanding a level of consultation Washington can never concede, by entering into an "understanding" with the USSR, however limited in scope, a Labour Government would not reduce Britain to a state of semi-alignment.

As the United Kingdom moves out of an older order, which it influenced and even moulded into a new and unfamiliar world not of its own making, it may find in semi-alignment not a total break with the past, but the possibility of a new beginning. That promise alone may hold an immense attraction for a party which will wish to channel its energies in social reform at home, not in the type of summitry in Moscow which Harold Wilson believed in 1966 could resolve the Vietnam war in the matter of a few days, or summit meetings in Guadeloupe where James Callaghan consorted with other leaders in an attempt to resolve the problems of an ever changing world.

If that is what the 1990s holds, then all our endeavours since 1949 may indeed, look wasted. Like Muggeridge's era sixty years earlier, our own age with its preoccupation with security, and its belief that only through common endeavour can the West prevent the catastrophe which consumed

Europe in 1939, may seem remote, if not rather absurd. Alas, we know how the Thirties ended. No doubt Labour's leaders are deeply concerned and committed men, but an obsession with one's own affairs to the neglect of everyone else's is a dubious obsession. At times its images and points of reference seem to be inescapably narrow, even naive.

A Not so Special Relationship: Anti-Americanism in the United Kingdom

Instead of appearing to offer some security against the uncertainties of an insecure world, association with the United States seems to have produced a state of desperate anxiety among a significant section of the British people. There is every sign that if it continues into the 1990s, British Governments however well-disposed to the United States will have to take account of the fact that the special relationship will not survive the century. Perhaps, it is remarkable that it has survived so long.

On the Left, American policy has become an extended metaphor for Western imperialism in all its forms; on the Right, the United States is invariably portrayed as an immature and unpredictable power, constantly seeking ways to escape from the dilemmas it faces, although in what direction is not always clear. Political parties, of course, do not always speak for their members, but in this case they appear to reflect a national mood.

In February 1986 a MORI poll conducted for *The Sunday Times* revealed that while one Briton in three regarded the United States and the Soviet Union as an *equal* threat to world peace, an additional one in five regarded the Americans as a much greater menace.[7] It is an attitude to be expected perhaps, of a nation which, no longer responsible for its own fate, seems to live in perpetual fear of the future. While it would be wrong to take opinion polls always on trust, in this case they do seem to have captured an authentic echo of fears which, although long suppressed, have long been latent.

Over the last twenty years, Gallup has regularly asked a sample of the British public how much confidence it has had in the ability of the United States to deal with world problems. In absolute terms, confidence in Washington has steadily eroded every year since 1977, the first year of Jimmy Carter's Presidency. The negative value of the index is now nearly twice as high as it was ten years ago. It is likely to decline even further if it is manipulated and exploited by the Labour Party for its own ends. Indeed, much of the support for its foreign policy agenda derives less from the intellectual coherence of its non-nuclear case than the extent to which the case requires a significant reduction in American influence in the United Kingdom.

One must not exaggerate anti-American sentiment, of course, or attribute every comment critical of the United States to crude anti-Americanism. As a rule, broad generalisations, are usually meaningless. On the left, those who feel that Reagan's America is a ruthless, uncaring society, a nation indifferent to the suffering of the Third World, or the nuclear fears of the First, unheeding before the fact, uncaring after it, often think of Mrs Thatcher's Britain in the same terms.

But the most disturbing feature of anti-Americanism in the 1980s (and the one that may be of most importance in the future) is that the phenomenon extends far beyond the Left, beyond even the Tory backbenchers, to Mrs Thatcher's own Cabinet. Writing in the aftermath of Grenada (1983), one of her own junior ministers, Alan Clark, voiced his deep misgivings over American policy in general:

> *Opinion in the West has to be divided between those who believe that the influence of the United States is benign and protective and those (among whom I count myself) who believe that, like the power of the 18th century monarchy, it has increased, is increasing and ought to be diminished.*[8]

The anti-American tone of many Tory MPs testifies to a deeply held need, all the more real for often not being acknowledged, to develop or restore a language of politics more appropriate to the 1980s than the political vernacular of the 1950s. Anti-Americanism may seem a dubious area in which to search for it, but it comes readily to hand. Whether it will yield any return is another question entirely. Poor Columbus set off for the Spice Islands and discovered America instead. Heaven only knows what the British people may find if they set off for an unkown destination in the invincible belief that they are rediscovering themselves.

The Miraculous Mandarins

In order to put the present antagonism towards the United States into historical perspective, to judge whether the special relationship can last, we first need to grasp the forces and forms which held it together in the immediate aftermath of the Second World War.

Until the late 1960s, the relationship was an unquestionable (if frequently questioned) political reality. Successive governments, Tory and Labour alike, remained convinced that without special access to the United States, Britain would speedily be reduced to the role of a supplicant, cooling its heels in the antechamber of history.

Looked at at the time, the relationship was far from self-deceiving. For the politicians it was part of the political framework which made possible the country's "graceful retreat" from power. The mandarins of the Foreign Office may have been less than "miraculous" but they succeeded, by brilliant sleight of hand, in effectively disguising the full extent of Britain's decline both from the British people and the world at large.

Clearly conscious in the late 1940s that the relationship would become progressively less "special" as the element of wartime reciprocity on which it was based gradually diminished, the Foreign Office set out with the clear intention of forging an interdependent set of links which would firmly couple the United States and Western Europe. As Thomas Brimelow put it in March 1946, the Soviet Union knew which of its former allies had become its most implacable opponent, not the strongest but the most astute. *"The one quality which most disquiets the Soviet Government is the ability which they attribute to us to get others to do our fighting for us . . . They respect not us, but our ability to collect friends.'*[19]

Twenty years on, the British continued to derive unique advantages from the relationship, particularly in defence, including a nuclear deterrent, Polaris, which was sold in the face of sustained opposition from Kennedy's Defence Secretary Robert McNamara, as well as a direct input into American strategic thinking which survived up to the SALT 1 agreement. *"There was no other government"* Kissinger later recalled when discussing the treaty *"which we would have dealt with so openly, exchanged ideas so freely, or in effect permitted to participate in our deliberations."*[10]

Unfortunately, the mandarins paid a high price for concealing the extent to which British influence depended entirely on a degree of political subordination which they were at pains to conceal not only from the public, but at times even from themselves. Suez (1956) was the last occasion on which Britain sought to maintain its complete independence, to carry out a policy in defiance of American wishes, in an area of acute sensitivity to the United States. Stanley Evans, one of the few Labour MPs who supported Eden, did so because he perceived that, if Britain failed, its "moment" in the Middle East would swiftly pass. In his letter of resignation to his constituents, following his abrupt "de-selection" by the divisional Labour Party, he ended with the telling observation that Suez had been a bid that failed, a bid to *"wrest a little elbow room within the Anglo-American partnership"*.

Suez, in fact, brought home to the political establishment a fact it had not always cared to acknowledge, let alone admit; that the relationship was not one between equals. As the height of the affair, Macmillan, in his role as Chancellor of the Exchequer, conspired against Eden by suggesting to the Americans that a run on Sterling would be the most effective way to stop the operation in its tracks, an act of betrayal which prompted Eden's biographer David Carlton to describe the Chancellor as the "Janos Kadar" of British politics, Washington's acceptable candidate for the Premiership when Eden stepped down, an analogy which was doubtless prompted by the unhappy juxtaposition of the Suez operation and the Hungarian Uprising.

Inevitably, as the mandarins found themselves on the defensive they became inclined to package and sell the relationship in terms which meant little or nothing to the public at large; Churchill's English speaking union, Macmillan's Atlantic Community, Evans' hope *"that the Americans will grant us the same benevolent twilight that the Romans allowed the Americans.*" Thirty years on, the exercise not only looks absurd, but also self-deceiving. As late as 1986, the inveterate American polemicist Noam Chomsky felt it still necessary to comment on:

> "*the remarkable "colonisation" of sophisticated British intellectuals who regard themselves as independent and critical, but in fact react to US power and propaganda in a manner reminiscent of some of the more absurd Anglophile Indian intellectuals under the Empire.*"[11]

All this has not been lost on the public, at a time when relations with the United States have entered the public arena. Since the ending of détente, and the deployment of Cruise missiles, the politicians have been forced to address the electorate, when before they saw no compelling reason to address it at all.

Mrs Thatcher must bear the blame for conducting relations with the United States in a language largely removed from public thinking, for failing to address public concerns, for neglecting to remind the British people that subordination to and dependence on the United States are not necessarily synonymous.

Instead, she has given the public an inflated view of Britain's own importance, with the inevitable consequence that anti-American sentiment has tended to increase whenever the Government has been publicly re-buffed. Far from communicating truths that have been concealed for far too long, the Government has found itself severely embarrassed whenever it has tried to challenge the United States directly. In this respect, her crude appeal to the special relationship has been not so much uncalculated, as miscalcu-lated. The British people could not help but notice how Lord Carrington's Middle East initiative in 1981 was shot down, the Prime Minister's opposition to the invasion of Grenada entirely ignored, Sir Geoffrey Howe's initial opposition to SDI dismissed out of hand.

By failing to communicate the realities of political life to the electorate in the 1950s, British Governments were bound to create problems for their successors as Britain's power diminished still further, as the bi-partisan consensus began to break down.

British Introspection

Long before the arrival of Mrs Thatcher, many Americans had begun to observe the absence of any real enthusiasm for the United States, the result of Britain's increasing remoteness from power. After 1970, no British Prime Minister could expect to increase his rating in the polls by forging a strong personal relationship with an American President. Even Harold Wilson preferred to talk of a "close" rather than "special" relationship, ever mindful of the shifting pattern of opinion within his own party.

In the United States anti-Americanism in Britain was taken to be an expression of faltering confidence, evidence of a reluctance to take risks, an unwillingness to recall dangers that had once been shared, but were now only dimly remembered. Still more acute observers noted that even those in favour of continued US-British alignment betrayed a telling lack of sentiment. They were more often moved by fear of the Soviet Union than affection for the United States. If they still referred to the special relationship, they did so because any other way of dealing with the Russians lay beyond their experience. As the Gallup figures showed, confidence in the United States was never higher than at the height of détente, when the Soviet threat appeared to have receded, when the British people no longer had to make a choice.

Ironically, the coming of the Second Cold War was also accompanied by an intractable recession which made the British even more preoccupied with the challenges they faced at home than the dangers which existed abroad. The wasting of the economy after 1979, the visible pauperisation of large sections of the community, the north-south divide, all trenchantly brought home the change in Britain's circumstances. Anti-Americanism was not only generated by a belated recognition of the country's reduced status in the world. It also became the expression of a more inward looking, introspective society which had little understanding of international responsibilities, which was inclined to find in unilateralism, if not neutrality, an escape from the realities of power politics to which both Superpowers were still "condemned".

With this change in circumstances, and the attitudes which attended it, disappeared one of the last props of the special relationship. Under Mrs Thatcher the British seem to have lost their "*special capacity*", as Coral Bell once described it, to see the world through American eyes.

The intense public opposition to the bombing of Tripoli in March 1986 revealed how deep the psychological incomprehension between the two countries has now become. As Italo Calvino observed in his last book, *Mr Palomar*, when discussing the gap between the generations, the difficulty of communication arises from the impossibility of transmitting each other's experience. "*We can exert no influence on what most resembles our own experience; in what bears our own imprint we are unable to recognise ourselves.*"

Forgetting their own past as an imperial power, the British people appear to have become reconciled to the status of a civilian power, invincibily wedded to the values which that status imparts: collective security, increased foreign assistance, the peaceful resolution of conflicts whatever the cause, the civilian proprieties which seem these days to be on the lips of every politician, irrespective of party. Inevitably, the United States has become rather an isolated figure in NATO, not only its world power, but also its only "imperial" one.

Distaste for power politics has now become one of the most notable features of British political life. Addressing a meeting of the World Development Movement in 1984, Labour's Shadow Foreign Secretary insisted that an attack on Nicaragua would be "*a major crime against international law recalling the worst excesses of colonialism.*" In the same year, the party's defence paper confirmed that, once in Government, it would be committed to a system of "*collective security through the United Nations*", a view that revealed how far it had travelled from 1966 when the United Nations was never once discussed during Denis Healey's momentous East of Suez Defence Review.

Even in response to terrorism, the use of force has been entirely ruled out. During the Commons debate on the Tripoli raid, Eric Heffer, at the time one of the NEC's principal members, and a former aspirant for the party leadership, described the President of the United States as "*one of the biggest international terrorists alive today*", a sentiment that found less forceful expression in the placards carried by children during a demonstration in Hyde Park depicting Ronald Reagan as "*Mad Dog No 2*" (a not so oblique reference to his own description of Col Quadaffi as "Mad Dog No 1").

If the language is more moderate on the Tory back benches, the sentiments are often remarkably similar. In 1983, only forty Conservative Members in a Parliament with the largest Tory majority since the National Government of the 1930s could be found to sign a motion congratulating the United States on the invasion of Grenada. One of the President's most consistent critics, the former Cabinet Minister Sir Ian Gilmour, has frequently accused him of "*fairly sleazy activities in Central America*" and condemned his administration for treating the Middle East as "*a place where votes can be won in the Mid-West and New York.*"

Given the strength of anti-American feeling on all sides of the Conservative Party, from the Thatcherites to the diminishing number of MPs who still look for inspiration to Edward Heath, and the greater number who would have earned Thomas Chatterton's praise for their ability to speak "*on both sides of a controversy*" at once, the deafening silence of the backbenches when the Prime Minister rose to defend her action in allowing bases in Britain to be used for the Tripoli raid came as no surprise to political observers. Mr Heath who had prevented American aircraft from using Lakenheath to resupply Israel during the 1973 Arab-Israeli war proved equal to the hour in his own condemnation of America's action, apparently oblivious to the fact that his own decision had been dictated by the threat of an Arab oil boycott.

So astounded was *The Times* by the Conservative party's response that it felt moved to comment:

> *It remains a remarkable fact about British political life in 1986 that a Conservative Prime Minister has to struggle so hard to defend an ally's use of its own aircraft and its own pilots to attack a common enemy of Western civilisation.*

It may indeed have been regrettable, but it was hardly remarkable, given what the American writer Irving Kristol has termed "the risk-aversive" nature of civilian power.

Over Grenada, even Mrs Thatcher could not bring herself to respond to the appeals of seven Carribean nations lest the picture of *HMS Antrim* taking part in an irregular invasion of a small Third World state might lead to a major clash with Britain's Commonwealth partners. Many of her own backbenchers shared her views, drawing the line at casualties, at international protest, at everything they could think of. As one Member of Parliament observed at the time "*Our commitment to democracy is as great as anyone's, but to make this the basis of an invasion is to seriously weaken the West*".

It would seem that civilian powers do not have much stomach for crusades, or missions, that civilian values leave little room for consideration of democracy or human rights. Intervention in the affairs of another country, when it involves the use of force, is unlikely ever again to meet with unanimous public support.

Like its partners in the European Community, the United Kingdom is much happier living in a world where there are few choices to be made, and no gambles to be taken. In the future, Britain may still have to recognise risks and even occasionally face up to them, but never take them itself. This is bound to make for almost permanent tension as long as it is associated with a country that looks at the world through different eyes – by necessity, if not always by inclination. Its desire that the United States should reduce its commitments to a minimum in Central America or the Middle East in the hope that Washington may be able to respond more "responsibly" to future events is hardly likely to commend itself to an Administration that is convinced that America's tendency in the past to react to events rather than shape them severely compromised its freedom of action.

As it is the United States, like the Soviet Union, probably feels that the "risks" it incurs are far less daunting than they may appear to those outside looking on. "*A great power like the United States*" writes William Deedes:

> "*is always more confident that it can contain a conflict than nations which have been relegated to onlookers. These dark fears were not part of our own mood when on our own initiative the ships were sent out on that hazardous mission to the Falklands. There is no bridging that psychological gap.*"

Indeed. But if the British people rallied during the war in the South Atlantic, their consistent and predictable criticism of every ensuing American military operation from Grenada to Tripoli surely betrays the awkwardness of a minor actor unexpectedly upgraded to a named role. Five year later, it is much easier to appreciate that the Falklands war was a last, despairing rally in Britain's retreat from power, a final gesture which brought it not within hailing distance of the future, but within range of the past.

The Commonwealth Conundrum

In Britain's case, these factors will probably be accentuated even more over the next few years by its membership of the Commonwealth, an arrangement which, like the special relationship, was probably a necessary part of the imperial disengagement, the methadone to the heroin addiction of empire, which eased the withdrawal symptoms, without reducing them entirely.

Unfortunately, the Commonwealth link has survived in a way that the special relationship has not, even though it has arguably always been less real. As Enoch Powell, one of the severest critics of both "myths" has argued, apart from a common history of British rule, the members of the Commonwealth have nothing else in common, "nothing else in their own eyes, nothing else in the face of the world, nothing else in verifiable fact, nothing else except a fiction British made for British consumption."

That, of course, is its strength over the public imagination. It is confirmation of the fact that the transformation from a world power to a European one has not lessened Britain's international reputation. In 1983 a Gallup poll found that eighty-three per cent of those canvassed wanted a closer relationship with the Commonwealth, a higher percentage than those who expressed a similar wish with regard to the United States or Western Europe.

It would appear that the British people even now expect their governments to play a world role, even if it means the exercise of responsibility without power, or subordinating the interests of a European power to the aspirations of non-European states much smaller than itself. Since the Commonwealth summit of 1977 Britain has been forced to lend its name to a whole series of quite unrealistic reports proposing major changes in the International Economic Order, such as the Arndt Report (1979) on constraints on economic growth, the Cairncross Report (1981) on protectionism, and most ambitious of all, the plans drawn up by the Commonwealth Secretariat in 1982 for a totally revised Bretton Woods system.

Britain, alas, is not the power it was in 1944 when, together with the United States, it drew up the first Bretton Woods agenda. By going along with these declarations, even Mrs Thatcher has encouraged expectations that she has been unable or unwilling to meet when the opportunity has actually arisen. It is because the British people, however, have come to believe that they are duty bound to argue on the Third World's behalf that they have been so critical of the Government's attitude towards the Cancun summit (1981), the 2nd Brandt Report (1983), Britain's withdrawal from UNESCO and its less than open-ended support for the Commonwealth's position during the United Nations debate on Africa's debt in 1986.

The fact that in every case Britain appeared to follow America's lead prompted the Labour Party to accuse the Prime Minister of being "*supine in her support of an American President*", as if the country had been denied by Mrs Thatcher its Third World mission. It is a convenient myth behind which to hide when it is becoming increasingly clear that Britain's interests and those of its Commonwealth partners are unlikely to converge very often, a fact which was rather embarrassingly highlighted during the debate over South African sanctions.

Or so it would appear but for one notable exception. As Britain's decline accelerates, so its experience and that of its Commonwealth partners may indeed begin to seem the same. To many Labour MPs, Britain has already become an offshore airbase for the United States, like the Philippines under Marcos or South Korea under President Park. Denzil Davies has often expressed fears about American attempts to subordinate the defence policy of a "*sovereign government*",[12] doubtless in the belief that what Mr Kinnock likes to call "*the Thatcher regime*" has already been suborned by the United States. As *The Times* commented after one of Mr Davies' speeches "*subordinate in his context is a very useful verb which obscures the very considerable difference between an ally's criticism and an attempted coup.*"[13]

On the radical Left there has always existed the view that NATO membership has entailed the militarisation of British society, with all the symptoms we associate with the term when discussing the Third World – the proliferation of bases, an economy distorted by military spending, a posture for the "military establishment" far stronger than is appropriate for a Parliamentary democracy or a European state.[14] More recently the soft Left has taken up the same message, perhaps most extraordinarily in an open letter to his constituents by Labour's spokesman for Health and Social Security, who accused Mrs Thatcher of deliberately contriving to subordinate the United Kingdom by agreeing that, in the event of war, large stretches of the country would come under American jurisdiction, that emergency government regional committees would transfer part of the nation to United States military command and that, under a further secret understanding, the Government had given permission to the Health Service to discharge up to thirty per cent of patients in NHS hospitals to make room for US casualties instead.[16]

The image of Britain as a Third World country in its relationship with the United States is a hazy vision which leaves many points of substance open to challenge and has the additional misfortune of being absurdly overdrawn. The Left is playing a part, knows it, indeed believes it to be one of its strengths. There are times when the Labour leadership needs to be reminded of the fact, unless it wishes in Government to translate its differences with the United States into an open confrontation.

The Thatcher Factor

As it is Mr Kinnock can probably ride on the crest of a quite different wave, the fact that Mrs Thatcher's policies have unconsciously acted as a catalyst in alienating the British people from the America she so much admires. Her close ideological identification with the economic policies of the Reagan Administration has politicised the special relationship for the first time since 1945.

From the time of Churchill's "historic compromise" – the Conservative party's acceptance of the Welfare State, which had been conceived and even debated in Churchill's wartime cabinet, there has never been a party-political affinity with the United States. Breaking with the post war consensus on almost every issue, Mrs Thatcher set out with the clear intention of "Americanising" Britain's economic culture, in a way that has opened up cultural fissures between the two societies which have long been latent. Writing thirty years ago, Anthony Crosland, the Labour Party's leading intellectual at the time noted that:

> *"anti-Americanism is an almost universal Left wing neurosis springing from . . . the need to find some new and powerful scapegoat to replace the capitalists at home, its utility in this role being much diminished under full employment and the Welfare State.*[16]

Industrial decline and high unemployment have merely reinforced the Left's case. The social casualties of Mrs Thatcher's revolution have made the British extremely wary of the Friedmanite principles on which the experiment has been based. They would probably be more critical still if they knew of Prof Friedman's own criticism of Mrs Thatcher's policies, or the Reagan Administration's private reservations.

Mrs Thatcher's policies have never been held in especially high regard in America. From the first, they were taken by the President's Treasury Secretary Donald Regan as a dire warning of where monetarism might lead if the Government so clearly failed to practise what it preached in terms of reducing public expenditure. As early as 1981, George Gilder, one of the main voices of the New Right, pointed to Britain as a "cautionary tale" of failing to combine a reduction in monetary growth with a real reduction in government spending.

In fact, Mrs Thatcher's "great leap forward" into a more entrepreneurial age inevitably met with intense opposition not only on the Left but also from within her own party, especially from those Conservatives who still believed in Churchill's historic compromise of 1951. Defeated and dejected on the backbenches, their representation rose quite substantially in the cabinet after 1985. If the Conservative majority falls to forty or so after the election the experiment may be quietly reversed, or brought to an end.

For there are clearly a large number of Tory MPs who appreciate that British society is probably far too conservative, or risk aversive, to take the American model model on trust, that there never has been a period in recent history when it attracted the uncritical admiration of all but a minority of citizens. Interestingly, a Gallup poll conducted in July 1942, only seven months after the United States had entered the war, found that less than forty-one per cent of those polled expressed any desire to become "more American". When the same question was asked forty years later the figure had fallen by more than half.

All that Mrs Thatcher has succeeded in promoting is a fear which the French successfully exorcised under de Gaulle – the fear of a *défi americaine*, or the further loss of economic sovereignty under the impact of an American capital invasion. In February 1986, a MORI poll discovered that sixty-eight per cent of those canvassed believed that American influence over the economy was already far too extensive. Hence the strong opposition within the Tory Party itself to the proposed Westland deal with Sikorski which claimed the careers of two of Mrs Thatcher's most prominent Cabinet Ministers, and the proposed sale of British Leyland's truck division to General Motors (including Land Rover with which the Ministry of Defence placed orders of twenty-five million pounds in 1986/7).[17]

"*They do not want to see our country and our industries handed more and more to American firms*" observed Edward Heath,[18], during the Leyland debate, a strange comment from a former Prime Minister who was never noted when in office for his sensitivity to public opinion. "*Why this Gadarene rush into the arms of American domination*" asked a writer in *The Guardian*.[19] It would appear that the prospect of American buy-outs is one that both Parties find disturbing. The fact that over the years US corporations have invested over $40 billion in the United Kingdom and at present provide one in eight jobs in manufacturing industry alone; that the British have only themselves to blame for the difficulties of British Leyland tend to be conveniently overlooked.

In politics, of course, none of these facts matter very much if an argument to the contrary can be made. Frustration is rarely rational and is anyway more likely to be more vividly expressed when people genuinely believe themselves to be exploited. In attempting the probably impossible task of reversing Britain's economic decline, Mrs Thatcher has merely accentuated the nation's perception of it, making the electorate more nationalistic, a development which in its Little England manifestation has taken the form of an aggressive anti-Americanism, the absurd but readily believed fear that the Government is intent on reducing Britain to the status of an off-shore tax haven for American corporations.

Conclusion

Anti-Americanism it is worth adding, is not unique to the United Kingdom. In the Federal Republic of Germany, Chancellor Kohl has been accused of "vassal-like fidelity" in his relations with the United States, of confusing "friendship with servility" by his opponents in the SPD, of being willing to comply with almost any American action,[20] a remark which recalls Denis Healey's description of Mrs Thatcher's "doormat diplomacy" in her relations with the United States.

Both in Britain and West Germany, anti-Americanism is part of a general crisis in the Atlantic Alliance which in recent years has become less value-based and much more interest-oriented for both parties. As European and American interests have begun to diverge, a valueless alliance may increasingly be seen in Washington as a marriage of convenience, even a *mésalliance* whose partners no longer share a common vision.

The difference between the two countries is that anti-American sentiment in the United Kingdom may have much graver implications for a government, whether Labour or Conservative, in its relations with the United States.

The support which the United Kingdom can still provide Washington – its vote in the Security Council, its willingness to deploy Cruise missiles *pour encourager les autres*, its offer of base facilities for 30,000 American servicemen and one fifth of all USAF pilots stationed overseas – the very foundation stones of the Anglo-American relationship which still render it real, if no longer special – are part of an edifice which the Labour Party has pledged to dismantle stone by stone, buoyed in this instance, at least, by opinion polls which suggest that it would be able to count on broad public support for every measure, except the last.

As for values, the threat may be more serious still. In Germany, the Government has tried to remind the SPD of its NATO obligations by employing words first heard in the Adenauer era – notably "reliability" and "trust" concepts which until recently found not echo in the Labour Party which was reconciled to close association with the United States ten years before the SPD came on board after the Bad Godesburg compromise. One of the strongest links between Britain and the United States was the values which they so clearly shared in common. It was significant that, in commemorating the special relationship, Henry Kissinger chose to speak of values rather than interests when he addressed an audience in London in 1982, reminding those present that it was beyond the psychological resources of the United States "*to be the sole or even the principal centre of initiative and response in the non-communist world*".[21]

If Britain chooses to turn its back on that historical legacy in the course of the next few years, the impact on American public opinion may be traumatic. All the evidence suggests that it will, whoever wins the next election, that Mrs Thatcher's departure from the political scene will foreshadow the end of one era and the beginning of the next. If future historians ever come to see the "sentimental relationship" between herself and Ronald Reagan as one of the relationship's high points, it may be in the sense that Arnold Toynbee saw the Antonine age, not as Gibbon believed the apogee of the Roman Empire, but *"the last flush on the cheeks of a patient dying of galloping consumption."*

Security Partnership With the Soviet Union?

Last October, Neil Kinnock told a meeting of the Socialist International at Bad Godesberg that when Labour came to power and removed all nuclear weapons from the country, he would invite Gorbachev to London to clinch a deal on disarmament.[22] Earlier, he had revealed that a Labour Government would take up the Soviet leader's offer to negotiate a separate nuclear weapons agreement with the United Kingdom, on the basis of an *"equivalent missile for missile reduction."*[23] Clearly were such an agreement to be reached, Britain would have travelled much further along the road to a security understanding with the USSR than Michael Foot proposed in 1983.

For the Labour Party, Gorbachev's offers are too attractive to ignore, too significant to pass up. In the Kingdom of Lilliput, when the King's clemency was declared, his subjects used to run for cover. Mr Kinnock's Britain may be so intent on running for cover before the sirens have even sounded their warning, that it may accept the Kremlin's assurances at face value, with profound consequences for the Alliance to which it will still belong.

For a mixture of reasons, some emotional, some political, Labour can be expected, if it ever gains office, to move towards a security understanding with the old adversary. In the first place it seems to have reverted to type, to have rekindled its old emotional ties with the Soviet Union which date back to the 1920s and beyond.

"In contradiction to every known principle of the human mind that singular people seems to have yielded a stronger and more ready assent to the traditions of their remote ancestors than to the evidence of their own senses."

No, Edward Gibbon was not referring to the Labour Party, to the extraordinary pleas for greater Anglo-Soviet understanding heard year after year at Labour Party conferences. Yet had his topic not been the defence of Massada in AD70 he might well have reached the same conclusion. The question which arises from Mr Kinnock's great enthusiasm for Mikhail Gorbachev (rather than President Reagan, whose Christian name he is assiduously careful never to mention) is whether it is a calculated response to the political fashions of the moment, or rooted in the Labour party's own past. One suspects it is a mixture of both. To the extent, however, that it is an echo of the Labour movement's commitment to the brave new Soviet society of the 1930s, which so enthralled H G Wells, the Webbs and Bernard Shaw, its unqualified enthusiasm for the Soviet Union together with its inherent distrust of the United States and all things American may remain a permanent feature of British politics until the end of the century.

The Labour Party emerged from the Second World War transformed from the Party of the 1930s, largely suspicious of Soviet intentions. In the period that has elapsed, the immediate post war years have grown too familiar, its images too stale. The questions raised by the war, in particular national attitudes to appeasement, the problems which faced Bevin in dealing with the only remaining totalitarian power, the surviving partner of the Nazi-Soviet Pact, have become obscured or overlooked, or are often suspected not to have existed at all.

In Gorbachev the Labour leadership has also discovered a man with whom it believes it can "deal" even more successfully than Mrs Thatcher. Gorbachev strikes a responsive chord in Labour hearts, with his grasp of detail, his consistent leadership, his historical perspective, his enthusiasm for reform. The Soviet Union is familiar to the Party in a way that the United States is not – a "lapsed" socialist society, to be sure, but a European power with European instincts, if translated into another idiom. It is from this unlikely perspective that the party once in government may seek to build a special understanding, unlikely because it accords so little to reality.

In its enthusiasm for the new leadership (which may of course not be entirely misplaced) the Party has chosen to totally ignore those "inconvenient facts" which Orwell spoke of in trying to explain the Left's blinkered perception of Stalin. The facts may have changed; the policies have not. The ruthless prosecution of the war in Afghanistan, the equally single minded attack on Soviet Jewery, which has been much more determined than under Brezhnev or Chernenko,[24] Gorbachev's not so admirable drubbing down of the British ambassador Sir Ian Sutherland over Britain's "refusal" to acknowledge the Soviet contribution to VE Day, throws light on a rather different Russia. Gorbachev's style abroad belies the fact that he himself is a product of the system that has remained essentially unchanged since Stalin. Style may be the man, but the man is not the system.

As we have seen, it is by no means clear that he will succeed in reforming the Soviet Union where Kosygin and Khruschev failed before him. That perhaps is not the point. Until there is clear evidence that the Soviet Union is moving towards some form of accommodation with the West, any precipitous British move towards Moscow is bound to undermine America's confidence in Britain as an ally.

Such thinking is most unlikely to discourage a Labour Government; indeed quite the reverse. For the Labour Party is now apparently quite convinced that it has a historic duty to encourage the reform process by removing Soviet fears of the Western Alliance, in particular its anxieties about American actions. Whether the United States has legitimate anxieties of its own is something which seems to concern it much less.

As Philip Sabin points out, in a recent study of public opinion, the collapse of détente and the abandonment of arms control in the late 1970s had a profound effect in convincing all shades of opinion that the threat of conflict between the blocs was very real, so real in fact that it was reasonable to ask which groups if any were *not* alarmed. What seems to have been the case is that the anxieties of the professional military establishment were based less on the fear of invasion than on political pressures or regional entanglements. In short the *"disagreement lay not over whether a danger existed but over what form that danger took".*[25]

The Peace Movement in the person of its main exponent Edward Thompson had no doubt on the matter. *"The United States"* he wrote in Protest and Survive *"seems to me to be more dangerous and provocative in its general military and diplomatic strategies which press around the Soviet Union with menacing bases."*[26] *The Economist* gave voice to a similar opinion, couched however in a Gallic paradox which is a hallmark of its style. There were two different responses to the Soviet challenge, it opined in an editorial in 1982; when the United States gets nervous it gets pugnacious, looks for quick solutions and expects others to agree. When the Europeans are nervous, they slide towards caution, calling for patience and compromise. *"Neither reaction is necessarily superior to the other; the point is they are different."*[27] Quite so. But even at the time, the Labour party under Michael Foot was convinced that American pugnacity was a much greater threat to peace than the Soviet challenge.

The quest for a security understanding with the Soviet Union is based on two simple premises: that it is Europe's responsibility to reassure the Russians about NATO's intentions, and that the Soviet threat itself has been grossly exaggerated by the military establishment for its own particular ends.

There is no quarrel with the need for restraint, or reassurance. Even Mrs Thatcher would agree with the West German Foreign Minister Hans Dietrich Genscher that Europe must, through political dialogue and co-operation, at least try to find various common interests which can be *"defined, utilised and protected."*[28] Where Genscher and Thatcher part company with the German Social Democrats is their instinctive opposition to bilateral deals with the Soviet Union, what Egon Bahr has called a policy of *"wandeldurch Annaherung"* – change through accommodation, of which the central theme is non-provocative defence.

Bahr's security partnership looks forward to the eventual dissolution of the alliances, through detente and mutual force reductions the creation of a neutral "collective security system" in Central Europe, guaranteed by the two Superpowers.[29] As the SPD Erhard Epple insists:

> One should not think badly of us when we consider security systems in which the heart of Europe will no longer be characterised by two different zones. Whoever thinks badly of us does so because we have our own interests. . . . It does not harm anyone if our interests happen to overlap once in a while with those of the Soviet Union[30]

Eppler summed up his new impartiality between the blocs by insisting that a decision not to deploy Cruise missiles would force both Superpowers to realise that West German support would depend upon their own behaviour.[30]

Since their deployment, the SPD has already gone far along the road to meeting Moscow half way. In 1985 it set up a working group with the East German SED to work out the technicalities of a nuclear "No First Use" policy, as a first step towards creating a nuclear free zone. The party also agreed a draft treaty for a chemical weapons free zone as well, although in the event it chose not to ratify it while in Opposition for fear of alienating the electorate before the 1987 elections. Its only concern, apart from hostile reaction at home, appears to have been Europe's response to such unilateral treaty making, not American opposition. That is why it attaches so much importance to the Labour Party's support for what Horst Ehmke has called the need for "*a security partnership between East and West, a partnership of survival*".[31]   There was a time when such giants in the Labour Party like Aneurin Bevan believed that the idea of socialist parties working together on an alternative defence policy was absurd – that it was "*a policy for hermits.*" Today's leaders have no such doubts or inhibitions; indeed they are already busy laying the ground, and preparing new lines of advance. The working relations between Labour and the SPD are now quite close, and likely to become still closer. As the SPD's former Chairman Willy Brandt remarked at last year's Labour Party Conference, its defence aspirations were both "*wise and far sighted*".[32]

The Labour Party has now joined a new group, the "European Socialist and Social Democratic parties of the Atlantic Alliance" whose first meeting in Oslo in September, despite ending with a ritual reaffirmation of loyalty to NATO, insisted that Europe "*could not delegate responsibility for security to others.*" In a guarded way, which *The Economist* would doubtless consider typically European the delegates even accepted the Labour Party's readiness to move away unilaterally from a nuclear posture, although in their final communiqué they adroitly avoided the codeword "unilateralism", agreeing that negotiations might be "*assisted by independent steps*" as well as multilateral actions.[33]

The next few years certainly hold out the very real prospect of a realignment of the Left in Europe, now that the SPD is likely to shift further left itself after its second defeat in the polls. Both Labour and its German associates seem to have already embraced what David Gress calls "*defence revisionism*",[34] the call for a radical restructuring of NATO's Armed Forces to deprive them of any offensive capability (even to counter-attack), and thus render them structurally incapable of posing a threat to Eastern Europe. Among the measures the SPD favours are the phasing out of attack aircraft, the reduction of tank forces, the development of greater reserves in place of permanent front line strength.[35] It is strategy which might have been lifted from the NEC's most recent defence paper.

One can only reassure the Russians, of course, if one is reassured oneself.

The Labour Party has no doubts on that score. Indeed, it is equally intent on dismissing the Soviet threat as exaggerated, or contrived. Fortified by recent academic studies, such as those from the School of Peace Research at Bradford, it believes that Soviet planners are much more likely to be aware of their own shortcomings than NATO's.

Many of those deficiencies are well documented: the fact that Soviet tanks tend to break down every 160 kilometres against NATO tanks every 250;[36] that Soviet firepower within a division may appear high on paper but, in reality, being short of spare parts and maintenance support, they are driven to deploy artificially large numbers of guns, including replacements, to achieve the required availability. Furthermore, their logistic backing is too slender to enable them to sustain the high rates of fire characteristic of the American forces. However, despite the evidence, this situation offers scant grounds for self-assurance, for the gravest weakness in NATO is its lack of conventional artillery and of sufficient stocks to provide ammunition for more than a relatively short war. This situation, in Britain at least, has its origins in the arrival of tactical nuclear weapons during the early 1950s – their advent being heralded as a glorious excuse to disband many of our artillery regiments and so save expensive manpower. It is difficult to calculate what it would cost to put this right to meet the needs of a purely conventional battlefield but the manpower bill alone could only be met by the reintroduction of National Service. To put the problem into some sort of perspective, the number of Allied artillerymen in Italy alone in 1945 was about half the present strength of the British Army. There were occasions in North West Europe when the number of Gunners supporting major operations outnumbered the infantry involved. To come closer to home, the shortage of gun crews in the Falklands was such that every available man, regardless of his proper trade, had to be pressed into service just to keep the guns firing – such is the price that has had to be paid for endless manpower reviews. Of course, it is not just a question of weapons and crews but of providing ammunition in the sort of quantities that the Arab/Israeli wars have shown to be essential in modern conventional warfare, together with the ammunition columns to move it and all the workshop back-up that a greatly increased force of artillery must have. So it is not just the armies of the Warsaw Pact who have a problem. All the loose talk about extra tanks and increased anti-tank weapons means little unless the vital question of conventional artillery support is properly answered.

Labour's whole case for defensive deterrence largely stands or falls on whether these assertions are true; that in regard to combat aircraft it is not numbers that count but the qualitative edge the West still enjoys – more advanced weapons, better avionics, the historic record that badly trained Soviet pilots have suffered disproportionately high losses against even apparently negligible opposition.[38] Essentially, Labour believes that the Soviet threat is a chimera dating from the Lisbon NATO Council Meeting of

1952 which mistook Soviet forces in control of Eastern Europe's civilian administration for actual combat divisions, and responded accordingly. In 1961, a Pentagon-commissioned study found that half the Soviet divisions were little more than paper units, with little equipment and fewer men. In 1965 the two Alliances were believed to have equal parity on the ground. Neither of these conclusions were ever officially acknowledged. Instead the force comparison tables issued by NATO have shown a growing conventional imbalance which takes no account of the size of divisions, the ability to re-equip, or the morale of Soviet forces, let alone their East European allies.[39]

All this may well be true, but it is unlikely to win Britain a greater hearing in Washington, or Brussels. For thirty years British defence has been designed to meet a Soviet conventional threat that has been considered more formidable than the threat the country faced in 1939, or 1914. To meet it, the country has spent more on defence per capita, more as percentage of GDP, more in absolute terms than any major European member.

As Britain's economic circumstances change in the next ten years, as economic reality finally intrudes into military thinking, one would expect a Conservative Government to justify its choices by reinterpreting the threat, a Labour Government to conjure it away altogether.

Unfortunately, books which seek to discount the Soviet threat, or studies of the military balance which seek to suggest that NATO is the stronger of the two blocs, fail in the end to convince because they engage in too much special pleading. Ultimately, they seem as oblivious to the need to keep an open mind as the officials in the Pentagon of whom they are often rightly critical.

Of course, there are eminent scholars who do not share NATO's perspective, or its assumptions. We could debate forces balances for a long time. But the fact that the debate would be interminable is actually symptomatic of why Labour's approach is so dangerous. For unlike the principles of physics, we have no way of determining whether any of the weaknesses in Soviet force structures would actually matter on the day; there is no way of testing our own strengths, short of a war which NATO's critics will never be called upon to fight. Their own contentions, no more than NATO's, are not subject to empirical verification.

The Services have always had to take account of numbers, of perceived intentions, of force strengths on the ground. History is replete with examples of countries which miscalculated their own power. The problem of human error is not reserved for offensive powers alone. The advocates of non-provocative defence have little to contribute except to remind us (quite rightly) that we must always take account of Soviet perceptions as well as our own. But the weight of evidence is that we have. We have banked our belief that the Soviet Union has no intention of going to war unless provoked to justify a chronic state of unreadiness in the 1950s, severe retrenchment in the 1960s, a reduction in manpower by half in the 1970s. The clearest indication that the brief reversal of this debilitating policy: NATO's three per cent real increase in defence spending in 1977, the Long Term Modernisation Programme the following year, above all the re-equipment of United States Forces in Europe under Reagan occasioned little consternation in Moscow, was its decision not to observe any NATO exercises after 1979, although it was entitled to by the Helsinki Treaty (1975). Fears of a sudden attack do not appear to have weighed very heavily on Soviet minds.

In the end, one suspects that unless the case for Soviet force deficiencies can be proved to be conclusive, the case for non-provocative defence is unlikely to sway opinion in the Pentagon. If a Labour Government embarks on that road, it can expect to travel it alone. For the foreseeable future, Washington's view is likely to remain that of Richard Feynman, a theoretical scientist who returned to physics after working at Los Alamos on the first atomic bomb:

> *I can live with doubt and uncertainty. I think its more interesting to live not knowing, than to have answers which may be wrong.*[40]

The Quest for Semi-alignment

There are many members of the Labour Movement who have learned enough in the years since the Party first committed itself to unilateralism to argue, not for Britain's withdrawal, but for what Mary Kaldor and others have referred to as its "conditional membership" of the Alliance. As she is the first to admit, the movement learned from its defeat in 1983 to recognise that it is increasingly necessary to seek ways of changing NATO itself, rather than threatening to opt out.[41] Anything more would scare the voters, leaving the Tory Party firmly in command of the middle ground.

It is already clear, however, from the Left's attitude towards the United States, and its commitment to search for, if not necessarily enter into, a security partnership with the Soviet Union, that Britain's membership under a Labour government would inevitably be more conditional than it has in the past. It is also clear that any decision to disarm unilaterally, or evict American bases, would put Britain on the same footing as some of the smaller powers, notably Norway and Denmark.

In addition, if the Alliance is already becoming less a society of nations than a group of states united by the mutual interest of the moment, then it may be difficult to describe many of its members as allies at all but rather as "associates", a term coined by Zbigniew Brzezinski, President Carter's former National Security Adviser, to describe how NATO might eventually evolve.

The deployment of Cruise missiles has undoubtedly sharpened this impulse. It proved a costly victory. NATO entered into the decision to upgrade its theatre nuclear forces in 1979 determined to show itself, as well as the Soviet Union, that controversial measures could be adopted and carried through. The deployment took place in very different circumstances. The unity of the Alliance was cruelly exposed, the loyalty of its members severely tested. In some cases loyalty grew into an expression of resentment, a determination never to go through the experience again. It is difficult to imagine that resolve evaporating within the next five years. Indeed it may be the only resolution the Europeans may ever show.

There are many in the Labour Party who would see this as a sign of Europe's coming of age, an end to the era of unquestioning support for extended deterrence. The Cruise debate, they would argue, has paved the way for an altogether different association, at once less formal but more secure, relying more on arms control and diplomacy, than on the principle of eternal vigilance in a nuclear age.

In short, there are several factors which suggest that were Labour to inherit power, Britain might find itself semi-aligned by the early 1990s, that its new status would be one of the constraints under which an incoming Conservative government might have to labour, even if the public at large might find something at fault in the new role, a faltering of purpose difficult to disguise.

One writer, with judicious academic restraint, has defined semi-alignment as a status in which "*states which are formally aligned . . . have made certain explicit reservations as to their degree of involvement in the alliance.*"[42] Clearly, in the British case, those reservations would relate to the non-deployment of nuclear weapons on British soil, the non-use of battlefield nuclear weapons in Germany, and the right (perhaps tacitly accepted) to insist on a level of consultation with the Soviet Union on nuclear matters on which no British Government has previously insisted.

Whether semi-alignment would necessarily be detrimental to NATO must remain a matter for speculation. Much would depend on external factors over which a British Government would have little control, in particular the extent it may push Western Europe and the United States into open confrontation, especially if it appears to confirm the Americans in their opinion that the term "entangling alliance" has taken on a very different connotation from that found in the history books of the past. As Ibsen once observed "*Friends are to be feared not so much for what they make us do as for what they keep us from doing.*"

It may not be enough for a Labour Government to manoeuvre with care, in the hope of containing a potentially disastrous breach with Washington by a judicious combination of pressure and conciliation. The problem is not whether the United States could live with a semi-aligned Britain (a very different prospect from a barely aligned Denmark), a country that could no longer be relied upon to take the lead in deploying theatre nuclear weapons as it did in 1957 as well as 1979, a power that has never before presented Washington's policy community with a "British problem".

The problem will really arise if the British insist on vetoing American actions outside NATO, or adding their voice to the chorus of anti-American protest which might follow another Tripoli raid, or limited military operation. For many Americans, alliances have become entangling, not, as George Washington predicted, because they have involved the United States in unnecessary confrontations on behalf of fickle or feckless friends, but because they have inhibited it from embarking on operations from which Europe would wish to publicly disassociate itself, or privately communicate its misgivings.

Once the United Kingdom abdicates its responsibility in the area where it has always been most onerous; that of nuclear policy, it cannot expect either to be listened to, or for its moral disapproval to carry any weight. It is not at all clear whether the Labour Party understands this, or much less cares. It is a reality that must be communicated to the rank and file of the party if a breach is to be avoided. Indeed, if semi-alignment means acceptance of a more muted role, a lower level of consultation with Washington, there are many Americans who might find the prospect far from unappealing.

Semi-alignment, will not, of itself, bring NATO down. It need not betoken the Alliance's progressive disintegration, merely a gradual loosening of ties, a return to the early pre-1951 era when the Alliance was no more than a non-reciprocal American guarantee to a purely European Alliance, the Brussels Pact. NATO will not disintegrate, it will evolve by a process of osmosis, taking on the shape of the environment in which it operates. It is difficult to imagine the Soviet Union passing up the opportunity by engaging in any action which would reverse a process that might only be arrested by ill-considered initiatives of its own. One suspects that the present Soviet leadership is far too astute for that.

If Britain is to remain a member of NATO, however, it will have to act in a manner consistent with semi-alignment. If the Alliance is to survive at all, it will have to act as befits what the philosopher Michael Oakshott has called an "*enterprise association*" in which the members are bound during the terms of their membership by agreed rules and procedures, in accordance with a guiding principle, the common good. Nations are always free to contract out; they are under no binding social contract. If by their very nature, however, enterprise associations are limited in time and restricted in scope, they do not allow maverick members to pursue their ends in the face of unanimous opposition.

That too is a political reality with which Labour will have to come to terms as it charts a unilateralist path in pursuit of a less demanding role. Conditional membership may be possible, even consistent with continued and active membership. But if the terms of an enterprise association do not prescribe the choices a nation may wish to make, they do prescribe the conditions of making them more strictly than Labour appears to realise, or at least is prepared to admit. Such associations, according to Oakshott:

"*do not specify performances; they postulate performances and specify procedural conditions to be taken into account when choosing and acting.*"[43]

The context is which a Labour Government makes its choices will have to be international, not national, multilateral not unilateral. It will have to lobby hard, and argue its case, and if possible find support from the semi-aligned countries that have already made that choice, notably Denmark, the Netherlands and Greece. Its problem is that some of the latter, notably the Dutch, have already expressed grave misgivings about a British Government acting in a way that might precipitate a major reduction in American forces.[44] Paradoxically, the semi-aligned have an interest in limiting the status to countries which by virtue of their size and history could not be expected to be anything else.

Whether it likes the fact or not, the United Kingdom is still tethered to its own creation. If it wishes it otherwise, it will have to slip anchor in the night, drifting along on the current of events, in waters as yet uncharted, in a direction as yet unknown.

5

Inadmissable Evidence: Party Preferences

IT is not unreasonable that Mrs Thatcher should fight her third election on the claim that she has been the only political leader in thirty years to have evolved an intellectually coherent and consistent economic programme, a radical new approach to Britain's long malaise in place of the petty compromises and fraudulent promises of the past.

Unfortunately, in the field of defence – apart from John Nott's abortive 1981 review, Conservative policy has been far from radical, merely predictably consistent. At times the Government has been beset by doubts, poised between endeavour and inertia, trapped in a mood of desperate indecision. Mrs Thatcher herself may have had a clear view of the Soviet threat before coming to power, but since 1979 she has developed no new ideas on how best to meet it. Instead, cost accounting has been the guiding principle and passion.

Despite a real increase in defence spending of twenty-five per cent between 1979–85, the inflow of extra cash has not been accompanied by the propagation of new ideas. During these six years, the Government's motto has been "business as usual", a rallying cry in war, a despairing riposte in peace from a party that so clearly has few ideas of its own.

As Britain has struggled to spend a fifth more on defence at a time when more has tended to buy increasingly less, three Defence Secretaries have come and gone, leaving George Younger an unenviable legacy. Whoever finds themselves in the Ministry of Defence (MOD) by the end of the 1980s will have a long way to go across regions as yet uncharted. No-one seems to know or especially care what may lie on the other side.

Francis Pym continued where the last Labour Government left off, his principal achievement in office being the decision to purchase Trident, a system that has proved so expensive that, according to a recent opinion poll, only thirteen per cent of Tory voters now consider that it is a reasonable purchase.[1] Sir John Nott embarked on a highly imaginative, if controversial review which had hardly been published and publicly debated before it was torpedoed by the Navy, fresh from its triumph in the Falklands war. The more flamboyant Michael Heseltine was given his head, only to lose it. His departure, early in 1986, was marked by almost unanimous agreement that his early promise had been left unfulfilled, in part because the Government had no new ideas to offer, in part because he had none of his own except the typical managerial solution of stretching limited funds still further, to the "horizon" and if necessary beyond.[2]

It has fallen on George Younger to square an impossible circle at a time when some difficult questions need to be publicly aired. Can Britain afford a nuclear deterrent as expensive as Trident when public support for the very idea of Britain remaining in the nuclear club has fallen by twenty-five per cent since the 1983 election? Can the country afford a fifty ship surface fleet when surface vessels were exposed as costly and vulnerable military assets during the Falklands war? Can it afford the new European Fighter Aircraft which promises to be the country's largest-ever equipment purchase when the RAF already has six fewer squadrons to show for itself since Mrs Thatcher came to office? Is there not an increasingly compelling argument not only for reducing the Falklands garrison as the Government has proposed, but abandoning the base altogether? Did not the war itself, far from heralding the onset of a brave new age, mark a last historical rally in the *longue durée* of Britain's imperial decline?

For the first time in years, the Conservative Party seemed to have produced a leadership that was prepared if not to reverse the decline, at least to arrest Britain's economic recession. A radical "New Approach" (the title of the Party's 1979 election manifesto) promised a radical re-structuring of the nation's political institutions. There has been little evidence of it in defence, apart from the Nott review. Well into its term of office, many were reluctant to condemn the Government untried. Experience suggests that they may have been far too trusting.

Compared with the bruising defence debates within the Liberal-SDP Alliance and the uncompromising alternative defence policies offered by Labour, the Government has proposed only more of the same. Throughout its eight years in office, its principal preoccupation has been one of style, rather than substance, to reassure the voters that the country is still on course, that there is no particular need to tack and jibe to the prevailing winds of political fashion.

A moment's reflection, alas, would suggest that this naval metaphor is not especially encouraging. For seven years Britain has been conducting its defence policy within the framework of a double hulled ship, the outer hull being its traditional role in NATO, the inner what the country can actually afford. Isambard Kingdom Brunel was the first engineer to design a ship which could transmit a strain-stress relationship between the two hulls. If the Conservatives insist on fighting the election, as they did the last, on the understanding that no real choices will have to be made, it may not be long before the ship of state founders under the strain.[3]

Some Conservative Heresies

The Monetarist Challenge

When the Conservatives first came to power in 1979, they were committed to reducing the level of public spending as a percentage of GDP, freeing the taxpayer from what was considered an unduly high tax burden. While acknowledging that the problems of implementation were severe, they did not accept they were insurmountable. Events would suggest that the Government laboured under a grave misapprehension, partly of its own making, in believing that the possibilities of success were more real than those of failure.

Of the four major economies in Western Europe, the British taxpayer is still the most heavily taxed. In terms of defence spending alone he has to find ten per cent more than his French counterpart, twenty per cent more than the average West German, 140 per cent more than the ordinary Italian voter.[4] In the view of many Conservatives, public expenditure still remains unacceptably high because the Government has spent far too much on defence. In terms of public spending, new possibilities may have been glimpsed, new lines of advance have not been prepared. The situation, in a word, has not improved for the better.

For many MPs on the Right, the MOD has remained the most profligate of all Government departments, enjoying a disproportionately high percentage of the Government's budget. When John Nott came into office, he found that the Service Chiefs had drawn up plans for the next ten years on the assumption that the three per cent real increase agreed by NATO's defence ministers in 1977 would continue indefinitely.[5]

The question that the next Conservative Government may have to face is how much of the defence budget to cut. Committed to reducing defence in real terms by just under £1 billion over the next three years (1987/90) from an estimated out turn of £18.75 billion at the end of the current financial year (1986/7), Mrs Thatcher may have to contemplate much more radical measures merely to hold the cuts at that level.

On the right of the party there is likely to be growing pressure for greater cuts in defence, rather than yet another ameliorative exercise designed to reassure the Service Chiefs and Britain's allies alike. Unless the next Conservative Government can reduce defence expenditure to something nearer the productive potential of the economy, there can be no major tax cuts. Unless defence spending can be brought down to the fourth rather than third largest item of government spending (after health and social security), there will be no hope of realising the Public Sector Borrowing Requirement (PSBR) levels which still remain at the heart of Mrs Thatcher's economic strategy.

Defence cuts are not only the context in which the present Government plans to set its economic policies over the next five years; they also form the context in which its critics on the Right have become to frame their own economic programmes.

In 1983 the Adam Smith Institute published a report on defence policy which still remains the monetarists' manifesto. Of the four principles on which it argued that defence programming should be based, two have already been adopted: the principle of efficiency and the principle of competition. The two others: the principle of choice and the principle of substitution have so far been evaded, to the consternation of many Tory politicians.

The principle of efficiency was a simple one. Unless the MOD went for lower costs, and competition in tendering it would never succeed in reducing defence inflation. The principle of competition was simpler still: unless State-owned enterprises were sold off and services usually undertaken "in house" contracted out to the private sector, the Ministry would continue to allow costs to escalate out of control.[6]

Since 1983, the Institute has seen many of its suggestions adopted, despite often intense opposition. Fixed price competitive tendering has forced state enterprises to bid publicly for Government contracts; there has been a limited amount of privatisation. So far, however, the Institute has not succeeded in persuading the Government to allow underspending to be carried through either in total or in large measure from year to year, with the procurement budget being fixed on a five year rolling basis subject to an annual review.

At the moment, the monetarists argue that the present system of budget allocations means remarkably little. Without being related to some standard benchmark it is next to useless. It may well be important to know that Britain's front line defence includes twelve armoured regiments compared with ten in 1981 and that the number of destroyers and frigates has fallen over the same period from fifty-eight to fifty-four, but such statistics tell us little about military effectiveness, and even less about whether the same degree of military capability could have been obtained more cheaply through more cost effective equipment procurement, or through a different balance between the forces employed. What the monetarists would like to see under the next Tory administration is the introduction of performance indicators that would bring input and output together in the form of unit costs related to some agreed benchmark, not necessarily past performance, but performance in the private rather than public sectors.

The Cabinet's failure to reform the budget process may not only be the result of a lack of intelligence and failure of political will – the reasons probably run much deeper. But the next Conservative administration may be much less resistant to pressing ahead with extended privatisation and further substitution. Civil airliners might be used for strategic airlift, RPVs might be preferred to a new manned aircraft (particularly the European Fighter Aircraft), ever increasing emphasis might be placed upon the Reserve Army at the cost of regular soldiers. Pilot training, the provision of transport, even weapons manufacture could be contracted out to private companies. The price of action may be much lower than the price of inaction.

The next Conservative administration may also wish to take the "civilianisation" of defence much further in an attempt to create a market environment that would mark a radical departure from the policies pursued by successive governments over the past forty years. Competitive procurement, leasing aircraft from the United States as the last Labour Government considered doing in 1978, buying from the lowest cost suppliers even at risk to combat performance could all be pursued in the name of greater efficiency. One proposal that the Adam Smith Institute made in its report was that the Government might provide subsidies to civilian transport firms to strengthen or modify existing designs for specialised military requirements. It also added that:

> The principle of civilianisation can also be extended to question the need for some specialist and expensive purpose built weapons eg, do we need expensive purpose built aircraft carriers when it it possible within days to convert merchant ships to perform this role?

So far such questions have gone unanswered. Much more worrying for the Services, given their present predilections, would be an attempt by a future Government to implement the first two principles outlined by the Omega report: the principle of choice and that of substitution. Instead of reducing the effectiveness of each Service, the report urged the MOD for once to choose between roles. Instead of struggling to maintain a conventional and nuclear establishment, its authors argued that serious consideration should be given to scrapping the second in its entirety in an attempt to keep defence spending under control.

Were the Institute's suggestions to be actually adopted, the Armed Forces would probably be found surprised and unprepared. Concerned with the need to reduce defence spending by £1 billion in 1983, it recommended that the BAOR be cut by half in favour of creating a force similar to that of the French *Force d'Action Rapide*. In arguing for a profound restructuring of British forces, principally by enhancing airpower at home, the Institute proposed that in return for a fifty per cent cut in the Rhine Army, the Government could create many more reserve units, using any savings which accrued on more spares and ammunition for a prolonged conventional war.

In addition to sweeping organisational changes in all three Services, the report also suggested that RAF (Germany) should be drastically cut back in the belief that defence, like charity, begins at home. Recommending that two more Tornado squadrons be allocated to the defence of Britain, it also called upon the Government to relocate five Jaguar squadrons from the 2nd Tactical Airforce in Germany.

In a word, the Party's monetarists seem ready to sell out everything and everyone in the Service of the only reality they appear to recognise: financial retrenchment. It may be an unattractive policy on which to stand for re-election when the Conservatives have the better of the defence debate, but it may well be an argument that will gain ground if the economy moves into a period of stagnation and high inflation.

Neo-Gaullism

Perhaps, even then the proposals just sketched could be conveniently dismissed as a political footnote, one of the "might have beens" of the Thatcher years, but for the fact that many of the propositions have become an article of faith among the party's neo-Gaullists.

On the question as to who the neo-Gaullists are, and whether they would recognise the description themselves, there is a striking lack of consensus among the politicians, reinforced by an equally striking lack of unanimity among academic observers. It is a phenomenon, however, which it would be unwise to ignore, or dismiss too lightly.

The view of the traditional Atlanticists is still informed by memories of the immediate post-war period, by the moral certainties of an earlier generation which drew very strongly on the lessons of the last war in the hope of avoiding the next. As a group, they look on the past with regret, and the future with dejection, deploring in particular the sense of moral purpose and common endeavour which the West appears to have lost.

By contrast, many neo-Gaullists tend to condemn the older politicians for their lack of political awareness, for ignoring economic realities, for constantly looking back to a past more remembered than real. Retrospectives are always fraught with danger, the most famous victim of them, as Saul Steinberg once observed, being the wife of Lot.

In an attempt to prevent NATO from atrophying from sheer inertia, many Tory MPs have begun to challenge the old orthodoxies. Many deplore the fact that, for years, the country has tended to hide behind large pronouncements and even larger gestures in trying to discharge a role beyond its means. In fairness, it must be said that neo-Gaullism does not call for the rejection of the trans-Atlantic bargain, only its revision:

> By awarding priority to the maintenance of British forces in West Germany (particularly the Rhine Army) at the expense of Britain's maritime forces, the Government is supporting an Alliance strategy which is in urgent need of change. The revisionist case is that, by making the choice of strategic priorities which it did in 1981 . . . the British Government succeeded not only in laying the seeds of an unnecessary and inter-service sterile argument at home, but also lost the opportunity which the need for further defence economies had created of initiating a major strategic review within the Alliance designed to look forward rather than to stand still.[7]

Any one familiar with the neo-Gaullist argument will recognise at once that they believe that the Alliance will only survive into the 1990s if there is a more precise understanding of national interests, if its terms of membership are more narrowly defined. They also want a new rhetoric and a new vision, free of the historical baggage of the 1950s. It is not a vision without values, but the values are those which appeal to Britain's maritime past, not its more recent continental commitment; it is not a rhetoric stripped of all emotions, but it does eschew the old appeals to burden sharing of the past.

In the words of Keith Speed, the Navy minister who resigned over the Nott review:

> ... countries must contribute to the Alliance their particular expertise, in many cases long established by history, geography, tradition and necessity. They must not be mesmerised to the exclusion of all else by NATO and Warsaw Pact countries facing each other on the central plains of Europe.[8]

It is the neo-Gaullists' fervent belief that only by returning to the maritime tradition can Britain's contribution to NATO be enhanced and underwritten. To quote the Tory MP John Wilkinson "*The Rhine Army is no longer either necessary to the military posture of the NATO Alliance in the strategic setting of the '80s or appropriate to the political circumstances of the Alliance, so different from those which led to the creation of this commitment in the early '50s.*"[9] It is striking how many neo-Gaullists believe that nationalism promises a greater commitment to peace than NATO's present allocation of burdens; how a division of responsibilities, as well as roles, is more likely to secure its future.

Both Wilkinson and Speed are clearly of the opinion that by the time Britain wakes up to the reality that it is still a maritime nation, it may find itself with only the rump of the Navy the Conservatives inherited in 1979. The belief that, in the same name of allied unity, the nation has sold itself short, is remarkable for the strength of feeling it evokes, not only among many of their fellow MPs but even such opinion formers as *The Times* which never misses an opportunity to remind its readers that "*the single most important consideration is that we are an island off the coast of Europe.*"[10] In constantly harking back to the Nelsonian tradition, the paper appears to be "*magnificently unprepared for the long littleness of life*" (De Quincy).

As heirs to a remarkable past, it would be strange indeed, if many MPs did not respond to further cut backs in the Navy with far more vigour than they did in 1981. The Conservatives, in fact, have a long tradition of expressing dismay at the scope of the continental commitment despite the fact that a Conservative Foreign Secretary, Anthony Eden, agreed to station an army on the continent of Europe in 1954.

Fifteen years later, Harold Macmillan thought that it was "*to be deplored that a commitment so contrary to British traditions, that is a permanent stationing of large bodies of troops on continental territory, should have been entered into without any corresponding arrangements or understandings as to the future developments of Europe, political and economic.*"[11] Even Mrs Thatcher has, on occasions, given voice to the same opinion though in rather more restrained tones. As long ago as the Summer of 1980, she told senior members of the Naval Staff that *"ultimately"* Britain would have to return to a maritime rather than continental role, even if for the time being it would have to concur with the *status quo*.[12]

In short, it is by no means impossible that the heresies of today might in time become the orthodoxies of tomorrow. It is a possibility that should certainly be explored. It remains to be seen whether a maritime strategy could be implemented in a manner that would retain the confidence of Britain's allies. On the question of whether present arrangements should be rejected for something else, the burden of proof surely lies with those who propose "revision".

The Labour Party

"Proceed towards the obscure and unknown through the still more obscure and unknown"
(Ancient rule of alchemists)

Labour's recovery from the nadir of electoral defeat in 1983 may well have been spectacular. Its recovery from the shock of discovering that Britain is a member of an alliance not necessarily on terms of its own choosing has been profound. In the intervening period it has advanced much further along the road to unilateralism than some of its critics have been prepared to admit. Under Michael Foot, Labour was not committed to kicking the Americans out of their nuclear bases, or immediately decommissioning Polaris, let alone taking the United Kingdom out of America's nuclear umbrella. Times have changed.

From an analysis of existing Parliamentary candidates, it is clear that after the next election the Party may significantly shift to the left. A third of all Labour MPS may be members of the Campaign for Nuclear Disarmament (CND). CND may be losing members every year but that is not of great moment in the political struggles that lie ahead. The Labour Party's commitment to a non-nuclear defence policy may represent the most readily obtainable common denominator among the majority of Labour MPs.

Neil Kinnock may not share the dislike of NATO evinced by the hard Left but his commitment to nuclear disarmament has never been in doubt. Cowardice and the betrayal of deeply held principles are not among his shortcomings, either as a man or as Party Leader. His political faults, such as they are, are strategic and conceptual, a failure to compromise, or make concessions in the hope of political return. In the final analysis, he is a product of the new Labour Party; he would not otherwise be its elected leader. When the times called for a man like Hugh Gaitskell, who was prepared to fight and fight again, Kinnock cut his cloth and went with the tide – the results may yet cost the Party the next election.

Commitment to Non-nuclear defence

It is easy, indeed fashionable on the Right to dismiss the Party's support for unilateralism as a further sign that it has been captured by the hard Left. Nothing could be more misleading. Some parties go astray in later life because they run out of creative ideas (like the Liberals before their revival in the mid 1970s, which was as surprising as the "sudden death" of Liberalism sixty years before). Others undergo a change of conscience like Labour in the late 1950s, which persuades them to abandon the principles on which they had previously campaigned. If Labour has changed direction once again, its reconversion to unilateralism can hardly be considered either inexplicable or unexpected. What is surprising is that the leadership's own conversion should have taken so long.

Even at the time of Gaitskell's victory, when the party reindorsed nuclear deterrence after a bitter struggle, the trade unions remained almost unanimously committed to CND. Unions like the TGWU never waivered in their allegiance as did many regional committees throughout the country. Some unions which had previously held back, like ASLEF, SOGAT and the ACTT actually joined CND at the time of its eclipse. In the light of such broad trade union support, the Party's eventual conversion to unilateralism should have come as no surprise once the nuclear debate was re-opened. When John Silkin, the Party's Defence spokesman entered the race for the deputy leadership his "discovery" of unilateralism at the advanced age of 58 secured him the vote of the TGWU, even though he went on to lose the campaign.[13] In that respect, the role of the trade unions, not the far Left, was the decisive factor in transforming the Labour Party after its defeat in 1979.

If the far Left, in fact, briefly reasserted itself in 1981, it failed to carry the day after Michael Foot's defeat. Disapproval of past compromises on socialism, the leadership's persistent failure to live up its own manifesto promises may have been widespread and deep rooted, but it was neither deep rooted enough nor voiced sufficiently loudly to prevail over a leadership that was still emotionally and historically committed to winning political power. As the Party shifted to the centre on economic policy and support for the European Community, largely as a result of trade union pressure, the far Left lost its hold on the NEC. By 1986 it found itself ministering to a diminishing congregation, served by small band of loyalists so bound to a set of received ideas that it was probably beyond salvation.

But if the far Left has been politically outflanked, the move towards unilateralism has proved permanent. Even if Labour loses the election, the nuclear debate will continue to preoccupy the Party faithful for years to come. In despair, it will probably turn inward, emphasising its distinctiveness as a community within the nation, passionately resolved to preserve its separate identity. Some may withdraw into themselves; others will continue to address the country in apocalyptic terms. Its proselytising instincts will not diminish.

In seeking to explain the commitment in terms beyond that of trade union support, perhaps we need look no further than the generation of MPs represented by Neil Kinnock who discovered that, while the poor might always be with us, nuclear weapons need not. It was brought up to believe that the arguments in favour of nuclear deterrence were self-evident and unchallengable. It was starved of the knowledge that most attracts young minds: that the importance of political life is the exercise of choice. The rejection of the bomb offered an escape from the past, an emancipation from the thinking of an older generation that seemed to lack the enthusiasm and passion for socialism that had inspired the 1930s generation of Cripps and Citrine. Kinnock and his peers entered the Labour movement in the 1960s when the politicians of the day such as Wilson and Brown seemed to prefer a managerial approach to socialism that had little appeal to the younger generation of MPs.

In the campaign for a nuclear free world, that generation found a role and a cause that gave their commitment to socialism a renewed sense of purpose. That was its attraction and its strength. As Peter Tatchell was later to write *"There is no point in even beginning to think about socialism or any other humanitarian ideal if we are denied a world in which to create it."*[14] Ban the bomb and the rest would follow. Defence policy once again held the foreground.

It is all no doubt very worthy, but the Party's metamorphosis has also been somewhat dishonest. Since it adopted unilateralism at its Conference in 1981, it has tended to become an enclosed order preoccupied with its own obsessions, a caste which seems anxious to avoid contact with the real world. It has shown little capacity to entertain genuine responses from the society it is meant to serve, or little genuine commitment to educate the public. It has left that to CND which, like all lobbying groups, has grossly distorted the case against nuclear deterrence in ways that have inevitably cast doubt on the Labour leadership's real understanding of the issues involved.

Kinnock, for one, of course would not agree. He has explained his views to the electors, and even visited the United States on three separate occasions to underscore his position. His is the enthusiasm, of the political fundamentalist who like Shaw's Caesar remains utterly convinced that *"the customs of his tribe and island are . . . the laws of nature."* It is an improbable claim on which to run for election, but upon his success in persuading the electorate of its validity may well depend the Labour Party's hopes in the polls.

The Civil Service

Regrettably (perhaps, for those who believe in open Government) the final determination of British defence policy is likely to lie less with the arguments, whether rationally or irrationally reached, than the willingness of the bureaucrats to implement a Government's decisions; indeed their capacity to understand the premises on which those decisions have been made.

Writing in the *New Socialist*, Paul Anderson argued that it was not inconceivable that a Labour Government would have to allow American nuclear weapons to stay in Britain even if it succeeded in dismantling its own deterrent. *"It is not inconceivable that a Labour Government, however robustly it asserts British sovereignty will fail to remove US nuclear weapons from this country."*[15]

Ever since the American Government intervened in the political debate at the 1986 Blackpool Conference, the Party has persistently been aware that the obstacles to carrying out its pledges may be great indeed. Nothing is to be gained by ignoring them, or dismissing them too lightly. There is little evidence that those called upon to execute the Party's policy will have any real sympathy for the task, or even understanding for what it hopes to achieve. Equally, even if Labour Ministers are not obstructed at home, they will have difficulty enough selling their policies to their European allies and the United States. If they fail, it may be impossible to claim that want of support at home explained their lack of success.

Before looking at the external obstacles the Party will face, we must first ask what opposition if any a Labour Government could expect at home.

In so far as the Party would be representing the establishment with the greatest challenge to post war defence policy it has hitherto seen, Labour Ministers will require far more than political will to prevail. In December 1985, the Shadow Cabinet asked the Oxford Research Group to carry out a preliminary study of the problems of implementing its defence policy. Its conclusions were sobering:

> There are no existing mechanisms for such a reversal [of policy], no procedures and few precedents. Labour will be confronting not a single, powerful and permanent establishment but a dozen establishments strongly opposed to some aspects of its policy.[16]

The Research Group was assiduous in identifying such groups, in particular the Office of Management and Budget that has been deeply involved in the Trident decision, and the much respected Strategic Systems Executive which has managed the British side of Polaris with great efficiency and which in 1984 succeeded in updating and extending the mutual defence agreement with the United States for a further ten years.

Even Conservative Governments have found obstruction and evasion in the past. Labour can expect far more opposition, especially the Fabian tactics of delay in which the Civil Service so excels. Its opponents in

Whitehall will not lose the will to resist; they will merely be driven underground where they will be far harder to deal with and far more difficult to identify.

All this is a very different matter from a major Whitehall rebellion. The bottom line, as the Oxford Research Group rightly pointed out, will probably be the future not the present – not the implementation of selective unilateralist policies which might one day be reversed, but a sweeping root and branch dismantling of Britain's nuclear structure – its ability to manufacture nuclear weapons. A Labour Government may meet with widespread opposition not because it attempted to challenge the prevailing NATO doctrine, or to terminate the special relationship, still less abandon Britain's nuclear deterrent, but if it challenged the long established principle of British politics: that the door must be left open for the reversal of policies by the Party in opposition.

There is no doubt that the scientific establishment would fight tooth and nail to keep Aldermaston open on the grounds that its scientists, once dispersed, could never be reinstated. There is equally no doubt that many Labour MPs would, in turn, contend that unless Aldermaston were closed, its plutonium stocks sold and fissile material fabrication facilities dismantled, Britain would continued to be regarded by the Soviet Union as a nuclear power.[17] Indeed if Dan Smith's advice were heeded the dismantling of the nuclear industry would have to be high on the next Labour Government's agenda:

> In general, a programme of conversion should minimise upheaval as much as possible. But in the case of research, development and management, the rule is the more upheaval the better. Design teams need to be broken up and dispersed... structures which maintain the current attitudes and approach of the arms industry will have to be demolished.[18]

As to whether such advice would be followed we can only speculate. David Fairhall, for one, believes it would be disregarded along with many other policies that the Left would like to introduce. At the end of the day, common sense would prevail. For Fairhall, a Labour Government would merely want to set an example in the hope that allies and enemies alike might follow in Britain's wake. "*The reality of [Labour's] proposed defence policy*" he argues, would be "*that our nuclear deterrent was on standby, not deployed, still available on notice if required.*"[19]

In the end, economic realities may, as always, shape even the most deeply held Party beliefs. Back in 1984, a Labour Party document accepted that a future Labour Government would have to retain a large number of scientists in the nuclear industry, even though the vast majority might be able to find jobs in the private sector. It went on to admit that even the latter could not be relied upon; that the status of engineers and scientists in modern Britain was low, that individuals might find difficulty in finding jobs of comparable responsibility and influence, that British industry had a deplorable record of successful R & D in the civilian sector and an even worse record of commercially exploiting good ideas.

The authors of the report eventually concluded that if the nuclear industry were to be closed down, the Government might have to adopt equally far reaching measures in other sectors, such as expanding university research and therefore the university system, transferring staff to new Government research councils and nationalising major engineering industries.[20] Struggling as it will have to, simply to find programmes that have been "underfunded" since Mrs Thatcher came to power, is likely to prove expensive enough without raising additional revenue for the wholesale "conversion" of the nuclear defence industry to non-military use. As one author recently concluded in the medium term, Aldermaston's expertise could be used by a unilateralist Government to dismantle Britain's nuclear weapons, which would be almost as skilled a task as building them in the first place. It would, however, be a one-off job.[21]

Service Chiefs

The civil servants will no doubt spend months, even years, discussing how Labour could implement its plans. The Service Chiefs are likely to be more direct, but more loyal. So far there has been only one Service resignation since the war when the First Sea Lord, Admiral Luce, followed Christopher Mayhew, the junior minister for the Navy, in resigning over the decision to abandon the aircraft carrier programme (1966). Such resignations cannot be ruled out, nor can the wholesale sacking of the Chiefs of Staff, an event which last occurred in peace time in 1937–8 when the War Minister Hore-Belisha dismissed the Chief of the Imperial General Staff, the Adjutant-General and the rest of the Army Council. It is more than likely, however, that instinctive acceptance of civilian direction will be seen as a more important principle to uphold than the nuclear deterrent in which some Service Chiefs, notably Field Marshal Carver, have never expressed much confidence.

The fiction of a military revolt is, of course, one that appeals to the Left's view of military establishments, especially British armed forces linked by history to the United States, and by inclination to the prevailing social order. Thus, Hugo Young, writing in *The Guardian* in October 1986 felt confident in predicting that a Labour victory at the next election would "*drive the defence establishment out of their foxholes from which they have so often preferred to see [defence] questions either not fully addressed, or else answered with nothing more than brutal appeals to precedent.*"[22]

Young was writing at the time of the Labour Party Conference in Blackpool which finally committed the Party to the strategy of "non-provocative deterrence". Interestingly, while journalists exercised all their ingenuity in devising apocalyptic scenarios of what might happen, were such a policy ever to be unilaterally imposed, the Services Chiefs remained deafeningly silent. Their retired predecessors did not. Indeed they were so vocal that, at times, it seemed that the public had been invited to eavesdrop on a private conversation between the individuals concerned.

Admiral of the Fleet Lord Lewin, who as CDS had been the Government's Principal Military Adviser during the Falklands war, made no disguise of the fact that the Services had given absolute priority for the past twenty-five years to an independent deterrent. Given this history, he warned, if Labour came to power the Service Chiefs would have to "*consider their position*" very seriously.[23] Sir Henry Leach, who had been Chief of the Naval Staff in 1982, insisted that had Labour been in power during his term in office he would have made known his profound misgivings to the Prime Minister.

Of all the issues in Labour's manifesto, the Oxford Research Group believed that none would cause more anguish for the services than the abandonment of Polaris, in particular because they would fear a crucial loss of confidence between the Royal Navy and its American counterpart where links run much deeper than between the respective services of any other NATO members. Equally important for the RAF would be its proposed role were a Conservative administration to be returned in 1992, pledged to reintroduce a minimum deterrent. Faced with a crash programme of constructing free fall bombs for Tornados, a medium term programme of air launched cruise missiles and a long term plan to rebuild nuclear ballistic missiles, financial constraints would probably make nonsense of any of these choices but the first. Only the Tornado option would be feasible and by the early 1990's there might be some doubt whether Tornados would get through.

At Blackpool, the Labour Party addressed none of these concerns. As it has regularly done for some years, the leadership chose to immure itself in an unreal world where trade-offs between Government and civil servants will not be necessary, where concessions to the military will not have to be made. Recognising, quite rightly, that Labour's defence programme represented "*the most radical proposal that Labour has ever put before the British electorate*"[24] the Party's chief Defence Spokesman Denzil Davies seemed reluctant to concede that precisely because this was the case, the ground would have to be prepared with great care.

In the end, of course, what Labour should be concerned about most is not "obstructionism" but the impracticalities of its own programme. The problem with Polaris, for example, is not bringing the boats back to port but what can be done (and at what price) to dismantle the missiles. It is already difficult enough to find anywhere to put low level waste. The nuclear waste will be the main problem.

The United States

Since adopting its policy of non-provocative deterrence, the Labour Party has gone out of its way to assure Britain's allies, particularly the United States, that its commitment to the Alliance is not in question.

Its statements have been models of Kinnock's style, re-assuring, well presented, superficially plausible. Their substance, unfortunately, is not totally convincing. Their proposals for "non provocative" defence remain incomplete, not to say misleading. Often they have shown remarkably little understanding of the concern aroused in Western Europe and Washington by the party's failure to spell out the consequences of its own actions.

What is required, is not some emollient performance belittling American concern, but an understanding of the very real uncertainty about Labour's continuing equivocation over higher defence expenditure, about the long term implications for the Alliance if its programmes were to be executed unilaterally, or after only the most perfunctory consultation with Brussels.

Kinnock's visits to the United States in 1986/7 failed to reassure his hosts. It is no secret that the Reagan administration despairs of the Labour Party; indeed one can see why. When looked at from Washington, the party looks all but defeated – the Right having shuffled dejectedly into the wings in the hope that, once in power, the old formulas can be applied, and the issues fudged completely. In the United States, Denis Healey and Roy Hattersley appear rather differently, refugees who have found in conventional deterrence a temporary haven from political reality.

Paradoxically, it is in the nuclear field that the United States may be able to adjust to Labour policy much more easily than in that of conventional deterrence. Perhaps it may be true of Britain, as Brzezinski believes to be the case with Germany, that the two countries have common interests and links which will make their courses converge, even without the formalised nuclear framework. It does not follow automatically that without the nuclear link, the United States and Britain would quickly diverge.

On Trident, the party is probably on fairly safe ground. Contrary to what many Conservatives claim, the Americans would probably be far from unhappy if Britain cancelled the programme. They are not at all happy that if it goes ahead as planned, Britain's conventional force strength may automatically be reduced, whatever the denials of the present Government. Some Ministers are already concerned that the Trident programme is due to reach its peak as a percentage of the equipment budget (1988/9) just when appropriations for the European Fighter Aircraft will have to be found. So far the Government has refused to place a single order.

Can Trident be scrapped at minimum cost to the Exchequer? At the moment, the Government is speeding up spending on the programme, in order to tie the hands of any possible successor. In September 1986, the first

keel of four intended submarines, *HMS Vanguard*, was laid. As much as
£500 million of improvements to the Faslane submarine base and the nearby
Coulport missile station have been completed. Development work has also
begun on the nuclear warheads at the Atomic Weapons Research Establishment at Aldermaston so that they will be ready when the first Trident
missiles are scheduled to arrive in the UK, probably within two years of
becoming operational with the USN in 1989. Warhead production accounts
for twenty-eight per cent of the Trident programme. So far £600 million has
been spent. If Labour were to cancel the programme, the production lines
would have to be dismantled.

The key to any cancellation is the financial penalties a Government would
incur. Vickers has negotiated a substantial penalty clause, guaranteeing it
125 per cent of the value of the contract – or more than £800 million if the
programme is cancelled before the order for the second submarine hull is
placed.

Labour's objectives, however, though fixed at this stage need not necessarily be defined. At first glance, the cancellation clause may seem daunting but
a Labour Government could at least retain the submarine hulls as part of a
nuclear powered submarine fleet. More attractive still, in view of its
opposition to building any more nuclear powered submarines (SSNs),
might be the option of selling the submarines back to the USN which is far
behind in its SLBM programme. Although smaller than the Ohio Class, the
British models would be able to carry only sixteen D 5 missiles, not the
twenty-four carried by their United States counterparts, the construction costs at Barrow-on-Furness are a third less than those at Groton. It
is not an opportunity that the United States Navy might wish to pass
up.[25]

The Americans are much more likely to be concerned about matters which
affect them directly. Twenty-five years on from Nassau, it is clear that they
have derived very little from nuclear co-operation with the United Kingdom, the British a great deal. As McNamara warned at the time, in claiming
otherwise Kennedy deceived only himself.

Since the Reyjkjavik summit (1986), it has been clear that if fifty per cent
cuts in strategic warheads are ever negotiated, the British will have a hard
time justifying not only an eight-fold increase in the number of their own
warheads but even the 128 which Younger has intimated the Government
intends to deploy. Only a few Trident warheads accurately targetted could
destroy the Soviet Union as a great power, while leaving the Soviet State
intact. In other words, the upgrading of the British deterrent has, as Gen
Seignious warned, brought to an abrupt end the period of West European
"*strategic irrelevancy*" which contributed to the strategic balance while
flattering the Europeans with the thought that they were significant nuclear
actors.[26]

If the Americans are not yet thinking of denying us Trident, that does not mean that they would not actually welcome Britain contracting out unilaterally. For many Americans, such a decision would be not so much an endgame as a refusal to play the game any longer.

If such were the case, they would be in no position to grumble about the cancellation of Polaris, even if the former chairman of NATO's High Level Group within the NPG, Richard Perle, used to insist that such a move would constitute a unilateral abrogation of Britain's commitments under the Brussels Treaty. Any commitment to phase out Polaris would be a serious course of action from which there could be no turning back. At this stage it is unlikely to meet with the unqualified support, let alone understanding, of the National Atomic Co-ordinating Offices and Joint Working Groups which have functioned quietly behind the scenes for twenty-five years. It is a choice, however, which might well meet with tacit American approval, even relief.

Since Reykjavik, the issue of Cruise has also become less immediate. If, as Kinnock claimed in a meeting at Bonn, the Superpower summit had validated "*the central thrust of Labour policy*", the Party may agree to mark time as long as progress on the removal of intermediate forces looks a possibility.[27] Mrs Thatcher may have told the Conservatives at Brighton that they had a historic duty to hold the line [28] but her own visit to Washington to warn the President of the dangers of reviving the zero-zero option while medium range missiles like the SS 21 and 22s remained, revealed that his Tory credentials were not quite as positive as the Prime Minister would have liked.

In what was seen as an important shift in his party's stance on nuclear defence, Kinnock told President Reagan on his third visit to the United States that the American missiles could stay as long as an agreement to scrap all intermediate nuclear forces was within reach. The problem will arise with its own rank and file whose impatience to scrap the missiles at once may get the better of their political judgment.

In March 1986, in one of his many attempts to square political circles, Mr Healey suggested that now the SS 20s might be bargained away at Geneva a Labour Government might try to trade off Polaris for a mutual cut in the Soviet arsenal. If an agreement proved elusive, Polaris would be scrapped all the same. Rather lamely, Healey insisted it was "logic chopping" to suggest that the Soviet Union would offer nothing if Labour was committed to abandoning Polaris anyway, not even as an exercise in political good will[29] Lame or not, the Left was far from happy with the "logic" of Healey's position. Robin Cook, one of his own Shadow Cabinet colleagues, disassociated himself from his remarks. Even Neil Kinnock claimed that he had been "mis-interpreted". Politicians are invariably the prisoners of circumstances but if they refuse to be influenced by them at all, they must not expect any remission of service. Whether Labour would avoid a rift with Washington may well depend on their willingness to be governed by the outcome of multilateral arms control talks. In the current climate, they have everything to gain.

Like its Social Democratic friends in Germany, Labour has also been quite unequivocal in its condemnation of SDI. A new age usually brings new perspectives and an era which has seen the Alliance weakened from within by unilateral American gestures may well find some of its members judging their conditions of membership rather differently from their predecessors.

In March 1985, Kinnock described even the Star Wars research programme as "*an embarkation on the arms race.*"[30] In a joint initiative with the German SPD, Labour tried to persuade the North Atlantic Assembly to condemn the programme later that year. The Labour Party's attitudes towards the Government's decision to tender for projects associated with the programme was perhaps accurately captured by Ian Aitken who scathingly wrote in *The Guardian* of Mrs Thatcher's ultimate betrayal: selling herself and Britain in exchange for a share in the technology, a decision which had finally reduced "*her Britannic Majesty's foreign policy to the level of market economics.*"[31]

Immediately before his departure for the United States in March Kinnock finally confirmed that Labour did not consider itself party to the secret memorandum of understanding drawn up between the US and British Governments in December 1985. The United States, for its part, is unlikely to make any fuss over Britain's departure from the programme, if indeed it goes ahead. Nor are those British companies who are already convinced that their market share is anyway likely to be minimal, that the Europeans will be denied project leadership in any of the programmes, that at most their role will be that of subcontractors. They may well be right.

But many British companies as we have already seen may need a great deal more persuading. At a time when practically every British development project outside the defence field is chronically underfunded, a decision to cancel the SDI Memorandum might be far more than a psychological blow. Many still hope that their involvement in SDI will provide them with a unique opportunity to gain access to key technologies without which they would never succeed in breaking through into the third industrial revolution. If the Americans have been increasingly wary of European participation in recent years, the effect of a British withdrawal from SDI, coupled by persistent criticism of the whole programme by one of their closest allies, may make them profoundly disenchanted with the European connection. The market place too has political imperatives which few Labour MPs appear to have grasped.

It is, of course, the issue of American bases in the United Kingdom which is most likely to provoke a major crisis between the two Governments. It was with the latter in mind, that Richard Perle accused the Labour Party's policy of being "*wildly irresponsible*". It could never expect the United States to accept risks entailed in offering nuclear guarantees to a country that was not prepared to accept any risks itself. On the eve of the 1986 Blackpool Conference Perle added that if Labour did not destroy the Alliance, it would none-the-less diminish its effective ability. Earlier in the year, the American ambassador, Charles Price, had warned the Party that, if his country were asked to remove all its nuclear weapons from Britain, it would come under intense political pressure at home to remove all its non nuclear bases as well, including NATO's entire force of FIIIs (115 planes in all) as well as the 110 A 10 anti-tank aircraft based in the UK.

Quite apart from the immense costs with which a Labour Government would be presented if it had to replace the cover afforded by the 300 planes in the United States 3rd Tactical Airforce (an estimated once and for all cost of £7 billion) Kinnock's personal enthusiasm for the policy has in no way been diminished. During his visit to Bonn, he insisted that the only issue dividing the two sides was the future of the FIIIS, and that, even in its opposition to the latter, the Labour Party was merely "*ahead of the times*", a claim which gave rise to the comforting illusion that, in time, the United States itself might catch up.

Unfortunately, the Americans continue to take a much less sanguine view of the matter. Most of the planes may well be "*long in the tooth*" as Mr Healey frequently protests[32] but one suspects he protests far too much. If they date back to the mid-1960's, so do NATO's short range nuclear systems on which it still relies. In addition, many of the FIIIs were brought over to Britain under the last Labour Government in 1976 because they were considered far too vulnerable to a pre-emptive Soviet attack in their former bases in West Germany and the Netherlands. Nothing in the intervening years has changed that position. Simply because the Labour Party has chosen to conjure away the threat by claiming in a recent defence paper that it had been "*contrived*" by the present Government[33] does not render it any the less immediate for our European allies.

During his visit to the United States, Kinnock found that the Reagan administration had no intention of denying American aircraft a dual-purpose role, or revealing whether they carried nuclear weapons. Rather than submit to such restrictions, they would pull out altogether, an option which Congressman Solarz warned would probably be taken by a Democratic administration as well. During his third visit to Washington Kinnock once again changed tack, suggesting that the removal of US bases and/or nuclear weapons would not be governed by a specific time limit, indeed that it might well be negotiated over a period of five years, or beyond the life of a single Government.

Whether the Party would find this acceptable is not at all clear. A recent Harris poll found that seventy-two per cent of all Labour candidates would be happy to see the closure of every American base in the country, whether officially designated nuclear or not. In that respect, the FIIIs were never the "*only issue*" separating the two sides, but the central one. In arguing otherwise the Americans were merely confirmed in their belief that Labour had become a closed shop through which its members were expected to work their passage by adhering to the belief that nuclear weapons, not Governments, make wars.[34]

The Labour Party and NATO

The United Kingdom has avoided making choices in defence for thirty years, partly as a result of a consensus (some might say conspiracy of silence) between the two main parties which has been underpinned and sustained by the advice of a bureaucratic elite which has been often unresponsive to the wishes of the Governments it has served.

The fact that the Labour Party now offers a radical break with the past is to be welcomed, not opposed. But does the party have the political will to stand by its pledges, to re-fashion the United Kingdom's commitment to the Western Alliance or will its policies be severely compromised and curtailed in a welter of mutual recriminations once it has achieved office?

Contrary to popular belief, both Michael Foot and Neil Kinnock have supported NATO, whatever their distaste for its nuclear doctrines. In 1949, Foot used his influence to persuade Tribune to support Britain's membership of NATO, much to the annoyance of his Left wing colleagues, 100 of whom voted against their own Government when Parliament debated the issue. For his part, Kinnock has been prepared to offset his opposition to nuclear weapons with a firm commitment to support the Alliance. An NEC paper published in 1985, while recognising that party policy would "inevitably" result in major changes in Britain's relationship with the United States, committed itself to changing Britain's role, not abdicating it entirely.

Like the majority of his colleagues in the party, Kinnock may want a better, safer world. Unlike many of them, he is committed to bringing the present into fruitful relationship with the past, to ensure that, just as in 1949, a Labour Government forged NATO, dragging an unwilling United States in tow, any administration of which he is leader will discharge a similar task forty years on, setting a lead which even Washington may have to follow. The reform of NATO means precisely that. Far from retreating into isolationism, Labour intends to argue its corner, confident that its own prescriptions are the only way of keeping the Alliance in being.

There is a wistful romanticism in its yearning to play a major role, to reform an institution that might never have been formed but for the initiative of a British Government, a wish to fight one's way back into history, not escape from it into a policy of neutralism or non alignment. It would be wrong to discount that commitment since it is shared by politicians of other persuasions as well.[35] It illustrates how even today Labour leaders are prone to delusions of grandeur.

Unfortunately, for all the seriousness of its intentions, the party has been unable to carry opinion either in Germany or the United States. With a CDU Government in Bonn and even a Democratic administration in Washington, the task is clearly beyond any one country, especially Britain. Much has changed since Ernest Bevin was Foreign Secretary. As the party marches along a well trodden path towards an improbable destination, the leadership probably knows in its heart that what it has to fear is not ambush by the Left or betrayal by the Right but actual arrival. For there is no sign at the moment that either Britain's allies or the Services would be persuaded of the wisdom of reform along the lines proposed: that of " 'non-provocative defence".

Non-provocative defence

The tragedy of the Labour Party in 1983 was that it chose to withdraw into a world of its own making, a private place of retreat in the belief that its defence policy could be entirely based on a visceral dislike of nuclear weapons. Instead of encouraging an open debate, the party presented the electorate with an ever shifting series of policies which lacked any common theme beyond an absolute commitment to nuclear disarmanent.

In an attempt to recapture lost ground, Labour has now produced the most comprehensive justification for conventional deterrence, a policy described by Denzil Davies as *"the most radical proposal that Labour has ever put before the British electorate."*[36] The question is how realistic is it; how much opposition is it likely to meet? The party may hold fast to a view of politics in which the Services are accessible to rational argument. It is one matter, however, to recognise that an argument can reveal an interest, quite another to imagine that it can create it. Davies himself knows perfectly well that no studies as yet have been made by the MOD as to how a policy of non-provocative defence would work. It is one of the paradoxes of British politics that the Labour Party has moved into the shadow of the next war before the Services have moved out of the shadow of the last.

Royal Air Force

This is clearly the case with the RAF which of all three Services may find Labour policy most disconcerting. At present, half its combat squadrons are armed with nuclear as well as conventional weapons. Of thirty-one armed units (in 1985) fifteen had a nuclear capability. Eight squadrons of Tornados, two squadrons of Buccaneers and one Jaguar squadron can operate in a dual role.

If a Labour Government pressed ahead with its plans, the long range Tornado would be restricted to conventional attacks against battlefield targets, in close support of Allied forces on the ground. Neither prospect holds out much appeal; indeed, it runs against the grain of thirty years of doctrinal thinking. Even if a Labour Government tried to avoid an open confrontation with the RAF, there are several reasons why it might find itself in conflict with the Chief of the Air Staff within months of achieving power.

Since the Second World War the RAF has never placed great faith in purely defensive warfare. The arrival of Tornados in RAF (Germany) was originally hailed as a quantum leap in capacity, not because of the numbers involved but because the new squadrons which arrived gave their pilots an opportunity to attack deep behind enemy lines. At the same time the airforce was promised a long range stand off missile which Labour has already announced it intends to cancel which could suppress enemy defences prior to an attack by manned aircraft.

In the late 1970's, the RAF refused to buy the American F 15, not only because it had no great interest in aerial dogfights but because it believed that the Government would allow it far too few to correct substantially a deficiency it did acknowledge: the thinness of its defensive screen. Equally short of strike aircraft, the RAF developed "nap of the earth" flying with its pilots flying lower than those of other NATO force (250 feet) so that they could get under Soviet radar and destroy enemy airfields and choke points on which both the first and second echelon forces would rely. That is why it still has the highest training standards in Europe; the missions its pilots are expected to accomplish are more ambitious than most.

Unlike the USAF, the RAF has also tried to fly out of range of Soviet missiles on the FEBA in the knowledge that at present it has neither the equipment nor the C3I capabilities to provide support to its own forces if they were engaged by surface-to-air missiles. Although its counter electronic measures have greatly improved, it still prefers to fly air patrols out of the range of the Soviet missile defences. What it does not fear are combat missions where its aircraft would be flying fast and low enough to fly under the enemy's radar. In the absence of numbers, the RAF has always had to think in terms of catching the opposition off guard, a philosophy learned from bitter experience in the last European war.

If Labour inherited power, all this would change. The full implications of its defence policy might well take time to reveal themselves but some decisions would have to be taken quickly such as the cancellation of the JP-233 cluster bomb, which has a specific denial not defensive role of cratering enemy airfields. The RAF has traditionally put its faith in cluster bombs; the USAF in precision guided missiles, a difference which has less to do with air doctrines than the availability of technology.[37] The difference after 1988 might be far simpler, but much less palatable, if the RAF is denied by its own Government the weapons it needs for striking deep behind enemy lines.

Such a Government would be asking for radical changes across the board, including the most difficult of all, a change in attitudes. To turn the RAF into a purely defensive force would be to challenge a prevailing set of values which has deep roots in past experience, which can be ignored by civilian advisers only at grave risk to service morale. In the event of another European war, the RAF might well be able to provide close air support for forces on the ground. To defend airfields, however, it will need far more than its present two Phantom squadrons. Most of its other aircraft are not able to provide defensive defence at all. In many of the comparisons between the sortie rates of NATO and the Warsaw Pact much play is made of higher pilot training, the greater serviceability of aircraft, and the all weather capability of Western planes.[38] All this may be true but it is unlikely to be of much comfort to British pilots.

In the end what will count in an extended conflict is "cumulative fatigue" which if unredressed may compound pilot error, and reduce combat effectiveness quite substantially. In defending airfields, the RAF would at present find quickly that the morale of its pilots might soon crack under the strain; that, at best, they would be unable to function optimally. During the Battle of Britain, in a very different air environment, and facing a very different adversary, the RAF found that the optimum level of sorties was only two a day.[39] It may be able to fly far more sorties at the moment, but its squadrons are far fewer. In this, as in so much else, the Labour Party seems to have paid little attention to past experience, or computations based on present performance. It has considered it enough to inject energy and urgency into the realisation of its own ideas, an option which may yet prove a recipe for disaster.

Finally, the air chiefs would have every reason to question whether deep cuts in existing force levels might not be the inevitable if delayed outcome of any major restructuring of the service. If offensive missions were abandoned entirely, there would be no particular reason for not reducing the total number of combat and support aircraft from 595 to 295. If, as Labour promises, it would spend more money upgrading air defence at home it could argue that it would be more cost-effective to invest more in surface to air missile defences, an argument which is in itself specious while increasing the number of AWACS early warning aircraft from six to ten for the limited number of manned aircraft still retained for intercepting Soviet aircraft beyond Britain's own air space.[40] It is not a prospect likely to appeal to Whitehall, however much importance is attached to home defence.

If the United States 3rd Tactical Air Force leaves, it may even be necessary to recall the British Air Force from Germany. Such a redeployment of forces may provide a transient reassurance to the British people that they could still be defended from air attack but it would be most unlikely to convince anyone else that Britain's conventional contribution to NATO would ever be the same again.

BAOR

The Army is also likely to be far from enthusiastic about Labour's plans, despite its clear commitment to maintain the British Army of the Rhine at its present strength (56,000 men). After all, a Party which has questioned the cost of Trident on economic as well as moral grounds (an estimated £12 billion over twenty years) is unlikely to find particularly attractive the cost of the Rhine Army over the same period (£46 billion).

For its part, the Army would like to make good some of the present deficiencies of the BAOR which the Conservatives have manifestly not redressed – to ensure at the very least that half its tanks will be provided with laminated armour by the end of the century, that most of the new armoured personnel carriers that it has been promised will actually arrive, that most of its artillery will be modernised, or upgraded.

Instead, it faces the disturbing prospect that the present leadership's commitment to the BAOR may be rather difficult to reconcile with the party's own understanding of non-provocative defence. Many Labour MPs like James Callaghan who have no illusions about the folly of the new doctrine, have no great commitment either to the Rhine Army which they would prefer to see halved, or pruned back even more radically to prevent otherwise substantial cut backs in the Royal Navy. Others, on the Left, have argued that under a system of non-provocative defence, the number of armoured regiments could be cut from nineteen to seven, the number of engineering units from twelve to five, the number of field and heavy artillery regiments by no less than half. We have already seen in Chapter 4 how woefully short we are of conventional artillery so that this proposal is proof positive, if such proof is needed, of the sheer idiocy of much of the Labour thinking on defence. For the record, it is worth nothing that when Callaghan last proposed cutting back the Rhine Army in 1981, the Defence Secretary contended that if it were to be reduced to between 25,000 and 30,000 men, or two not particularly strong Army divisions, the 25,000 men brought back would probably have to be disbanded to save costs.

The full meaning of conventional deterrence has not escaped the Service Chiefs, even if it has escaped Mr Davies. No doubt, like many of his colleagues, he is a deeply concerned and thoughtful man, but his image of the next war is inescapably narrow. Even Denis Healey, the most distinguished of Britain's postwar Defence Secretaries, cannot escape the criticism that his view of non provocative defence may already be out of date.

It is all very well to base a policy on:

> ... the Clausewitzian principle that defence is much stronger than attack because you are fighting on your home ground, you can create obstacles in advance of an attack, you have inner lines so your inner lines of communication are much shorter ... [41]

The main problem a Labour Government will face in its debates with the Army is not that it has adopted a tendentious critique of present NATO strategy but that the situation has changed so radically that the hypotheses drawn from the critique have lost much of their meaning.

Defensive deterrence is not a novel concept; it has been around for a long time. Unfortunately, it happens to run against the grain of present Soviet thinking; it is an idea behind the times, not ahead of them, an idea which may ironically have had its day, even if the Shadow Cabinet has not noticed its passing.

What the Labour Party proposes is an anti-tank defence, based on physical obstacles, large reserves and highly mobile decentralised army units able to mop up the exhausted enemy forces with the latest anti-tank weapons.

Unfortunately, it is not only the number of Soviet tanks which is of such concern to NATO, but the increasing number of airborne assault brigades which could be used to leapfrog fixed defences. As its confidence in armoured forces has declined, the Soviet military has adopted a new concept, the Operational Manoeuvre Group based not on a tank division but a mixed tank and airborne formation designed to paralyse enemy forces and avoid precisely the battle of attrition on which the Labour Party has now set its sights. At a time when NATO has so few highly mobile units of its own, it is rather disconcerting to find Soviet military writers already dismissing the tank force as the unusable deterrent of the 1990's, while rating the combat effectiveness of an airborne brigade (sixty assault helicopters and 1900 men) as equivalent or even superior to that of a tank division (with 10,000 men and 500 combat vehicles). The "rotary wing revolution" seems to have passed Labour by [42] just as the onset of tank warfare did in the 1930's. It is somewhat depressing to think that political parties like the nations they lead are condemned to recall the future, while forgetting the past.

Royal Navy

The Royal Navy will also need some convincing if conventional deterrence is to be sold to the admirals as well. In the 1982 Parliamentary debate on the defence estimates Callaghan was led to observe that when he listened to the speeches from his own front bench he began to feel "*we are becoming a Navy party*", an observation which elicited from Labour's defence spokesman John Silkin the reply "*We are.*"[43]

From a man who shortly afterwards discovered the virtue of unilateralism after thirty years in political life, the commitment was pretty vague. The promise to maintain a surface fleet of fifty ships contained in the party's most recent defence paper, compared with a probable post election Government target of forty-seven may well be welcome. But then the Navy will not be getting the ships it wants. Instead of nuclear powered submarines it has been promised diesel powered ones; instead of major surface ships, frigates with smaller hulls. If that is indeed what is on offer, the present balance of the Navy will be seriously affected; it will certainly be prevented from playing a more active role in defence of the Northern Flank or relieving some of the seventy frigates and destroyers from the US 2nd Fleet which will be required for convoy escort.

Since Labour is also adamantly opposed to any out of area operations or even the flag showing exercises sanctioned by the present Government, one of the CVs may also be decommissioned or sold off in the next defence review. Indeed if Britain were to dispose of an offensive fleet altogether, it is not inconceivable that in the early 1990s a Government in its second term might go for more radical measures still, abandoning all the carriers and amphibious ships, all thirteen destroyers and all but twelve frigates which would be retained for convoy duty. Large replenishment vessels such as tankers could be replaced by merchant shipping if needed; anti-submarine missions could be undertaken by helicopters and aircraft based on land. Of thirty-one diesel powered submarines, only sixteen might be retained; the rest could be sold for scrap, or exported to the Third World, the conscience of Labour MPs always permitting.[44]

As an apocalyptic scenario, all this may well be debatable. One matter is not. A purely defensive role would justify cuts in surface ships far more sweeping than those originally proposed by the Nott review.

The central point of divergence between the Navy and a Labour Government will be the fate of the SSNs, an issue likely to be contested as bitterly as was the future of Britain's aircraft carriers in 1966. To date, Labour is committed only to discontinuing the programme, not phasing out those already in service. The contention that they are too expensive for a power of Britain's modest resources, and take too large a slice of the defence budget; that in addition they have already set back the conventional submarine programme with delays for the Upholder class is a fair one, if a trifle contrived. But like so much else to do with conventional deterrence, the argument against SSNs cannot be demonstrably proved; it is not self-evident even though it may well be true.

In the end, where naval arguments may fail, economic considerations may prevail. If Trident is scrapped, Vickers will have to continue building SSNs if it is to have any hope of survival and if its entire workforce is not to be pensioned off. Fifteen years ago, the company solved its commercial problems by concentrating on defence work, primarily building submarines to the exclusion of merchant shipping and heavy engineering. Diesel powered contracts would not make up for the loss of the Trident order or nuclear powered submarines. The only alternative – reconversion to civilian use, as argued by the Barrow Alternative Employment Committee, might capture the imagination of the Left with the prospect of building wave-powered generators and tidal barriers for the Mersey and the Severn estuaries, but it is unlikely to appeal to a Government whose energies will be largely devoted to bringing the unemployment figures down to the levels promised in its manifesto.[45]

In the end, the Services might swallow many of their doubts and misgivings if they could be convinced that the next Labour Government would ever find the money to hold defence spending at its current level of five point five per cent of GDP, the absolute minimum if conventional deterrence is ever to prove more than a transparent attempt at political escapism. Unfortunately, there is every reason to doubt whether this would be the case.

Many who advocate a non-nuclear defence posture do so, after all, not only because of their distaste for nuclear weapons but because of a concern now voiced quite widely, that Britain's economic decline has made it increasingly difficult to fund the type of welfare society they took for granted in the comparatively affluent 1960s. Would another Labour Government, like the last, countenance a high cost conventional programme like Tornado which in a single financial year (1976–7) cost Britain more than the Health Service? The defence paper which Denzil Davies commended to the party at Blackpool was the result of a compromise within the NEC whereby he was allowed to keep only "some", not all of the cuts saved from the cancellation of the nuclear programme. It also contained a little noticed clause which pledged that even these savings would be released from the defence budget by 1991 at the latest, "*international circumstances*" always permitting.[46]

Squaring circles may well be a politicians' stock in trade, squaring principles is a more hazardous and dubious undertaking. In the light of Roy Hattersley's spending plans, Labour will face an uphill struggle as it is to match its pledges on defence with its economic promises. Merely restoring the pre-1979 level of public spending as a percentage of GDP would require a significant reduction in the defence burden as a proportion of national spending from the eleven per cent to which it rose in the last Labour Government.

Every week the Shadow Cabinet is reminded of the cost of defence equipment by weeklies like New Socialist or The New Statesman which have been assiduous in pointing out that the £80 million replacement cost for a frigate could build four 300-bed hospitals, or eighty new secondary schools. In 1982, Labour Research, an independent television research organisation, produced a report claiming that the MOD's £1.8 billion bill for R & D compared absurdly favourably with the £107 million budget for the Medical Research Council, and that British Rail's electrification programme at £825 million cost £75 million less than the development programme for the advanced Harrier jump jet.[47]

It is easy enough, of course, to put these figures in perspective. Commenting on the claim by the Labour Party's Defence Study Group in 1977 that the price of the Frigate *Ambuscade* could have provided a new 500-bed hospital in Bangor, Gavin Kennedy observed:

> The expenditure of even £600 million in regional employment aid in the United Kingdom is at the expense (among other things) of employment projects that could run

in Calcutta or anywhere else where the contrast in living standards with the UK as a whole is vastly greater than any living standards within the UK itself.[48]

But since the Defence Study Group published its report there have been three developments which have sharpened the debate about defence expenditure within the Labour movement, which Kinnock and his colleagues cannot afford to dismiss too lightly.

If the average citizen has always lead a life of quiet desperation, in Thoreau's words, until recently that desperation was at least tempered by an understanding that the standard of living was improving every generation. Today the gap between the UK and the Third World is actually beginning to close for the first time in 150 years. In the 1950s and 1960s health statistics showed a progressive improvement. Today twenty six per cent of the population is officially classified as "deprived". If the slums of the 1930's have disappeared "*millions are living in sordid depressed quarters of old cities of the kind the rest of the advanced world would no longer tolerate.*"[49] While infant mortality has continued to fall, there has been a dramatic rise in comparison with our partners in the European Community. Indeed, within a few years it is set to rise in absolute terms for the first time since the National Health Service (NHS) was established.

Ignoring such statistics will not be easy for a Labour Government still committed to high defence spending. It will be made less easy still by the need to be seen by its own supporters to reverse the demise in social services specifically identified, not with the nation's historical decline, but the actions of Mrs Thatcher's Government. Between May 1979 and June 1983 (during Mrs Thatcher's first term in office) each day saw twenty-eight fewer teachers, five less NHS beds, 312 fewer houses built. Inevitably, this picture, however distorted, has already given rise to the question: what is there to defend?

As Peter Tatchell has argued with great eloquence, the greater the degree of social inequality and injustice within society, the more people will feel that they have nothing worth defending. "*What is the use of people putting their lives on the line if, at the end of it all, their only reward is a return to the dole queue and the dereliction of the inner cities,*"[50] a question of course, which was first asked after the Great War failed to produce a Land Fit for Heroes.

Faced with Tony Benn's plea for "*a major diversion of resources from the means of death to the means of life*"[51] Kinnock and his Cabinet will find it difficult to hold the line, especially in the face of opposition from the trade unions on which the party has traditionally relied at its annual party conferences for the massive block votes in favour of continued NATO membership. This is the third change in the social climate that the Callaghan Government did not have to face in the 1970's when it embarked on defence cuts which appeared "trivial" to the then Health Minister, David Owen.[52]

The NEC's plans for spending more on conventional defence are ambitious, so ambitious that they are bound to unsettle the rank and file of the

Labour Movement which has always been opposed in principle to high defence spending. What Kinnock is asking for is that most difficult of all changes, a change in attitude every bit as radical as the change he expects from the Services. To turn Labour into a non nuclear but pro-NATO Party would be difficult enough, given the struggles within the Alliance that doubtless lie ahead. In attempting to bring about this change at a time when the party may be engaged in a contentious debate about high defence spending or the diversion of resources to the social services may prove impossible even for the most astute of politicians.

The Labour Party's defence policy finally fails to convince because it seems to be seriously at odds with Kinnock's real mission – not the reform of NATO, but the rescue of the Welfare State after the alleged battering it has received from Mrs Thatcher. Labour may well have taken Britain into the Alliance in 1949 but it was also the first country to create a Welfare State. One would expect its leadership to fight with much greater vigour to keep Britain in the first rank of welfare societies than to prevent its demotion into the second league of NATO powers.

Coalition politics

Since the formation of the Liberal-Social Democratic Alliance the British have had to live with the prospect of a split vote, a hung Parliament, a realignment of political parties. It is not a prospect for which they would opt from choice, wedded as they are to old party loyalties, but it is one which they have to take into account at the next election. If it appears that the Conservatives may be in power indefinitely, and that Labour will once again squander its electoral advantage on a defence policy unacceptable to all but a minority of voters, tactical voting might possibly bring about a coalition government.

The prospect, it should be added, is still rather remote. It is most unlikely that the Alliance will capture the 200 or more solid Labour seats in the inner cities which will probably continue returning Labour MPs for the rest of the century. It has apparently found equal difficulty in capturing the middle ground in the Tory marginals, ground which the Labour Party itself must capture if it is to have any hope of regaining power. According to an opinion poll commissioned by LWT, the Labour vote is already twelve points up in these seats since the election, largely at the Alliance's expense.[53]

If the vote in 1987/8 is very close, however, if the Conservatives crash as badly as the Attlee Government did in 1950, its hour may yet come.

The continuing economic crisis will probably be the single most important political reality over the next few years. If the public sees it not as a temporary reverse but the end of a secure life that has been artificially buttressed by oil revenues and high public spending, the election of a centrist government may prove far more attractive than it does at present. For the electorate the formation of a coalition would be less a vote of confidence in the future, than a failure to imagine any alternative.

The reason why the Alliance probably won't succeed on this occasion is the same as the last; no-one knows precisely where the two Parties stand. As soon as the Alliance was formed, it began to generate frictions almost as harmful, and debilitating, as those within the Labour Party which had led David Owen and his colleagues to withdraw. Since then its promise has been more rhetorical than real. The Alliance may have great potential in principle for raising questions never asked, indeed for providing compelling and challenging new answers, but its potential can only be realised if a clear policy line is enforced by the leadership. As it happens, the two Parties have worked ever since in different, often conflicting, directions.

In the run up to the last election, one party announced that it was committed to Cruise, and other to its cancellation. The Liberals were enthusiastic for a nuclear freeze, the SDP was not. Owen wanted no early use of nuclear weapons, Steel no first use. Neither could agree on the future of Polaris. As a leading SDP member admitted at the time, the two Parties had reached their conclusions by "*different routes*";[54]

Knowing that, as the next election approached, this polite agreement to disagree would seem increasingly remote and unreal, that the discrepancy between principle and reality would no longer be so easily ignored by the voters, Owen decided to force the issue at last year's SDP Conference. The vote against abandoning Britain's nuclear deterrent by a decisive margin of three to one did much to restore his personal authority in the Alliance, and the country at large. As John Cartwright, the SDP's defence spokesman wisely remarked "*If we are seen to be putting our political interests before the defence of Britain we shall not get the confidence of the public and nor shall we deserve it.*"[55]

The Conference's decision to keep open the option of replacing Polaris or extending its life marked a decisive break with the unwritten understanding of the past four years not to raise awkward questions. By highlighting the divisions between the two Parties, as well as within them, Owen hoped to force the unilateralists' hand. The resolution presented the SDP's partners with a challenge, not a threat, a challenge to play the role of a full participant in the defence debate, rather than a passive observer unwillingly dragged along in the slipstream of Dr Owen's own utterances. A means had apparently at last been found to translate Owen's many soliloquies on defence into genuine partnership exchanges.

In the event, the policy came horribly unstuck at the Liberal Party Conference. By defining joint policies, there was always the threat of exposing the deep ideological differences between the Parties. All the Liberals had to do was to approve a thirty-six line resolution, thirty-two lines of which reiterated previous Liberal policy. Only the last four lines called for a European dimension to Britain's deterrent – a serious quest for an Anglo-

French partership as a way of replacing Polaris if its replacement was considered desirable. Steel lost the vote by a large enough margin to plunge the Alliance's standing in the polls to the lowest ratings it had achieved since the 1983 election.

The decision of the delegates was all the more surprising when we consider what the SDP formula actually was; a promise on the deterrent which was hardly a promise at all, but a qualified response to the electorate's clear wish to maintain a deterrent, other than Trident. Indeed, if the Liberals had actually accepted the formula, the electorate would have had great difficulty deciding where truth ended and wishful thinking began. Against a Labour promise to scrap the deterrent altogether and a Conservative pledge to continue with the Trident programme, the Alliance would have kept everyone guessing as to whether it would ultimately be abandoned by default rather than choice.

An Alliance Government might well have concluded that Polaris would have to be phased out by 1995, ten years earlier than David Owen suggested, especially if such a step could be justified as assisting the United States in its search for an arms control agreement. There was little likelihood of spending twice as much as the Trident programme on building eleven new SSNs for a submarine-launched cruise system which the SDP favoured. Even the European option which the Alliance leaders raised with the French prior to the conference season might have looked less attractive once Owen and Steel were in office. The only possible missile, the submarine launched M5, would only just have begun development and would not therefore have been available on the same time scale as Trident. Chirac may have expressed some interest in Anglo-French co-operation, but if he had been serious, he would have reversed years of French thinking. It was, after all, Giscard D'Estaing who first raised the question of replacing Polaris at the Guadeloupe summit in 1975 precisely because the French wanted two centres of nuclear decision making in Europe, not one.

If the formula, therefore, offered the prospect of only extending the life of Polaris until the system was phased out because of ageing hulls, and unstable reactors, it may in reality have marked a significant step on the road to unilateral disarmament.

In the meanwhile, the two Parties have shored up their relationship. Having taken the party to the brink of the abyss, and looked into it, the Liberals decided to draw back. Steel now has the endorsement of his party in outlining the Alliance's price for a coalition with either of the two parties. The Conservatives would have to drop Trident, Labour its opposition to the retention of Polaris while an alternative is discussed. When Steel spoke, however, of the need for Kinnock to abandon plans for *"chucking away our defences and endangering NATO,"*[56] it was still not clear how high Polaris figured on the agenda.

The Alliance will go into the election offering nothing more than the timid compromise of a coalition which is itself caught in two minds, between the belief that abandonment of the deterrent will never win public support and the fear of seeming to be a high defence spending party, even more wedded to the old NATO orthodoxies than the present Government. The disarray of recent months does not preclude the possibility of a real meeting of minds in the future – but to suggest that the Alliance will ever be able to offer the voters a real alternative is probably to indulge in wishful thinking. The grim irony of the Alliance is that it is the supreme example of consensus politics. Its attempt to refashion the mould of British politics has so far failed because it has never had the courage to move beyond the bounds of the British political experience.

What will happen after the election if the Alliance loses ground substantially, is another matter entirely. If Steel retires, as he says he may, the Liberals are likely to lurch further to the left. The Liberal MPs who voted against the Party defence policy at the last conference, MPs like Simon Hughes (Bermondsey), Michael Meadowcroft (Leeds West) and Archie Kirkwood (Roxburgh and Berwickshire) are hardly likely to throw in their hand with the Conservatives, or be particularly happy with the Party's present subordination to the SDP's defence policies. If the SDP does badly in the polls, the Liberals may even be tempted to contract out of the Alliance in the hope of another Lib-Lab Pact which sustained the Callaghan Government during its last two years in office.

Their defence policies would not be far removed from Labour's anyway. Indeed unlike Labour the Liberal Party's commitment to unilateralism has never wavered since 1957. Only a constitution which enables the party leader to veto conference resolutions, and write his own manifesto, has enabled Steel to accept the retention of Polaris as a purely tactical measure. Under the leadership of someone like Paddy Ashdown, the party's real voice may be heard for the first time. A series of straw polls, taken by the Party Chairman in 1984, revealed that the majority of Liberal MPs wanted a policy of conventional deterrence, preferably non-provocative in intent.[57] Ashdown himself believes that, if Europe is to escape total dependence on the United States, it will have to take more responsibility for its own defence. "*That NATO's deterrent would then be exclusively American should not worry us. After all, this is the present situation anyway.*"[58]

If the Liberals did move along the unilateralist road, the SDP would either have to join them, or opt out of the Alliance itself. Before 1983 there were signs that its nerve was clearly failing, that at heart its commitment to nuclear deterrence was more equivocal than David Owen's. As recently as January 1984, the Council for Social Democracy only narrowly defeated a demand for a complete nuclear freeze and a policy of No-First Use, having earlier vetoed a resolution calling for the non-deployment of cruise missiles. Owen may be a leader who, by temperament as well as choice, wishes to mould the future rather than passively respond to events, but quite soon the situation may not be of his own making. His own future may be closely tied to David Steel's.

In short, the agreement the two leaders have patched up is not a settlement of the issues which divide the parties, but a temporary arrangement to minimise the effects of the dispute on the Alliance. If it does not survive the next election, there is a clear possibility that the Alliance itself will not survive either, or that the SDP will have to follow the Liberal line on defence, an ironic outcome. The Labour Party's defence policies would at that stage no longer prove an obstacle to a coalition. The future, in fact, may well be Labour's for the asking, provided that it does not throw it away, as it did in 1983 by ill-considered policies and dubious public posturing. In such circumstances, given the nature of the first-past-the-post system, we could hardly condemn as "opportunists" or "disreputable politicians" men who sought simply to seize an unexpected opportunity by using their political skills.

6

The Audit of War: Defence Budgeting

"We fear the future not without reason. We hope vaguely, we dread precisely. Our fears are infinitely more precise than our hopes."
(Paul Valery)

FOR forty years, defence has been carried on largely independently of public opinion, sometimes, as with the deterrent, independently of perceived challenges or threats. The overriding constraint has been economic necessity: whether it has taken the form of Sterling crises, balance of payments difficulties, or the offsetting costs of the Rhine Army. The next review will be no different, quite the reverse.

The present Government, for all its radicalism in domestic politics, has been remarkably consistent in its *approach* to defence. Even the Nott review, as David Greenwood remarked after the Falklands war, did not change Britain's priorities. It merely involved an "adjustment" of the defence budget from the short to the medium term.[1]

The adjustment, of course, has not worked; which is why another review will almost certainly follow in 1988. As the Commons Defence Committee noted two years ago, the Government would have to choose between roles if a future defence budget fell markedly short of the resources available to meet commitments. The basis of the choice, when it comes, will as usual, be economic necessity, not political choice. As the Committee further predicted, budgetary, not military, constraints would probably force "*a hurried reconsideration or elimination of a major commitment.*"[2]

Thereafter, Britain is more likely to be influenced by other constraints for the first time in recent history: by the intrusion of the public into the political debate, by reperceptions of the Soviet threat, by the progress or non-progress of arms control, by at least some of the developments and trends which I have tried to sketch as the context within which future decisions may have to be taken. In this respect the ninth defence review when it comes may be very different from any we have seen since the Sandys review of 1957, which assumed that the future could be secured cheaply and effectively by nuclear deterrence and practically nothing else. Arguably it was the most foolish and damaging review of the post-war era, a British version of the future crammed with British images, an extraordinary exercise in wishful thinking which proved an arresting, if hardly necessary reminder, that British military thinking has been notoriously out of step with the times.

Unfortunately, the Sandys review offers no reassurance that we will be any more successful in reading the runes in the 1990s, than the next Government will be in casting them.

Conservative Government and the 1988 Defence Review

Were Labour to come to power tomorrow and turn its mind to more radical policies on defence than those which the Government is offering, it would find that some hard thinking about the future has already begun. Mrs Thatcher's Britain has not stopped still since 1981, even though there has been little public discussion of radical reform either within the Cabinet or on the backbenches. There is in fact a growing awareness of change and flux, a recognition that new challenges, if still elusive, are very real; that many of the manifesto promises are not, in fact, realisable within the public spending limits which the Treasury has set.

Trident

Immediately after the Reykjavik summit (November 1986), Mrs Thatcher had to move quickly to secure President Reagan's continued support for the modernisation of Britain's nuclear deterrent. What worried her, and her Cabinet colleagues, was not what the President had said on the spur of the moment about eliminating all ballistic nuclear missiles, but what his successor might say in 1989 when the first Trident missiles are actually tested. If the purchase were ever unilaterally cancelled, it might create a crisis between the two countries similar in its impact to that which followed the cancellation of the Skybolt programme in the early 1960s. It is doubtful whether the decision this time would be reversed. Britain, though still important, is no longer America's most important ally.

At the NATO Foreign Ministers' meeting in Brussels last December, only a month after Gorbachev and Reagan had conducted their abortive exercise in summitry, the United States confirmed that it had abandoned its wish to look at the future of ballistic missiles. It saw no set of circumstances in which the option would be feasible. But once opened, Pandora's box is notoriously difficult to close. As Cesare Pavese once remarked, if you are ever forced to look into the abyss, the only course of action is to go into it and meet the future head on. It would be highly surprising if the Government has not prepared the ground for a major U-turn on Trident.

Although there is no evidence that the United States would put pressure on a Conservative Government to reconsider its position, to purchase Tomahawk instead, it is as well to remind ourselves how vulnerable the

United Kingdom already is to American pressure, which could take a more subtle form than outright refusal to supply the missiles.

The Americans have always ensured that Britain never developed the technology to manufacture ballistic missiles of its own. The Polaris deal offered an opportunity which they have not let slip. British companies carrying out repairs on the missiles do so under strict US "supervision".[3] Any British company bidding for subcontract work on the Trident system must be "approved" by the United States Navy. Such approval could quite easily be withheld.

The British may be making their own warheads for the system, but they have to be tested in the Nevada desert. In addition they do not have enough plutonium. They have even been forced to cannibalise some of their older nuclear weapons to arm the existing Polaris fleet. The H-bombs which were carried by the Vulcan bomber force in the 1960s have all been dismantled, so that their plutonium could be recycled for the Chevaline multiple warhead system. Even with two nuclear reactors, operated by British Nuclear Fuels at Sellafield, working at full capacity, Britain would still not be able to make up the difference. True, the new plutonium plant at Aldermaston will be complete within the next few years but two of its four bays will be needed to upgrade the WE 177 tactical bomb, now reaching the end of its design life, if the British intend to continue to manufacture their own tactical nuclear weapons.[4]

Perhaps, most important of all, Britain could find itself disadvantaged at any time before the mid-1990s if the US Joint Strategic Staff at Omaha chose to "revise" the arrangements under which Trident is meant to be targeted. Unlike Polaris, precise satellite intelligence is absolutely essential if Britain is to make use of Trident's much improved accuracy, which is the only justification for buying so expensive a system. No doubt Britain will have codes for targetting her own missiles in an emergency, but they would be largely useless if the Americans ever withdrew all access to the intelligence which has been promised. The mere suggestion that such an eventuality might arise should be enough to make the Government reconsider the whole question of whether Trident is worth the expense.

Could the Government go for Tomahawk instead? Very much so, providing it acted quickly. The Vickers design department has confirmed that the lead time for installing Tomahawk in the Trident hulls which are already being built would be three years. In principle, the Government would have until 1992 to make a decision, since the maximum life for Polaris now appears to be 1995, not 2005 as once thought. In practice, the Government could either adapt the two hulls for the existing SSN fleet or sell them back to the American Navy, expanding the planned nuclear power submarine programme to take twelve vertically launched Tomahawks per boat. If the Government chose to opt for a minimum deterrent rather than a Super-power force (in content if not scope) there would be no need to deploy the

400 Cruise missiles that it considered before taking the decision to buy Trident in 1980.

In reality, the Government would probably find itself pulled by opposing forces. On the one hand, it might begin to doubt America's willingness to honour the agreement Mrs Thatcher reached with President Carter on her first visit to Washington in December 1979. On the other hand, such considerations are likely to weigh equally heavily with regard to purchasing Tomahawk, which the United States Navy has just launched successfully in its vertical launch mode. British Aerospace would probably be able to build Cruise missiles itself (and would certainly welcome the opportunity), but it would represent a completely new technology for British industry and require the Navy to adopt new techniques.

Even if both managed to rise to the challenge, the Cruise missile option would represent yet another high risk area for the defence industry, a programme whose costs for the warheads alone could in the end even outrun Trident's. If a Conservative Government did opt for Tomahawk or the Cruise option in a different form, its reasons are more likely to be political, rather than economic.

Another Nott Review?

Like the majority of its supporters in the Tory Party, possibly even the junior Navy minister, Keith Speed, the Royal Navy was completely caught out by the Nott review. Addressing Parliament in January 1981, the Defence Secretary had insisted that the Government intended making no "*apocalyptic choices*". MPs heard only the first word, not the last. When Nott went on to argue that the Government had no intention of making "*a stark choice... between a maritime capability and the central front*" they went away even more reassured.

Public euphemism, of course, as Paul Fussell once maintained, has been "*the special rhetorical sound of life*" since 1914, a disturbing political phenomenon since euphemism urges us to ask no questions. Had this not been the case, the Government's critics might have asked whether the target of maintaining fifty frigates and destroyers was not itself unrealistic even at the time.

By 1989 there will be no way of keeping fifty ships in being. All the cuts that can be made will have been completed; the provision of support services; competitive tendering for new equipment; the reduction of on-shore personnel; the freezing of pay. All the Government will be able to do is reduce the front line surface strength of the Navy to forty-seven ships in service, without formally abandoning the commitment to maintain fifty overall.

Every indication suggests that the Government is moving in this direction, despite its protestations to the contrary. The fate of the Type 23 programme is a case in point. Although the first was ordered in 1984, only two tenders were invited the following year. If the number originally agreed is cut substantially, the Navy will have to live with all the problems of an ageing fleet. If cuts in cost are made (such as replacing their expensive EH 101 helicopters for the less expensive Sea King) the Navy will find itself with modern platforms but obsolescent weapons.

Of course, a Conservative Government could try to avoid political controversy by continuing the deception for as long as possible, 1991 by Malcolm Chalmer's reckoning. In a paper published last year he suggested that "*about fifty escorts*" could be maintained until the mid-1990s by ordering only nine new escorts between April 1989 and April 1995 while retiring all but five of the existing twenty-three Leander class frigates. In the long term, however, such a rate of ordering, would even make it impossible to maintain forty-seven or more escorts until the end of the century.

The Government would either have to accelerate its rate of ordering, perhaps by going for a cheaper model than the Type 23, or accept that the number of escorts might have to be reduced to forty.

Chalmers believed that, unlike 1981, the Government would not grapple with the problem head-on by making the choice between quantity and quality but allow the situation to develop of its own accord. As he concluded, perhaps rather cynically (but not without cause), such an option would allow the orders for the eight Type 23 already planned to be completed at a slow, and therefore inexpensive, pace:

> It would leave open the option of pursuing one of the alternative low-cost designs for frigates that are now a focus of intense discussion. And even if such efforts proved unsuccessful, the Government would know that the repercussions of its policies on the size of the Fleet would not be felt until well after its stay in office had expired.[5]

It is also possible, of course, that the Government, recognising that it might not be able to spin out the Fleet's demise for as long as Chalmers predicts, might decide to go for another "Nott review", to choose now rather than later to reduce the number of major surface units to forty-three by 1995, and focus on the submarine fleet as Nott originally planned.

Indeed one Navy authority believes that, at the present rate of ordering and deletions from service, the Fleet in 1990 will have only thirty-four frigates and destroyers of reasonable age, plus five Leander class frigates which would be twenty years old, and some even older, making a total of thirty-nine in all.[6] To increase the number beyond that, several more of the Leander class the last of which was commissioned in 1973 might have to be run on until the end of the century.

This analysis may possibly be too pessimistic. But what the Government would have to ask itself is whether it could justify the cost of maintaining forty-seven escorts simply to avoid the kind of political controversy which followed the 1981 Review.

To begin with, the cost of the naval equipment budget is running at the moment at a staggering £2 billion, having doubled in five years. As the 1986 Defence White Paper revealed, while the equipment bill for the Army and Air Force had fallen by ten per cent and five per cent respectively, the Navy's had risen by seven per cent (not only because of Trident). Indeed, in 1986, the Government spent more money on the Royal Navy than any other administration had done in the previous twenty years. The Navy has not been particularly discriminated against by Mrs Thatcher as many of its supporters claim; it is merely that the naval procurement budget is spiralling out of control.

Secondly, there is a limit to the amount that could be saved by engaging in more competitive tendering, introducing more fixed price contracts to replace the cost plus formula of old. Certainly there is room for improvement, but not as much as the cost cutters often imagine.[7] What the Government may be moved to do is to end the present system of allowing the Navy to design ships itself. By allowing the Navy to lay down only minimum specifications, and then encourage British industry to design ships specifically for export, it may even be possible to maintain more than 47 ships in being, though not of the navy's own choosing, and possibly not of NATO's as well.

Thirdly, the present Government has learned the folly of phasing out periodic refits for ships that are likely to find themselves in the front line. During the Falklands war, the decision proved a false, even fatal, economy. If the decision had not been taken in 1981, ships like the *Cardiff* would have received Type 1022 radar in place of its obsolescent Type 965 which, when actually tested, proved too slow in passing the data to its SeaDart missiles' own target tracking radar. The *Sheffield* only went down because it had not been given up-to-date ECM equipment. Rather than go for "invisible" cuts which are politically less contentious, the next Government may find the courage to abandon the Type 23 programme (the only major warship now on the drawing board for the next century) and go for smaller corvettes which may not only be better armed, but also more likely to survive in an open or closed sea environment.

In fact, the Government could justify a further cutback in escorts by taking up the argument that in the next war, not only would large convoys be too vulnerable to protect, however many frigates were deployed, but that an integrated air defence would be unnecessary if each merchant ship were given its own air defence system. Area defence is expensive; self defence much less so, especially if container ships or tankers were given their own Seawolf missiles, their own ECM systems, possibly even their own command and control centre.

Some naval experts are now arguing that if the Royal Navy were to form its escorts into two "support groups" whose sole task would be to keep open certain identified sealanes and not to escort convoys at sea, more economical use could be made of surface vessels. Indeed the shift of emphasis in helicopter operations from screening a convoy to forward defence, may suggest that the Type 23 design is unnecessary. Each of the two Groups might only need twelve frigates and destroyers, a carrier and several fleet submarines to patrol two designated sealanes.[8] Whether the argument is convincing need not really concern us. The very fact that some members of the Navy are in broad agreement with its thrust might be enough to provide the politicians with the expert opinion they need.

There would be a curious irony of course if the next Conservative Government were to pursue such a course with the Nott review as its inspiration, even guide since it might also feel it necessary to cut back the SSN programme which the former Defence Secretary believed to be the key to the future success of anti-submarine warfare.

As early as 1964, Harold Wilson spoke of the nuclear powered submarine as the capital ship of the future, the "battleship" of the modern age. It was not until the late 1970s, of course, fifteen years later that they received Harpoon torpedos which have made them a formidable anti-submarine weapon. Before that they had only the updated Mark 8 which first went into service in the 1950s and could only be used against surface ships. While he was Navy minister (1968–70) David Owen became a passionate advocate of the SSN fleet, one of the few causes to which he has remained true ever since. In his book *The Politics of Defence* he argued that, by giving undue emphasis to the surface fleet, the admirals had jeopardised the valid case for a specialised British naval contribution to NATO, a contribution which no other member except the United States could make.

Owen has continued to argue for a force of twenty-three SSNs (six more than planned), a figure which in a more recent book Captain Moore has commended as just sufficient to allow the Navy (at the expense of some surface units) to become once again a major naval force, with submarines with 80 per cent of the capability and a third of the cost of the latest US generation of nuclear powered vessels (the SSN 21s).[19]

Costs, unfortunately, put even this number far beyond Britain's reach. Unless the Government intends to drop the Trident programme it is difficult to see how it could ever be realised. It is true that the Government ordered a nine fold acceleration in SSN construction in September 1984, but the order happened to overlap with the Trident programme. On average, it takes five and a quarter years from the date of order to the date a Trident submarine enters service. This means that the three SSNs ordered three years ago should be completed at about the same time that the first of the Trident submarines is due to start its preliminary trials before its commissioning in 1992.

The average time between the placing of an order for a nuclear powered submarine and the start of work at Vickers yard at Barrow on Furness is just under two years. This means that the shipyards will have three submarines in an early stage of construction in 1988, the year the company intends to start work on the second of the Trident hulls. In addition, Vickers will have a new class of diesel-powered submarine under construction, with others on order. Only if the Trident programme is cut back, or abandoned, will the Navy get the number of SSNs promised.

More alarming, the Government seems to have given serious considera-tion to reducing the present SSN fleet by as much as a third, so that less than seven will actually be at sea by 1996. In documents that were leaked from the MOD last September, this was not the only subject of discussion which seems to have exercised Ministers' minds. The papers appeared to show that the Government's interest in ASW operations, which had possibly been over-emphasised under Nott had now been substantially downgraded. The proposed cuts in ASW R&D as well as the torpedo programme,[20] may indicate that the next Conservative Government may even find as much difficulty in defining the Navy's role in the twenty-first century as it did in 1957. For some Conservatives it would appear that its blue water capability, along with its traditions, may fast be becoming relics of another era.

The Case against an Out of Area Capability

Mrs Thatcher came to power firmly committed to maintaining Britain's ability to prosecute military operations outside the European theatre. It has been a commitment to which she remains committed, although the force at the Service Chiefs' disposal may often appear less than convincing. Indeed, even the exercises in which Britain has taken part such as Operation Swift Sword in the Gulf last November appeared to many observers as another example of what Edmund Burke once termed Britain's abiding passion for *"amusing itself with the puppet show of power."*

Following the Oman expedition, the Chiefs of Staff produced a major report of the strategic deployment of British forces out of area. It concluded that the deployment of armed forces was better than it had been before the Conservatives came to power. Several developments showed it might become better still: the on going programme of improvements in the RAF's air to air refuelling capacity had further enhanced the services' ability to move a powerful force at short notice, including the whole of the 5th Airborne Brigade within thirty-six hours.

What the Chiefs of Staff wanted to see in the near future was the creation of a proper mobile military force along the lines of the rapid deployment force that had been established in 1959 and which had deterred an Iraqi attack on Kuwait a few years later. What they did not make clear was the cost of such a commitment. On paper, at least, it would have to be far larger than the 10,000 strong RDF that the Government established a few years ago for minor military operations in the Caribbean and East Africa, a force made up largely of Royal Marines with no heavy equipment, and only a minimum of light armour. What the Service Chiefs clearly do not envisage is drawing down on the Rhine Army as *The Times* proposed a few months earlier, in a leader which suggested that if the troops were brought back from Germany they could be based in the United Kingdom "*where they could add to the country's capacity to provide a mobile reserve for out of area operations.*"[10]

Unfortunately, *The Times*, did at least have logic on its side. Any significant contribution to a RDF of the kind the Service Chiefs propose would probably equal the cost of the Air Defence of the United Kingdom. A proper mobile force, believes Keith Hartley, would have to consist of a carrier and supporting escorts, possibly five in all with two squadrons of helicopters on board; at least 5000 troops, together with three strike squadrons, and a sizeable transport fleet.[11] At a time when the Government is already cutting back on several items, in a losing battle to trim defence spending, the prospect of a mobile force looks increasingly unrealistic.

At a time when more money will have to be found to enhance the Air Defence of the United Kingdom, without reducing the effectiveness of RAF (Germany), the Government is unlikely to find the money to buy the Adverse Weather Air Delivery System radar which would enable the thirty Hercules which have been "stretched" to take more troops to fly in close formation in poor visibility.

Under Defence Review pressure in 1974, the RAF gave up its Belfast heavy lift capability because it was surplus to NATO requirements. In the event of a crisis in the Far East, the Air Force, with its present fleet, could lift 500 troops a day over a ten day period, with no tanks, and only the minimum number of helicopters (Pumas in the case of Hercules; Chinooks in the case of Belfasts under civil hire). These days the normal method of transporting spares (urgent or otherwise) is by civil carrier. It is cheaper, faster and, on the whole, more reliable.

Operation Swift Sword showed that the Air Force would be able to lift twice the number of troops at twice the rate to the Gulf – a more likely theatre of operations – to be sure – but one which might require a larger force, more heavily armed. At present, given the more immediate priorities the Air Force faces, there is really no justification for expanding or refitting an airfleet that still has an estimated flying life in excess of fifteen years. All that can be justified is "stretching" half the Hercules fleet, a task which has now been completed, to what purpose is still not quite clear.

The Navy has even less of a case for retaining an out of area capability beyond that of maintaining "a balanced fleet", a concept Britain can probably no longer afford. As Sir John Nott remarked last year, the concept of global reach is a nostalgic wish for the days of empire by a Service which should have come to terms with the imperial retreat earlier than any other since it was Admiral Fisher himself who recalled the battleships to Scapa Flow. Nott remained firmly of the opinion that Britain could no longer afford to maintain two operational carriers (with one permanently in refit) since in terms of men, equipment and aircraft they would draw down on the resources in more urgent demand elsewhere.[12]

As his immediate successor Michael Heseltine put it more bluntly during a conference on the future of British naval power in the '90s:

> ... naval power is formidably expensive. Is power projection really cost effective? Is this the sort of thing a medium sized naval power should be doing; or perhaps, is it the only thing it should be doing?[13]

If the latter, then the effort would be on a scale that would daunt any Government, even the most nostalgic.

The Global 86 exercises, in which Royal Navy ships took part, led by the aircraft carrier *Illustrious*, showed just how overstretched the Navy would find itself in a global crisis. The highlight of the tour was meant to be the Rimpac exercise with the United States Pacific Fleet last June, in which *Illustrious* was to have taken part with two allied carriers. Unfortunately, a fire aboard the ship two months earlier had forced the Admiral in command to transfer his flag to a Type 22 frigate.

Such mishaps of course, are the normal hazards to be expected of modern ships in difficult conditions. It seems clear however, that the Navy's present deficiencies with regard to the projection of naval power overseas are now so manifest that only a major change in priorities could redress the balance.

In the event, it is most unlikely that a Conservative Government would wish to draw attention to Britain's diminishing role in NATO. As SA-CLANT has recently reiterated he is currently fifty per cent short of the destroyers, frigates and diesel powered submarines considered necessary to prevail in the next war at sea.[14] In the last ten years, the United Kingdom's contribution of the first two categories of ships has fallen by nearly a third; the number of British frigates within the NATO area in a permanent state of readiness by half.

It was statistics such as these which dissuaded the Government from building up to eight corvettes in 1985, officially described as "*enhanced offshore patrol vessels*" to complement the Navy's overstretched force of frigates. Sir Lindsey Bryson, the then Controller of the Navy responsible for warship construction, had made out a strong case for the ships two years earlier on the ground that they would enhance the out of area role. When the admirals studied the plans more closely, they realised that the ships could only be built if the orders for the Type 23 frigates were substantially reduced.

Presumably, the next Government would face the same dilemma. Indeed in the ninth defence review, if not the next, Britain's out of area capability, together with the Royal Marines, who provide the kernel of the much smaller RDF, may well be dropped by a Conservative Government whose gaze, by necessity perhaps, rather than choice, may no longer be fixed on distant stations of palm and pine, but the latest balance of payments figures.

Privatisation, Competition and the Quest for Efficiency

With such grim forecasts in mind, one thing seems certain: the Government will push ahead with its schemes to privatise as much of the defence industry as it can, and open the rest to more active competition.

In the past seven years the MOD has had the better of the argument. It has won just about every battle with the Treasury since 1979, and can boast a twenty-four per cent real increase in its budget as a result, an annual increase up to 1985 of one per cent more than the official three per cent NATO target which the Alliance adopted in 1977 to narrow the gap between its own spending and that of the Warsaw Pact.

This was all the more surprising given that high defence spending was totally at variance with monetarist thinking, which believes that it tends to "crowd out" other components of demand. Throughout this period, the Treasury argued that high defence spending was continuing to displace output, by crowding out resources such as skills in high technology and research and development which usually remain scarce, even in a recession. Over the long term, this supply side-effect appears to have become more pronounced than ever with every one per cent rise in defence associated with a corresponding one per cent fall in the share going into investment. And it is investment of course, which is thought to be the key determinant of the long term growth of labour productivity and national income.

Probably, if it hadn't been for Mrs Thatcher's determination to honour Britain's commitment to a three per cent real growth in spending, the Budget would have been cut within the first two years of her first administration. Once on the high spending road, it was difficult to stop, especially after it became an election winner. That was certainly the case in 1983. It may well be the case today.

It did not escape the Treasury's attention, however, in the last election year that the net cost of Britain's defence commitments overseas (£1.4 billion) exceeded its current account loss due to EEC Budget repayments. The current account of the balance of payments is still one of the main constraints on Britain's economic performance, as it had been throughout the post-war period, because of the nation's propensity to import more as demand expands. This constraint either emerges in the form of government deflation and low growth or a sliding exchange rate and higher inflation. If the defence costs to the current account in 1983 had miraculously disappeared, national output would have been £2.5 billion higher – an increase of 0.75 per cent on GDP.

Next time round, the Treasury is likely to expect the MOD to come up with much greater savings, simply to contain the defence budget at £19 billion, not reduce it (which may well happen) by £1 billion or more (with all that this would mean in a massive reduction in the equipment budget, or slippage in the introduction of new programmes).

What room is there for greater privatisation? Back in 1984, David Greenwood felt confident in arguing, very little. In defence, the concept, he suggested, was distinctly unattractive:

> "*Certainly in the serious business of deterring the Queen's enemies the personal insurance option is not available. And the notion of privatisation has no appeal at all.*"[15]

Echoing these sentiments, the Labour Party described the Government's plans as an "*unwarranted extension of privatisation into an area concerning national security.*"[16] Since then, however, much has been achieved. Warship refitting has been contracted out to private firms, an activity which was once the sole responsibility of the Royal Dockyards. The management of non-military stores for the Armed Forces has been contracted out at two depots. Industry has been given the job of servicing the RAF's few remaining Hunter aircraft, as well as providing engineering support at training stations, such as Shawbury, for its Gazelle and Wessex helicopters. The Government intends that it should also be given the job of repairing thirty per cent of all Army equipment. All air charter contracts are now open to tender, while the movement of Army equipment by air may be opened up next year.

In principle there is probably no limit to the process. It remains to be seen whether the MOD will judge these pilot schemes a success or not. But then the Ministry, already short of project management skills, may be hard pressed to monitor them itself.

If the Conservatives are returned they will probably find more opportunity for cost cutting in more open competition for government contracts or, where this is not possible, ensuring that the contracts involve incentives as well as penalties to promote more efficient production and early delivery. Michael Heseltine was particularly anxious to eliminate cost plus contracts where the contractor is paid his cost plus a margin of profit whatever happens to the project itself. In an effort to introduce greater competition into areas where there are only monopoly suppliers (such as British Aerospace) the Government has considered making it obligatory for prime contractors to contract out more than seventy per cent of their work to competitive tender, a practice which has long been pursued in the United States.

There are other areas which the Government has already looked at, areas in which new initiatives can probably be expected if it is returned in the forthcoming election. It would like to put the representatives of small companies on the boards of Government research establishments, and to break once and for all the stranglehold of the relatively few large scale manufacturers such as Vickers and GEC. Whether it will be successful will depend on its willingness to force through measures which are still far from acceptable even to companies who accept the principle of open competition and recognise they would be the first to gain if forced to improve their export performance.

There is certainly a long way to go. According to a report published two years ago by the Comptroller and Auditor General, in 1983–4 thirty-six per cent by value of non-competitive contracts involving some incentive pricing had still not been fixed when half the work was done, seventeen per cent had not been fixed when the work was already three-quarters finished and seven per cent had not been fixed when the contract was completed.[17]

The problem with competition is that it is not the universal panacea its apologists often make out. When the sole British manufacturer of tanks, Vickers, rebuilt the Royal Ordnance factory at Leeds to equip a seventh regiment with Challenger tanks, the lack of domestic orders forced the company to close its own tank assembly plant in Newcastle. Competition may be admirable in principle but it can only really be effective in areas where demand can sustain more than one producer. If Britain's armed forces continue to contract over the course of the next ten years, this problem is likely to be thrown into even greater relief.

As Sir Frank Cooper has argued, tackling defence procurement may well require more radical measures still, such as manufacturing more weapons systems under license (which would maintain jobs, while reducing excessive expenditure on R&D), more effective multinational collaboration and a reduction in R&D costs which the Conservatives last tried to tackle seriously in the 1956 Defence White Paper.[18] If all these remedies were to be adopted, the United Kingdom would ultimately produce a narrower range of equipment, but far more effectively than it does at present.

Unfortunately, none of these remedies are likely to appeal to the next Conservative Government or figure very prominently in its planning. Not for the first time, a British Government will probably defer taking a decision, knowing quite well that it has only bought itself a reprieve. At one time there may have been something grimly heroic about refusing to face reality. Today the exercise seems merely intellectually impoverishing as well as politically self-defeating, if depressingly in tune with the ages.

Labour Government and the 1988 Review

At times in the last few years Margaret Thatcher and Neil Kinnock have both resembled figures in a morality play, one representing the old orthodoxies in the defence debate, the other expressing enthusiasm for a brighter (even safer) future. Both are dealing in certainties – the certainties of their own convictions. Labour believes in itself, its instincts, not least the credibility of its policy of conventional deterrence. Where the facts may be insufficient to warrant its choices or where they may suggest different policies altogether, all the resources of the political art will be needed to sell its ideas to the Services, and to enable the Party to hold them itself.

Yet the deeper convictions of the Labour leadership are more muddled and ambiguous than may first appear. To the rank and file, Labour's mission may seem clear cut and inescapable, but it may look less than self-evident to those who will have the responsibility for carrying its policies out. This ambiguity will doubtless be reflected in the compromises the Party will have to make once in office; probably no more so than its first Defence Review. Like that of 1975 it will certainly be controversial, politically quite new. It is doubtful, however, whether it will be a grand conception, or even an entirely honest one. As always the electorate is likely to be duped.

A Coastal Navy?

Labour has always insisted that the money saved on Trident will be spent, not on more schools or hospitals, but more ships and submarines. Whether through perversity, or some of the old patriotic instincts reasserting themselves, Shadow Defence spokesmen have been peddlng this line ever since John Silkin first stumbled upon the plight of the Navy.

For all its ludicrousness, this is a very persuasive argument, simple, easily accessible, decidedly the fillip the Navy needs. If the Party finds itself more than ready to take refuge in its certainties who can blame it?

The certainties, unfortunately, are all too false, if not a little foolish. Scrapping Trident will not buy twenty-one additional Hunter killer submarines (SSNs) as Silkin suggested five years ago,[19] or Keith Speed's ninety new Type 23 frigates.[20] A frigate costs £100 million; an SSN £100 million more. If you divide these into the total cost of the Trident programme, then the manpower costs alone would be more expensive. Trident involves only four submarines, with 800 men to support each ship. Once it is in place, it will take an increasingly smaller percentage of the Defence Budget, as Polaris did in the 1970s. The cost of frigates and submarines are escalating all the time, which is why the Navy can afford so few.

If it comes to power, Labour will find soon enough that the practical alternative use of Trident money, if it is thought of as a potential source of funds for the augmentation of other programmes," *is not in financing the re-instatement of things which have already been expunged from future plans ... [but] in insuring against yet more excisions from programmes in being.*"[21] In other words, simply keeping fifty frigates and destroyers at sea would be far more costly than the party imagines.

The first thing Labour may do is to cancel the Type 23 programme. It may be committed to a large surface Navy, but not necessarily an ocean going one. It may start by looking again at the offshore patrol vessels which Sir Lindsay Bryson called for some years ago, only to be told by the navy that there was "*no place*" for them in the existing budget.[22]

Phasing out the frigate fleet would be one way of resolving the old and hitherto still unresolved debate about whether it is cheaper to design a multi-role ship or a specialised one. Multi-role vessels tend to cut back on weapons, speed and damage control. Limiting roles may be cheap but a cheaper platform is not necessarily the best or the cheapest way of deploying weapons. Even were the problem of the weapon/platform ratio to be solved to the Navy's satisfaction, the admirals would still have to decide every time how many ships they would need for any particular mission.[23]

Specialisation – defining a role then designing a ship around it – happens to be much easier for in-shore vessels. Here the arguments as Ravel once said of musical notation may be *"complexe, mais pas compliqué"*. Take mine-sweeping. Hunt class MCMVs can hunt for mines and also destroy them. They do not need a vast array of defences to protect them against submarine or air attack; they could even rely, if necessary, on shore-based airpower.

Coastal defence has been neglected by successive Governments for so many years that Britain has fewer than seven Island class craft, plus two larger Castle class off-shore vessels which will be expected to work with seven minesweepers in wartime. This is hardly an impressive force for a country which has 270,000 square miles of sea to protect, including a coastline 7,700 miles long. Apparently, the present Government has found no other method of protecting shipping in coastal waters except by convoy-ing them from port to port, even though the Navy estimates that, at best, it will be able to keep only a minimum number of ports open in the face of a determined Soviet minelaying campaign, with the few naval vessels and auxiliaries it will have at its disposal.

At least some effort has been made in recent years to redress the balance in the Navy's favour. In June 1984, the Government ordered fourteen patrol craft for the protection of major commercial ports in wartime. In addition, a series of twelve fleet mine sweepers are in the process of construction, the first of their kind to be commissioned since 1945.

Even so, more could be done. Once in office, Labour may decide to build many more multi-role Hunt MCMs (mine counter measure forces), River class minesweepers and a new class of Single Role Minehunters (SRMHs). The Russians now have new deep water mines like Cluster Bay and Cluster Gulf intended particularly for use against Allied submarines and deep draught tankers. It is doubtful whether contingency plans to rely on commercial trawlers and even cabin cruisers for minesweeping operations are any longer feasible, however successfully they were used during the last war.

The demands of the other services will inevitably mean that the next Labour Government's ship building plans may have to be highly selective. In the spare and haunted landscape that faces it in coastal waters, it may well decide to give priority to a new generation of in-shore and off-shore vessels, at the expense of programmes like the Type 23. Certainly it is inconceivable that a Labour administration would ever authorise another generation of large ocean going vessels.

Such a decision must also be set against the background of growing concern about the dwindling number of diesel powered submarines available to operate in the shallow waters of the North Sea. Under the last Labour Government Britain's diesel powered submarine fleet was cut by half in favour of building more SSNs. The same priorities were originally accepted by the present Government, which planned to phase out the Oberon class without replacing it with another model. For all the interest shown in submarines, the smaller versions have had a distinctly checkered history. They are now beginning once again to come into their own.

Oberon will now be replaced by the Upholder class, the first of which will be commissioned next year. Of the Oberon submarines themselves, a total of nine will be modernised to keep them operational into the early 1990s. Committed to abandoning the construction of any further nuclear powered submarines, Labour may be tempted to take these measures a step further. Instead of building many more Type 2400 at £120 million a time, it may opt to buy the German Type 211 (at 3,500 tons) or build a similar version itself. The latest German design has a fuel cell system, with a performance of seven knots over twenty-four days, a great improvement on present designs.[24]

When taken together, these developments show a clear trend towards a coastal fleet. In the last few years, the British seem to have discovered something about the world around them and a great deal more about themselves. The very scope of the threat that Britain now faces in its own waters, rather than in the north in the Norwegian sea, or further still in the Eastern Atlantic, may explain the apparent slowness of the Navy itself in making the mental adjustments required to incorporate the North Sea into its field of vision. It is as if, at some point in the late 1970s, the mental shutters came down; as if the admirals preferred to retreat into the half-light of the traditional world of large surface ships and global deployments.

Under Labour, the global deployments will certainly come to an end, perhaps abruptly. The Navy's response is unlikely to be muted. The desire not only to rediscover but redress the balance between the coastal and blue water Navy may be a strong and necessary one. But Labour will not make amends by overstating the case.

Amphibious Forces Scrapped?

If there is such a thing in military circles as a sacred cow quite beyond criticism, it must surely be the Armed Forces' amphibious capability. Yet even here the Services are not free from the economic constraints which have dominated British defence policy for several generations. In discussing the need to replace the Royal Navy's two assault ships, the Commons Defence Committee expressed the fear that the decision, when finally taken, would probably depend "*far more on whether it will be financially inopportune than on whether the military case for the capability has been made out.*"[25] If the Labour Party is intent on scrapping the Navy's carriers, it may also be tempted to scrap its two assault ships, and six logistical landing craft as well. Even the present Government has deferred taking a final decision on whether to replace the assault ships (at £800 million) or abandon them in favour of flying the marines to their most important theatre of operations: Northern Norway.

Of all Britain's non-nuclear commitments, the defence of Norway may be the most important to the country itself but will it be seen as important enough to squander so much money on amphibious forces when there are more urgent priorities closer to home? Anxious not to forfeit Norwegian goodwill, the commitment will probably remain, but in a form the Norwegians are unlikely to find particularly reassuring. Given that the latter have finally consented to allowing the Marines to pre-position equipment in the country, a case could be made out for flying the troops in.

Superficially, after all, the airborne option may seem quite attractive. It would be faster to move troops by air, than by sea, although it would also be more provocative and therefore difficult to square with the Labour Party's present understanding of deterrence. As Liddell-Hart once wrote "*the use of an airborne force or any landbased force is a more irrevocable step, since its commitment is more definite and its withdrawal more difficult.*"

Added to that there are technical difficulties which weighed heavily on Michael Heseltine's mind when he came to look at the future of amphibious operations. Airborne forces are narrowly limited in vehicles, heavy weapons and the ammunition they can carry. If they have to wait for these requirements to arrive by sea, they will lose their main advantage: speed of intervention. In Norway even prepositioned equipment is unlikely to be positioned in the right area at the right time. There is only one main road linking the north with the south, which could be rapidly interdicted by 400 close support aircraft, not to mention the 100 attack helicopters the Soviet Union would have available for military operations in the region. In other words, air reinforcement would need to be early, comprehensive and specific to a particular sector, a policy which the Norwegians themselves, having long practised a policy of non-provocative defence, might well find unacceptable.

Such considerations, while not overriding, may lead to a compromise. Instead of building two new amphibious ships, the next Labour Government might choose a makeshift option instead, arming a couple of container ships at a third of the cost, crewed by twenty-five not 500 men. In principle, each would require only a minimum armament of Phalanx guns for use against sea skimming missiles; and high velocity missile systems against low flying aircraft.

Since the Marines would need at least eight helicopters to take off simultaneously, carrying 240 soldiers, the containers would have to be adapted accordingly. Given the present range of heavylift helicopters, the ships which might carry them could proabably remain over the horizon. The idea of converting merchant shipping in this way is actually very attractive. The trouble is that we will have very little merchant shipping left by the early 1990s if the attrition of the Merchant Marine continues at its present rate.

The Restructuring of the Rhine Army

Even if Britain managed to carry European opinion, non-provocative defence could not be introduced overnight. Its introduction may take ten years not five according to the Bishop of Salisbury's Commission on The Church and the Bomb (or even as many as twenty according to one of the commission's members).[26] A Labour Government would have to move with caution, but not that cautiously. Within the lifetime of a single Government, certain hard decisions about the continental commitment will have to be made.

The Party is committed to maintaining the Rhine Army at its present strength. If it has doubts about its manpower levels, they have been held in check, partly one suspects because most of the arguments for restructuring the force are based on the understanding that the increased deep strike capability of the Tornado squadrons, which RAF (Germany) has only recently acquired, would now enable all but two armoured divisions to be stationed in the United Kingdom.[27] Since the Tornados would not be allowed a deep strike role, such arguments would probably have little appeal.

On the other hand, if Britain is to develop a non-provocative posture, there is no need to continue the armoured personnel carrier programme, or the further modernisation of the army's tanks. If the six artillery regiments will certainly receive their Precision Guided Missiles, their SP 70s in place of the largely obsolete 105 millimetre Abbot guns, it is not clear whether every armoured regiment will get the Challengers it has been promised.

Tanks will have their role reduced to dug-in artillery, or movable fixed defences. As artillery they would be absurdly expensive for so limited a role; but withdrawing them from service prematurely would be more expensive still. What the next Government will have to decide is the future of the tank force itself; what will replace the Challenger; will there be any need for a replacement at all?

In the past the British have opted to replace the whole fleet at one go, rather than engage in half fleet replacements, like the Germans (who of course have far more tanks). The policy has been cost effective, but not necessarily wise. Indeed, by the time the new tanks are in production, they have already begun to look rather old.

The Rhine Army only got Challenger so early because of the cancellation of the order by Iran. In normal circumstances, the Army could never have afforded to place orders for so many, or expect to receive them so soon. As a result, it has been able to retain its ageing Chieftains in armoured reconnaissance units and provide its main armoured regiments with a tank which is at least the equivalent of the Soviet T-80.

Even a Conservative Government would have to look very carefully at the next generation, the MBT-2000, which by the time the last of them comes off the production line in 1995, may be inferior in fire power, mobility, and even armour protection to the next generation of Soviet tanks. Since the Army could have opted five years ago for a better design in partnership with its allies or on its own, using new gas turbines to get higher output per engine, a Labour Defence Secretary might be able to throw much of the onus for a decision not to go ahead with the MBT-2000 on the Army itself.

But even if the next generation tank is cancelled, the dilemmas a Labour Government would probably face would be far from exhausted. If the Army is to receive more defensive weapons, especially more artillery or precision guided missiles, it will need more men to fire them, something the Labour Party has probably not taken into account. Cuts in manpower under the last Labour Government (16,000 men) led to a thirteen per cent increase in the ratio of weapons to troops, and a shortage of men which was felt most acutely by the Royal Artillery. In 1977 the Army's Rapier missile units, which required seven men per system, had to make do with five (a quite inadequate number in war). In the Royal Armoured Corps, the number of tanks increased by more than fifty per cent while crew levels continued to fall.

If the new weapons are to shape and transform Britain's military role in Europe, by removing the necessity for battlefield nuclear weapons, they will not necessarily make the continental commitment any cheaper. An unexpected change in Britain's economic fortunes could well change a Government's view of the Rhine Army in terms which might force it once again to explore the possibility of a new round of German subsidies to offset the foreign exchange losses of maintaining 56,000 men. (66,000 if we include RAF) (G). When the last offsetting agreement expired, these losses amounted to no less than £661 million (1979–80). The current losses are just under £1 billion. Despite the strength of the Deutschmark, which has added to the cost, Bonn continue to maintain that co-operation on the joint production of aircraft and other weapons systems has made such offsetting arrangements quite unnecessary.

But the argument may soon be about to change in Britain's favour. There *is* a case that can be made out for a greater German contribution to British costs, one that is non-partisan as well as intellectually coherent. All the present German arguments address only the immediate situation, the state of NATO today. What of the situation in a Europe where Britain had agreed to maintain its conventional commitment to its allies by voluntarily surrendering its own nuclear deterrent?

It is a question to which an answer has actually been provided by the

American academic Todd Sandler, whose study of the trade-off between public and private goods in the field of defence economics suggests that offsetting agreements of the kind Germany used to provide should be seen as a tax transfer between two allies, not as a subsidy at all.

Sandler divides military goods into two categories: deterrent and protective. Deterrent weapons carry with them the threat of retaliation; protective weapons offer the promise of defence. In a purely non-nuclear alliance, protective weapons would not only become the major military commodity traded between the Allies; the existence of such an alliance would substantially change the nature of the "trans-Atlantic bargain".

Deterrence, after all, is indivisible. Arguably, Polaris, although a purely British deterrent, nominally committed to NATO, deters the Soviet Union from attacking not only Britain, but also Germany as long as there are British troops on German soil. Protection, however, is very much divisible because the probability of survival once an attack occurs is not equal in all territories. In addition, protective weapons tend to be spread very thinly. The forward deployment of the Rhine Army and the Tornado squadrons committed to the 2nd Allied Tactical Air Force may accord with the concept outlined in the 1981 Defence Review that "*the forward defence of Germany constitutes the forward defence of Britain itself*" but it is not a view shared by all. The continental commitment, particularly in an age of conventional deterrence, is likely to throw into relief the lamentable state of Britain's own air defence, and its present inability to patrol its own coastline even more markedly in the past.

As Gavin Kennedy notes, the specific deployment of protective weapons makes the thinning costs more visible, not less. Those allies that press for a specific commitment from allies that might gain more immediate protection by keeping their forces at home should in principle be charged user fees. It is an argument that leads him to the inescapable conclusion that "*Germany could be charged for the BAOR or (assuming political clearance) provide that ground force itself*".[28] It is not an argument which is likely to appeal to Bonn, but it may be one which a Labour Government might wish to employ either to reduce the capital cost of the Rhine Army, or even to argue for a completely new division of responsibilities which would require Britain to redefine its role in the Alliance for the first time since 1954.

Such academic arguments apart, if Labour did cancel Trident it would be able to claim (however speciously) that it had done so to secure a safer world, a more secure defence, and to maintain Britain's conventional commitments to its allies. In return for such a "sacrifice", it may have the right to claim something in return. The Alliance, if it is to survive, may have to rely less on tacit understandings that joint defence projects will continue to offset the Rhine Army's cost to the nation, and more on explicit claims, formulated rights and open argument. This is not a matter of academic analysis, but of recognising political reality. If conventional deterrence were to become widely accepted, NATO would no longer be the same alliance, or able to function in the same way.

Opting Out of the European Fighter Programme

Whichever Party wins power, it will immediately face the daunting prospect of participating in the European Fighter Programme; daunting because each aircraft will cost more than £200 million, and each pilot costs at least £10 million to train, even though, in the event of war, the life expectancy of both the plane and its crew would probably be no higher than six days. John Nott was totally against the EFA on the grounds that it was both unnecessary and too expensive. He only agreed to provide funds for a "demonstrator" aircraft. It was Michael Heseltine who rushed off and signed up for a commitment costing more than Trident, without even bothering to examine what the RAF's requirements actually were.

Britain will have to reflect on its participation in the programme much more than it did with Tornado fifteen years ago. Cheaper aircraft will be available, and more will be developed between now and the end of the century. It may still be too late for British Aerospace to build the P110/Advanced Combat Aircraft on which it has worked for ten years or longer. Had it been in power, Labour might have gone for the US AV8B jump jet as a replacement for the RAF Harrier, just as Denis Healey preferred to buy the F111 in 1965 rather than the much more expensive TSR 2. When the time comes in 1988–9 to place orders for the EFA, a Labour Government might opt for the US F 18, perhaps built under licence in Britain.

Governments cannot afford to shrink from painful choices in the name of European co-operation, although it is understandable that they should wish to postpone them as long as possible. The next Government, however, will not have long to make a decision unless it plans to put its hopes in new technology, which is already beginning to allow unmanned aircraft to do, if not everything a manned plane can accomplish, most of what is expected of traditional aircraft, at a fraction of the cost.

Whatever option it chooses, a Labour Defence Secretary is most unlikely to opt for the European Fighter. Indeed, he may find himself in the fortunate position of having some aircraft surplus to requirements if the aircraft carriers go the way of the Ark Royal in 1979. When the last of the old carriers was decommissioned, its Phantom fighters and Buccaneer bombers were handed over to the RAF. At present, a total of sixty Sea Harriers are either in service or on order, and their mid-life update has already been agreed for 1987–91. It may be tempting if the three carriers are sold, or de-commissioned to transfer them to RAF (Germany).

Once updated, they will be able to carry advanced medium range air-to-air missiles, and a new radar which will give them a *"beyond visual range"* interception capability. There would be nothing intrinsically implausible in placing the Sea Harriers in Germany since they were originally a modified transonic ground-attack aircraft designed to provide close support to land forces, not to engage in aerial combat at sea.

The reallocation of the Sea Harriers would not resolve the problem of buying a new generation tactical aircraft for the 1990s but it would increase the RAF's front line strength in the United Kingdom while enabling it to discharge its responsibilities on the continent at no additional cost. Above all, it would provide a Government with time to study the options available for buying off the shelf from the United States, or providing the Army with a more comprehensive missile defence rather than close air support by manned aircraft. The decision to contract out of the EFA therefore should not necessarily be dismissed as yet another choice that had been postponed when times were hard. The hard times might mean, on the contrary, that the aim of thinking a decision through, and making sure it is the right one, is more important than ever.

The Imperial Recessional: Part 2

In the mid-1960s, a Labour Government took the decision to withdraw the troops from East of Suez. They returned but have periodical exercises in the hope of convincing a disbelieving world that Britain is still a world power. For twenty years, the British have maintained a substantial out-of-area capability which proved itself so effectively (though only just) in 1982. It was the Falklands war, and the absurd cost of maintaining a garrison to parade a commitment we can probably no longer honour, that seems to have convinced the Labour Party that the capability itself should be dismantled once and for all.

As the Party's defence paper argued last year, a Labour Government would concentrate exclusively on Britain's "*legitimate defence interests within the NATO area.*" It would abandon the rest, by negotiating a treaty with Argentina, cancelling any future "flag showing exercises" in the Pacific and the Indian Ocean, reducing the Army's airborne brigade so that it was capable only of deploying in Western Europe, and ensuring that exercises such as Swift Sword in Oman were never again mounted. In this the party was only being consistent with its 1982 discussion paper on foreign policy which devoted a whole chapter to the American "threat" in Central America, not a line to the threat to Europe's oil supplies in the Gulf, apart from a promise that the next Labour Government would withdraw support altogether from Britain's closest ally in the region: the Sultan of Oman.

Not content with abandoning the Gulf and the Falklands to whatever fate may await them, Belize too could expect little assistance from the former metropolitan power. During a debate in the Commons in October 1984, Denzil Davies refused to commit his party to the former colony's defence, explaining that the defence treaty between the two countries was "*an extraordinary agreement*" by one state to another in an area so far removed from the United Kingdom and its vital interests.[29]

The Labour Party has doubtless been alarmed by the extent to which British forces have been used out of area under the present Government, having clearly believed from its own faltering of purpose over Cyprus in 1974 that such operations had entered political folklore. In the last few years, the British have not only fought a war in the South Atlantic, they have sent peace keeping forces to the Sinai, and to Lebanon in a vain attempt to bolster the authority of the Lebanese Government, from enemies internal and external alike, patrolled the Gulf during the interminable Iran-Iraq war, and helped the United States Navy clear the Red Sea of mines which may have been placed there by the ever unpredictable Colonel Quadaffi. Indeed, there has been so much activity, on however limited a scale, that some political commentators have openly speculated whether the retreat from east of Suez may not have been a terminal event, but a passing phase, one of history's many false trails.

There was even a time not so long ago that the Labour Party itself became carried away at the thought of an East of Suez role. As John Silkin once argued '*We need a surface fleet to fulfil our obligations to the Third World nations who look to Britain rather than the United States or the Soviet Union for protection.*'[30]

That Silkin's aspirations have met with little response is hardly surprising when one recalls that Britain's "re-entry" East of Suez has not been on its own account but as an ally of the Americans. Unlike 1973, when the Royal Navy began the clearance of the Suez Canal on its own, the ships went to the Red Sea in 1984 with the United States Navy. Unlike the British exercises in the Gulf with the Dutch and French in 1972, the two British patrol vessels in the Gulf in 1984 had to co-ordinate their activities with the American carrier group led by the *USS Midway*. Like the Navy itself, the supporters of an out-of-area presence have tended to focus too exclusively on Britain's own contribution without giving any consideration to the context in which the contribution has been made.

The reason it has proved unacceptable to Labour is the American connection. Of necessity, the British role seems to have been restricted to areas where the United States can provide protection, or reinforcement or the promise of assistance if needed – in the Sinai, as part of a diplomatic effort to underwrite the Camp David process; in the Levant as part of a five power peacekeeping force, in Beirut protected by the sixteen inch guns of the *USS New Jersey*; in the Gulf and the Red Sea, as part of a joint naval operation from which both Italy and France chose to disassociate themselves, in order to maintain a semblance of independent action.

There are two principal reasons why an East of Suez role would be scrapped by Labour. The first is that it would be seen as a necessary contribution to Britain's emancipation from the past. Indeed, were it not for its role as a "client state" of the United States, a role quite different from that in 1958, when the two countries last intervened in their respective spheres of influence, Lebanon and Jordan, our interest might be with the mirrored reflection of an historical phenomenon rather than with the phenomenon itself. Sending peacekeeping forces to the Lebanon for no particular purpose may seem a high price to pay for retaining some remnant of political influence in a region where the British "moment" has long since passed. As Peter Foot wrote of the Gulf patrol:

> The fact is that British forces are once again patrolling the area because the United States expects them to do so, the British Government does not expect the Americans to get it right without the benefit of British counsel, and because the United Kingdom does not wish to appear less of a world power than France.[31]

Labour's second objection would be that Britain's dependence on Washington has changed very little since the Suez crisis, when it was expressed in the form of a United States veto and a run on Sterling which brought the operation to an ignominious end. To that extent it already sees Britain as a surrogate of the United States, not an ally. This is not just an exercise in typological description, an example of "butterfly collecting" as Edward Leach called it in a different context. Labelling is at least useful if it helps us to understand the extent to which the British have deceived themselves if they imagine that they could pursue their interests independently of the United States. To reverse Chou-en-lai's remark about détente, Britain and America may be lying in the same bed, while dreaming different dreams but, in this case, the British have no choice of sleeping partner.

On this particular occasion, there seems much to be said for the Labour view. Its premise may be erroneous, but the conclusions it has drawn from it seem sensible enough. Britain's East of Suez role, does indeed appear to be nothing more than an historical rally in a continuing retreat, another alibi for not confronting the real problems of European defence co-operation. It is an eloquent commentary on the role that historical myths still play in political life; it is not, alas, an accurate index of the country's true military standing.

Post 1993 Years

Britain's commitment to the defence of the West has been the result less of clear cut strategic planning than instinctive reactions on the part of a nation to the challenge it identified in 1949, indeed some years earlier, before the Soviet Army had reached Berlin. It has always been both a national interest and an international obligation, one that achieved a higher degree of political consensus than perhaps any other issue since the war. If that consensus has broken down, it is merely a symptom that the country has begun to redefine its national interests to take account of the public interest as well (the fact that spending on the citizen – in the form of housing, schools or hospitals has been cut drastically in the last few years to pay for an absolute increase in defence spending).

It is not a new phenomenon of course. In 1950 Attlee chose to abandon the last phase of the National Health Programme to pay for re-armament. Such sacrifices are unlikely to be made again. Britain's defence spending last year was once again higher in absolute terms than that of any other European ally. It was higher per head. It was higher as a proportion of national income, a vivid reminder of the country's apparent willingness to "pay for its decline".

Since the 1950s, defence spending has been financed primarily at the expense of future rather than current consumption. The largest cuts in private and public spending have been at the expense of capital investment (which fell by twenty-eight per cent between 1979–83, at the same time that defence spending rose by twenty-four per cent). It seems inevitable, which ever Party finds itself in power, that there will be a major cutback in defence spending as a percentage of GDP. At five point three per cent it is already far too high.

We have already seen that by the end of another Tory administration the figure will probably have been reduced to four point nine per cent. Ironically, the Labour Party actually intends to maintain spending at its present level, although to work after 1991 towards reducing it by as much as a third, to bring the United Kingdom into line with its European partners.

In every general election since 1974, the Party has promised to cut back the level of military spending to three point five per cent of GDP (which at present prices would save £6 billion or so a year, enough to provide much higher investment in manufacturing industry, housing and the social services). For the moment that objective has been set aside by a leadership that believes it is in a strong position to demand that the Left accept a continuing high level of spending as the price for nuclear disarmament. After 1993, however, the leadership may have to make concessions itself.

I have not attempted to provide an outline of the ninth defence review as precisely as I have the eighth because predictions must start from a programme in being. We don't know whether the parties will follow the course I have suggested. But clearly any attempt to reduce defence spending over a period of three to four years to three point five per cent, following the structural disarmament which will already have taken place in the intervening years, will have a profound impact on defence policy. It will mean not a choice within roles, but between roles; it will require a major redefinition of Britain's defence interests; it will mean much harder choices than John Nott faced in 1981 when, as the Prime Minister stated, the debate was "*not about reductions but about how to spend the increase*",[32] An increase which clearly was not enough at the time to maintain the existing programme in being.

It seems that there are two radical measures which a Labour and Conservative Government could both adopt, if they believed that the international situation still merited a high level of defence spending. Neither may offer a solution to the problems that Britain confronts at present but they may perhaps shed some light on the questions the politicians will have to ask in the future.

Before we consider these, there is one reform which cries out for implementation, which ever party comes into power. Every year, millions and millions of pounds are wasted through the gross inefficiency of the existing Defence Procurement system. If there were greater stability amongst Service Operational Requirement staffs and if both the Services and the Procurement Executive would settle for a level of true adequacy rather than the endless search for perfection, abandoning the all-too-visual attempts to beat the existing boundaries of technological possibility, we could hope not only to put an end to the saga of failures about which I have already written but have reliable equipment at a better price.

The Rhine Army

Although Britain will not be obliged to maintain an army on the continent after 1994, the pressure for it to continue to do so is likely to be quite high. It is always possible that the Army will be called home, but retained as a reserve, ready to be airlifted to the front at forty eight hours notice. But the arguments which already make this an unattractive option, are unlikely to seem any the less forceful in 1993.

The net saving of basing the troops in Britain is unlikely to be great, except in terms of foreign exchange, a problem which may be resolved along the lines I have already suggested. The cost of barracks, and training areas would be quite substantial, not to mention the serious equipment problems which dual basing would undoubtedly raise. Either two complete sets of unit equipment would be needed, one in Britain for training, the other in Germany for operations, or else everything would have to be airlifted at the cost of maintaining an airborne capability out of all proportion to the size of the armed forces involved.

Whatever solution to the problem is finally adopted, there are some harsh realities to be faced before any sort of sensible decisions can be made. The first is that it is effectively impossible to train a mechanised corps like the present 1 (British) Corps in the United Kingdom – the necessary space simply does not exist unless valuable agricultural land were to be taken over to provide the huge training areas needed. The second is that no amount of airlift could ever move an entire corps to Germany from this country, even if the heavy equipment was stockpiled – the movement problem is prodigious. Third, the whole idea of stockpiling is an illusion. Not only would the cost be prohibitive but the difficulty of keeping the stocks fit for immediate use is enormous and the risk of failure high. The matter has been studied again and again and the conclusions reached have been identical in each case.

If the British Army of the Rhine is to be brought home, it would have to be completely re-roled as a light, highly mobile force with a high complement of helicopters and of anti-tank weapons of all sorts. It could then fulfil a vital role in Germany as a hard hitting mobile Army Group reserve – something so badly needed in the light of current Warsaw Pact tactical philosophy, which seeks to engage the whole depth of any force opposing them simultaneously. Such a force could just be trained in the United Kingdom, given that we retain the use of the Canadian training area at Suffield. Furthermore, it would be ideal for the Home Defence task, should the need arise in the longer term.

It has been suggested that a British Government might seek to restructure the Rhine Army, avoiding the crippling costs of maintaining the present family infrastructure by rotating brigades every three months and expecting soldiers to spend six months out of every twelve away from their families. Quite apart from the movement costs and the stress caused by such repeated upheavals, the effect of such a policy on readiness would be disastrous. In any case, restructuring has been tried before and found wanting. The reshaping of BAOR into four smaller armoured divisions after the 1974 manpower cuts was not a success. Having eliminated the brigade level of command, the MOD had to return to the brigade formation in 1981. Paradoxically, the human problems of keeping an army in a state of high morale in peace demands more manpower on the ground than the same units need in war. Individual units may be able to cope but only at the cost of many hours of what is effectively unpaid, unacknowledged overtime and stress which may eventually be reflected in declining figures for enlistment.

This problem might be alleviated (if not necessarily solved) by broadening the base of the armed forces, either through greater use of reserves, or by re-introducing a limited form of National Service.

Already Britain pays an inordinately high price for much smaller armed forces than any other NATO member. Excluding only Canada, Denmark and Luxembourg it has a lower percentage of the population in the Armed Forces than any other country.

Although the Territorial Army is still smaller than in the 1960s, when its strength was well over 100,000 men, its importance has if anything increased. In the 1960s it operated on the idea that it would have weeks in which to bring itself up to a fighting pitch; now a substantial part of it could expect to be mobilised in forty-eight hours. Britain's order of battle on mobilisation would consist of at least one third part time soldiers. On exercises they have proved their value. In 1980 they "*showed up better than most Allied regulars*" according to Sir John Hackett.[33] By 1990 the TA strength will have reached 86,000. For the first time it will also have elements of the Army Air Corps equipped with Scout helicopters.

The Royal Auxiliary Air Force has also been given a much greater degree of responsibility than its old task of defending airfields. Since last April, its members have been able to fly aircraft themselves as pilots, navigators or engineers aboard VC 10 transports or Nimrod Mk 2 ASW aircraft. In the United States, members of the Air National Guard fly Mach 2 fighters as complicated as Lightnings or Phantoms which could be made equally available to reserve pilots in Britain.

Even if greater use is made of reserve formations, however, it seems almost inevitable that Britain will have to give serious consideration to reintroducing National Service if the Rhine commitment is to be retained in the future. If the Grigg Committee, which was set up in 1957 to examine the factors effecting recruitment was correct, in its opinion that conscription was difficult to sustain during a period of permanent employment, at a time of endemic unemployment National Service could surely be introduced without incurring the usual economic costs.

If national (not military) service were made compulsory, (if the citizen could opt for social work or military employment) then the Armed Services could be held at a higher level than the inter-war median which has still not been reached. If a balance were preserved between regular and conscript troops, substantial savings could be made on pay and pensions. That the United Kingdom is the only European NATO power with an All Volunteer Force is an anomaly; that it is the highest spender is more anomalous still.[34]

Lend Leasing

Another measure which could be taken, if equipment costs continue to soar, would be to forgo building frigates and aircraft ourselves, leasing them instead from the United States. As recently as 1979, the Government gave serious consideration to filling the air gap at home by leasing three squadrons of F4 Phantoms from the United States Air Force in Germany (having dismissed the idea of paying McDonnell Douglas to re-open its F4 production line which it had closed earlier in the year). In the event, an additional Lightning squadron was formed by bringing the planes out of the reserve. In addition, further aircraft were found by fitting the Sidewinder AIM 9 missile to Hawk trainers.

The only other planes which the United Kingdom could have leased eight years ago would have been US F15s, or 14s. This option too would have been expensive. Neither plane had ever been serviced in Britain. The lack of technical expertise, plus the transfer of spare parts, together with the modification which would have been necessary to replace their Phoenix missiles, which the Air Force could not have afforded, with SkyFlash, would inevitably have made any leasing arrangement prohibitively expensive.

If the British felt able to press ahead with Tornado replacements instead and make do in the interim with aircraft of their own manufacture, a decision not to take part in the EFA programme could create a situation in a few years time where the leasing option might not only be attractive, but even necessary. As an editorial in Flight International noted at the time of the F15 discussions:

> "*British military aircraft procurement since the 1950s has tended to be one long story of promising projects cancelled for reasons thought good at the time. Only a handful of designs such as the Harrier show what might have been. Given this sort of track record, only a brave man would totally discount the possibility that [the F15s] might one day sport RAF colours*".[35]

Only a brave man would predict that the country might not end as it began in 1940 when the Atlantic world was spawned, reconciled to a policy of lend-lease, with the Americans supplying the "tools to do the job", whether in the form of F 18s or even M1 tanks, which would be of little use outside the European theatre. History may not follow any particular pattern, but it is often cyclical. When approached with an open mind, it invariably reveals how the process has a habit of repeating itself at the most unexpected moments.

Conclusion

All things being equal, it seems highly likely that the world of the mid-1990s may not seem entirely remote from that of today. Even after the expiry of the Brussels Pact there may well be a Rhine Army, progress in the MBFR talks notwithstanding. If the situation in Eastern Europe continues to remain volatile, if the American commitment is substantially cut back, Britain's contribution to the common defence may well turn on the continental commitment much more than it does at present.

If the scene that I have drawn suggests that Britain will still have a Rhine Army in the late 1990s, a substantial fleet (though only a coastal one), an air force more impressive than the 1930s, I would not wish to suggest that this is a tale whose end is implicit from the very beginning. There is no way of knowing. Yet is seems equally false to suggest that all futures are equally possible, and that by mere force of will or political choice, a government can alter the drift of history in accordance with its own particular philosophy. Most societies are conformist by nature. Political choice seldom prevails in matters requiring radical alterations of deeply conditioned attitudes and social beliefs.

It has been my sole object in this chapter to attempt some analysis of the manner in which the two parties may attempt to proceed, to suggest certain interim conclusions about the costs of their respective policies and to indicate some lines of research which could be profitably pursued.

In the end it is important to recognise that all exercises in futurology tend to be self-defeating since we can only extrapolate from the present and only come to terms with the future when it is already our past. The tools of the political scientist do not allow him more than a glimpse of the future. Like Cassandra it is the fate of academic observers to be disbelieved. Peering into the future as T S Eliot concluded is invariably frustrating:

"For last year's words belong to last year's language. And next year's words await another voice."

APPENDIX TO CHAPTER 6

Two Ways Forward

The outlines of policy and decision making reflected in this Appendix suggest a possible sequence of events based upon the courses open to the two main parties discussed in this chapter.

A CONSERVATIVE ADMINISTRATION (1988–93)

Strategic Nuclear Forces	4 Polaris boats to be phased out by 1995 Trident cancelled; Tomahawk instead
Home Base	Continued modernisation of air defence (primarily missile defence)
Eastern Atlantic	47 frigates/destroyers, down to 43 by 1993 Leander programme stretched; Type 23 cut back SSNs down to 15 Carriers phased out
Europe	EFA programme cancelled in favour of BAe P110 MBT-2000 orders cut Rhine Army maintained at 55,000 RAF (G) pegged at present levels
Non NATO roles	Falklands garrison phased out 1991 Fleet exercises in Indian Ocean/Pacific reduced Marines scrapped, together with RDF

A LABOUR ADMINISTRATION (1988–93)

Strategic Nuclear Forces	Polaris decommissioned; Trident cancelled US bases remain under a bilateral 5 Year Treaty (re-newable)
Home Base	Air defence enhanced: Tornados brought back from Germany Coastal Fleet expanded (including diesel powered submarines)

	If no offsetting agreement with FRG, one division BAOR re-located to UK
Eastern Atlantic	Type 23 programme abandoned; new corvettes instead SSNs pegged at present numbers Carriers sold or taken out of service
Europe	Rhine Army levels remain same until 1991 RAF (G) given Sea Harriers EFA abandoned; no new tactical aircraft MBT-2000 programme cancelled Assault ships decommissioned, together with Royal Marines
Non NATO roles	Falklands garrison withdrawn; plus forces from Belize Gurkhas pensioned off, but Hong Kong garrison maintained No Fleet exercises "out of area" RDF scrapped

7

Towards a Conclusion: The Death of the Past

"The great exponent of perseverance, William the Silent, Prince of Orange, never wavered in the face of every hardship and disaster . . . The immortal sentence in which he epitomised his life cannot be repeated too often. It is not necessary to hope in order to act, or to succeed in order to persevere."
(Dean Acheson *Present at the Creation* (New York: 1969) pp 727–8)

WHAT I have tried to accomplish in this book is to suggest what the shape of British defence policy might look like in the mid-1990s, whichever party finds itself in power. I have tried, somewhat impressionistically perhaps, to suggest the context within which the next Government may have to work, and the constraints under which it may have to labour. I have attempted to outline the preferences of each party, and the direction they may chart out of necessity or choice. What the parties promise in their manifestos can, at best, provide us with only a rough idea of the course they will probably follow.

The defence choices I have outlined might change quite radically if external events, or economic crises, or more subtle shifts of power within the parties themselves were to provide greater room for manoeuvre than I have suggested. Ultimately, politicians, like the philosophers admired by William James, exist to make distant things seem near and near things distant. Illusionists, of course, go out of business if no one trusts their illusions, but British politicians have been practising the art for longer than most.

There has long been a school of thought that the United Kingdom has declined over the last forty years because it has lived beyond its means, because it has pursued a role within NATO, and in the early days outside it, which was clearly beyond its resources. The historians of decline have spoken of the "*Collapse of British Power*", the "*Long Recessional*", the "*Descent from Power*" (to mention the title of only three books), terms which have conjured up the ghosts of opportunities lost, and choices avoided, which have led to the dilemma we now face.[1] The problem is that there are now so many analyses and interpretations from which historians have failed to reach any agreement that we may already have reached the stage forecast by Mark Twain that "*we shall soon know nothing at all*" because scholars "*have thrown so much darkness on the subject.*"

172

The past, as such, offers no prescriptions. One of the cardinal mistakes of political scientists is to search for them on the basis of the limited understanding they have of past events. That is why I have no prescriptions of my own to offer, why I prefer to remain a detached, if not entirely dispassionate, observer. I have not attempted to suggest alternative defence policies because I do not believe that my own private world, any more than that of many politicians, will survive the pressure of events which even now cannot be predicted.

That, of course, has not discouraged academics of more radical sensibilities from appealing to the past for support. Indeed far from being "*a foreign country*" it has become familiar territory which many are happier to revisit than to travel in hope towards a future as yet unknown. Ironically, history has actually fixed them in some of their most self-confident postures.

Of the many contemporary analysts, perhaps Malcolm Chalmers has been the most persuasive in arguing that the dilemmas I have sketched were not inevitable, that they might have been avoided, but for a whole generation of civil servants and politicians who preferred to parade a series of commitments which could not be honoured, and to issue a series of promissory notes which could not be cashed. In defence of this thesis, he cites Sir Richard Clarke who was involved in overseas financial policy in the late 1940s when Attlee decided to cling on to Britain's Great Power status, whatever the cost:

> *"Thirty years later, when one sees the relative success of Germany, Japan and France which were forced to make great social and economic changes, one cannot be absolutely sure that our right long term course was to display remarkable ingenuity and to retain the status quo.''*[2]

Over the years Chalmers has pursued this line of argument with remarkable consistency, charting the various turning points when choices might have been made: Thornycroft's call for reduced defence spending, Owen's criticism of the 1975 review for the cuts that were *not* made, rather than those that were, a decision which convinced many on the Left that:

> *"By 1978, if not before, the Labour Party was politically incapable of generating its own concepts of defence policy. Instead, it operated a pale imitation of what the Conservatives claimed they would do when back in office.*[3]

Temperamentally, the British have always found it difficult to arrive at clean, clear-cut decisions without accompanying them with qualifying formulas which have either subverted, or weakened the line of action they have intended to pursue. As one of the few studies of British military thinking concludes *"military thought, being exclusively pragmatic, has failed to devise any long range proposals for a grand design that might have helped the political radicals to re-assess British military policy.''*[4]

The other point of view has been put equally cogently by David Greenwood who has argued that in real terms Britain has not declined; that manpower cuts have been dictated by defence inflation and structural disarmament which the country has not been alone in fighting; that the British Armed Forces are more professional, even better equipped today than at any time in their history; that one has only to compare the success of 1982 with the military shambles of Suez (1956) to see what improvements have actually been made. On the whole his message is upbeat, if resigned. What has happened over the past thirty-five years is merely a "restructuring" of Britain's forces, not an absolute decline.

If one accepts Greenwood's line, then the next defence review will see further adjustments in the defence budget, and continued cuts in force levels, a process which could continue indefinitely. If one accepts Chalmer's argument, then something can and should be done while time permits, a view which, from a very different premise, has been taken up by Conservative MPs as well in the person of the neo-Gaullists. It is not particularly remarkable that change rather than continuity should hold out such appeal for many members of the party who have found in Mrs Thatcher a leader whose policies have certainly polarised opinion to an extent no other politician has succeeded in doing in the past thirty-five years.

It is, perhaps, only fair at this stage to come clean and state my own belief that they will be no more successful than the radical Left; that continuity, not change, will be the central theme of the next ten years in terms of muddling through as best we can, that this may even be the desirable option. Like the politicians of the 1950's the Governments of the future will not be oblivious to our changing circumstances, but they may find the decline easier to come to terms with if it can be prolonged.

Like Paul Kennedy, I consider that the management of Britain's decline has been an exemplary lesson in how to retain political influence as long as possible by *not* facing up to political realities, by evading choices, by electing Macmillans not Thornycrofts, Heaths not Macleods, Gaitskells not Bevans, soft rather than hardnosed politicians who have been singularly adept in not taking hard, if necessary, decisions. As Kennedy remarks (in a passage he believes has relevance for the leaders of the Soviet Union and the United States now that their own societies have entered a period of protracted decline):

> *Keeping a declining British . . . omnibus going along the road for such a long time is a fair art, and not one that should be entrusted to persons who are liable to shoot the passengers, who don't know how to service and oil the machine, and who have the nasty habit of trying to crash into oncoming vehicles.*[5]

In the forerunner to this book I accepted Kennedy's analysis while equally accepting that the psychology of the declining power was not to choose but to wait upon events. Writing in 1986, it seemed to me that it might have been preferable, if choices between roles had been made twenty years earlier, if

British Governments had discharged their responsibility to take hard decisions and stand by them. But I also concluded that the radical choices that were now on the table, whether unilateralist or neo-Gaullist in inspiration, might well reflect the psychology of the declining power even more than the choices that had not been made.[6]

I now believe that, even in the 1950's, the best the out and out reformers could have done was to have introduced piecemeal administrative reforms, making choices within roles rather choosing between them, an endeavour which, while worthy in itself, would have altered attitudes in the Services and Whitehall very little, and in the nation at large even less. A number of more radical measures, if well administered and applied in happier circumstances, might have yielded better results, but the nearest we came to this was the disastrous Sandys review (1957) which did irreparable harm to the Air Force for nearly a generation. If ever implemented, radical measures might have wrought greater damage on the Services than any they were designed to repair. There is very little evidence that British society was ready to receive them.

If we are ready for them today then root and branch reforms will not save the situation, or restore British influence. Setting an example by unilaterally disarming, or "revising" the trans-Atlantic bargain will merely bring our decline to a head much faster than carrying on as we have. The Left would welcome such an outcome seeing in it our "emancipation" from the deadweight of a past, perhaps more imagined than real. Others might see it, as a relatively painless adjustment to a "little England" posture, painful only if carried out too abruptly, inevitable perhaps in the context of a much wider development: the marginalisation of Western Europe.

Given that a Europe left behind in the Pacific age will still, in per capita terms, be wealthier than any other part of the world but North America, still able to live off its historical capital well into the twenty-first century, the Swiss or Swedish model may well not be a bad one, but it will be a radically different world from the world we have known for 300 years. If our current high defence spending may be the price we have to pay for reading history, what of a country that cannot make it at all?

It is because no-one can be sure what will happen before the century draws to its close that it still seems worth paying a price of admission, to have some say in the events that will shape our future, aware that I am that such an argument carries an unfortunate resonance of the old plea for a seat at the top table. If this study does convey a message it is a simple one. If riding the tide seems to have been a not entirely unprofitable strategy, and certainly not one that can be explained by indifference to Britain's changing circumstances, perhaps we should carry on as we have for as long as we can.

It was General Hackett who once observed that *"an Army's best qualities are shown when it is losing."*[7] Possibly, the same may be true of countries in an advanced, even terminal state of decline. To fight even in the face of certain defeat requires more than courage. If, by chance, our decline can be reversed, it will be all the more important that we are allowed by our Governments to fight on.

Notes

Introduction

1. See review of Jonathan Schell's *The Fate of the Earth* in the Sunday Times, 20 June 1982.
2. G. J. Reiner, *History: its purpose and method* (Boston: Beacon Press 1950) p. 255.

Chapter 1: The Acceptance World (1945-87): The Present Impasse

1. Harold Macmillan, *The Blast of War (1939-45)* (London: Macmillan 1969).
2. Sidney Pollard, *The Wasting of the British Economy: British Economic Policy 1945 to the present* (London: Croom Helm 1983) p. 37.
3. Cited Avi Schlaim, (ed) *British Foreign Secretaries Since 1945* (London 1977) p. 27.
4. See Denis Healey's *Canberra Speech 1965*. Cited Christopher Mayhew *Britain's Role Tomorrow* (London; Hutchinson 1967) p. 19.
5. Martin Edmonds, *"Planning Britain's Defence 1945-85'* in Martin Edmonds (ed) *The Defence Equation: British military systems-policy, planning and performance since 1945* (London: Brasseys 1986) p. 14.
6. *The Way Forward* (HMSO: Cmnd 8288) 1981.
7. *The Guardian*, 24 November 1982.
8. George Urban, *A Case for Coherence: assumptions and aims of British foreign policy*. Occasional Paper No. 4. Institute for European and Strategic Studies (London 1984) p. 13.
9. Cited Eric Grove, *"The Royal Navy: the Fleet comes home"* in Edmonds *The Defence Equation* op. cit., p. 81.
10. *The Guardian*, 22 December 1982.
11. *The Guardian*, 1 July 1986.
12. ibid.
13. *Statement on the Defence Estimates 1986* (HMSO: May 1986).
14. Lord Hill-Norton, *Return to a National Strategy* in Joyn Baylis (ed) *Alternative Approaches to British Defence Policy* (London: Macmillan 1983) p. 118.
15. *Naval Forces*, 5:6, 1984, p. 44.
16. *The Daily Telegraph*, 3 May 1985.
17. *The Way Forward*, op. cit.
18. Sir Henry Leach, *"Britain's Maritime Forces: the Future"* RUSI Journal, September 1982, p. 12.
19. Cited Malcolm Chalmers, *Can the Royal Navy Retain "about 50 frigates"*? Defence Information Group Briefing Paper, July 1986, p. 4.
20. Lord Carver, *"Getting Defence Priorities Right"* in Baylis Alternative Approaches to Defence Policy, op. cit., pp. 183-4.
21. *The Daily Telegraph*, 24 August 1983.
22. *Janes Fighting Ships 1983-4* (London: Janes 1983).
23. *The Times*, 7 January 1977.
24. See Geoffrey Till, *"Strategy in the Far North"* in Clive Archer/David Scrivener, *Northern Waters: security and resource issues* (London: Croom Helm 1986) p. 74.
25. *"Lehman, Seeking Security"* International Defence Review 15:5 1982, p. 303.

26. *The Times*, 3 February 1987.
27. John Mearscheimer, *"A strategic Mis-step: the maritime strategy and deterrence in Europe"* International Security 11:2 Fall, 1986, p. 7.
28. ibid, p. 6.
29. David Hobbs in Archer/Scrivener Northern Waters, op. cit., p. 95.
30. *Defence Attache* No. 4 (1985) pp. 9–10.
31. Keith Speed Sea Change: the battle for the Falklands and the future of Britain's Navy (London: Ashgrove Press 1982) p. 182.
32. *The Daily Telegraph*, 20 January 1984.
33. *The Guardian*, 13 May 1985.
34. *The Sunday Telegraph*, 2 November 1986.
35. *The Times*, 17 August 1983.
36. Combat Reconnaissance Tracked Vehicles.
37. Edwin Bramall, "British land forces: the future" *RUSI Journal*, June 1982.
38. Michael Elliot-Bateman, *Defeat in the East* (Oxford University Press 1967) p. xii.
39. R. A. Mason, *"Towards the Next Anniversary: the RAF looks ahead"* Defence, March 1979.
40. Neville Brown, *The Future of Airpower* (London: Croom Helm 1986) p. 156.
41. Mason, *"Towards the Next Anniversary"*, op. cit., p. 164.
42. *Flight International*, 5 August 1978, p. 395.
43. *Allied Forces Germany* (House of Commons Select Committee on Defence 93) 1984.
44. Lord Carver, *A Policy for Peace* (London: Faber and Faber 1982) p. 29.
45. *The Times*, 6 February 1985.
46. ibid.
47. David Greenwood, *The Trident Programme*, ASIDES 22, Summer 1982, p. 41.
48. *The Independent*, 4 December 1986.
49. Paul Stares, *"The Future Credibility of the British Independent Deterrent"*, Defence Analysis, 1:2, 1985, p. 138.
50. Martin Ince, *The Politics of British Science* (Wheatsheaf 1987) pp. 88–9.
51. *The Times*, 22 April 1982.
52. R. P. Smith, *"Defence Costs"* in John Roper, (ed) *The Future of British Defence Policy* (Royal Institute of International Affairs: 1984) pp. 143–8. Smith writes about defence inflation: *"to use an evolutionary simile, it resembles Cope's rule of phyletic size: that body size tends to increase fairly steadily within evolutionary lineages until the family dies out. Weapons tend to show a similar trend. I am sure contemporary defence economists would have been making dire predictions from extrapolations of the length of the surissas, the thickness of fortress walls, and the weight of knightly armour. The predictions are inappropriate because the family gets displaced"* (pp. 147–8).
53. *The Sunday Times*, 11 September 1982.
54. Philip Geddes, *"Admiralty Scorns New Frigate"*, The New Statesman, 17 September 1982.
55. Malcolm Chalmers, *"Trident and Britain's Defence Programme"*, Defence Analysis, 1:3, 1984, p. 220.
56. Giovanni de Briganti, *Royal Air Force (Germany)*, Armed Forces International, December 1984, p. 56.
57. ibid.
58. *The Guardian*, 25 April 1983.
59. Keith Hartley, *"Defence Procurement and Industrial Policy"* in Roper *The Future of British Defence Policy*, op. cit., p. 180.

Chapter 2: Farewell to Arms? The Political Context of Decision Making (1988–95)

1. K. J. Coutts, W. Godley, R. Rowthorn, T. S. Ward, *The British Economy: recent history and medium-term prospects* (Cambridge: Faculty of Economics 1986) p. 18.
2. *Medium Term Projections on Alternative Policy Assumptions*, National Industrial Economic Review No. 118, November 1986.
3. David Greenwood, *"Managing the Defence Programme and the Budget"*, Three Banks Review, June 1984, p. 61.

4. Sidney Pollard, *"The Wasting of the British Economy"*, op. cit., p. 4.
5. Philip Sabin, *The Third World War Scare: a critical analysis* PhD Kings College, London, August 1984.
6. David Capitanchik, *"The Changing Attitude to Defence in Britain"* Centrepiece 2 (Aberdeen: Centre for Defence Studies Summer 1984) p. 9.
7. David Widgery in Louis Mackay/David Fernbank, (eds) *Nuclear Free Defence: Symposium 1985* (London: Heretic Books 1985) p. 45.
8. See my *"Politics and the Peace Movement in Britain"* in Phil Williams, (ed) *The Nuclear Debate: issues and politics* (Royal Institute of International Affairs 1984) p. 63.
9. A. J. P. Taylor (et al) (eds) *Churchill: Four Faces and the Man* (London: Allen Lane 1969) p. 59.
10. Cited Paul Kennedy, *"Why Did the British Empire Last so Long?"* in Strategy and Diplomacy 1870–1945 (London: George Allen and Unwin 1983)
11. Taylor, *Churchill: Four Faces and the Man,* op. cit., p. 151.

Chapter 3: Journey Without Maps: The International Context (1988–95)

1. Octavio Pax *One Earth, Four or Five Worlds: reflections on contemporary history* (Carcener 1985) Commenting on America's past role *"outside history"* Paz writes *"I nonetheless believe that the fascination that decadence holds for Americans lies not so much in its philosophical and aesthetic charms as in the fact that it is the gateway to history."* (p. 22).
2. Zbigniew Brzezinski *"The Atlantic Crisis: a Personal View"* Atlantic Quarterly 1:1 (1983) p. 97.
3. *The Guardian,* 6 September 1981.
4. *The Listener,* 30 October 1986.
5. Pierre Lellouche, *"Europe and Her Defence"*, Foreign Affairs, 59:4, Spring 1981, p. 814.
6. Pierre Hassner, *"Intra-Alliance Diversities: NATO in an age of hot peace"* in Kenneth Myers, (ed) *NATO: the next thirty years* (Boulder, Colorado: Westview Press 1980) p. 384.
7. *The Washington Post,* 19 February 1983.
8. Anthony Cordesman, *The Gulf and the Search for Strategic Stability* (Boulder, Colorado: Westview Press 1984) p. 258.
9. For a discussion of the MI tank see my *US Military Power in the 1980s* (Macmillan 1983) pp. 85–7.
10. Department of Defence Appropriations for 1985. *Hearings Before the Subcommittee of the Committee of Appropriations, House of Representatives, 98th Congress, 2nd Session (Washington D.C.: 1984)* p. 694.
11. D. E. King, "The Survival of Tanks in Battle" *RUSI Journal,* March 1978, pp. 26–31.
12. *Strengthening Conventional Deterrence: proposals for the 1980's Report of the European Security Study* (London: Macmillan 1983) pp. 32–3.
13. Cited, *"E.T. – Where to Now?"* International Defence Review, March 1984, p. 718.
14. Dan Smith, *The Defence of the Realm in the 1980's* (London; Croom Helm 1980) p. 78.
15. *International Herald Tribune,* 6 March 1984. This is not to suggest that American commanders do not believe that they would not be able to sustain defence on ground of their own choosing. The Commander of the US 8th Infantry Division believed in 1981 that his forces would have a 6:1 advantage in the Fulda Gap (the most difficult of all the places through which to launch an attack. In some places it is only 30 kilometres wide.) *Defence Week* 2:38, 17 August 1981, pp. 4–7.
16. For both comments see Michael Harrison, *"Our Atlantic Quagmire"* The Washington Quarterly 5:3, Summer 1982.
17. Debate with Eugene Rostow *East-West Papers No. 2* (East-West Foundation 1986).
18. Eugene MacCarthy, *"Look No Allies"*, Foreign Policy 30 Spring 1980.
19. Maxwell Taylor, *Precarious Security* (New York: Norton 1976).
20. Melvin Kraus, *"It's Time to Change the Atlantic Alliance"* The Wall St. Journal, 3 March 1983.

21. In 1983 Sen Levin described half the NATO members of having *"failed the basic test of political and military will"*, Defence Week, 5 July 1983.
22. *The Times*, 17 November 1984.
23. E. P. Thompson, *"The Image and Reality of War"*, New Society, 23 August 1984.
24. Cited Geoffrey Barraclough, *An Introduction to Contemporary History* (Penguin 1964) p. 76.
25. In February 1944, Roosevelt sent a Memorandum to the State Department: *"I do not want the US to have the post-war burden of reconstituting (Europe). This is not our national task at a distance of 3500 miles or more. It is definitely a British task in which the British are far more vitally interested than we are."* Cited in David Reynolds *"The US and European Security; a reappraisal of the "isolationist" tradition"*. RUSI Journal, June 1983, p. 19.
26. For the "Atlanticism" of the 1950's and 1960's see Kees van der Pijl *"The Making of an Atlantic Ruling Class"* (London: Verso 1984).
27. Cited Richard van Alstynse, *"The American Empire: its historical pattern and evolution"*, Historical Association (1960) p. 25.
28. Lawrence Eagleberger *"The Transatlantic Relationship: a long term perspective"*, NATO Review, 32:2, April 1984.
29. *The Washington Post*, 22 May 1985.
30. Zdenek Mlynar, *Night Frost in Prague* (London: 1980) p. 92.
31. *The Wall Street Journal*, 16 February 1982.
32. Jonathan Dean *"MBFR – Past and Future"* in Derek Paul, (ed) *Defending Europe: Proceedings of the Conference on European Security Requirements and the MBFR talks*, 6–7 May 1985 (London: Taylor Francis 1985) pp. 88–90.
33. J. G. Keliher *"The Negotiation on Mutual and Balanced Force Reductions"* in The Search for Arms Control in Central Europe (New York: 1980) pp 89–90.
34. At the Guadeloupe summit, the United States formally asked Helmudt Schmidt to request the modernisation of Europe's theatre nuclear forces, wishing to avoid the outcry that had arisen from its own initiative in deploying them for the first time in 1957.
35. *The Times*, 4 February 1987.
36. *The Times*, 25 October 1986.
37. *The Sunday Times*, 26 Octoer 1986.
38. John Garnet *"Limited Conventional War in the Nuclear Age"* in Michael Howard, (ed) *Restraints on War: Studies in the Limitation of Armed Conflict* (Oxford University Press: 1979) pp. 84–5.
39. Thomas Callaghan, *"The Structural Disarmament of NATO"* NATO Review, June 1984, p. 21.
40. Hugh Green, *"Prospects for European Arms Co-operation"* in John C. Garnett, (ed) *The Defence of Western Europe* (London: Macmillan 1974) p. 99.
41. Cited Stephen Kirby, *"The IEPG: the Failure of Low Profile, High Politics"* Journal of Common Market Studies, 18:2, December 1979, p. 178.
42. K. Seitz *"SDI: The Technological Challenge to Europe"*, The World Today, August/September 1985, pp. 154–7.
43. N. Trotter, *"The Protectionist Wedge"*, Air Force, December 1983, p. 53.
44. *The Guardian*, 19 November 1985.
45. *International Herald Tribune*, 15 October 1985.
46. ibid.
47. Cited Christopher Coker, *"The Western European Union and European Security"*, in Robert Jackson, (ed) *Community or Discord: crisis and response in the Atlantic Community* (New York: 1985) pp. 155–77.
48. *The Times*, 4 October 1984.
49. See *Application of the Brussels Treaty. Reply to the 28th Annual Report of the Council* (Assembly of the WEU 29th Session) Doc 948, 18 May 1983, p. 12.
50. *The Sunday Times*, 28 October 1984.
51. Bernard Burrows, *The Security of Western Europe* (London: 1972) p. 43.
52. *The Financial Times*, 2 April 1985.
53. *The Times*, 23 April 1985.

54. *The Financial Times*, 24 April 1985.
55. *International Herald Tribune*, 3 October 1984.
56. *The Times*, 3 December 1985.
57. Dominique Moisi *"The Limits of Consensus"*. Atlantic Quarterly, 1:2, Summer 1982, p. 33.
58. Cited in George Thomson, *"The Politics of Anglo-French Nuclear Weapons"*. The Round Table April 1972, p. 158.
59. Pierre Gallois, *"The Raison d'Être of French Defence Policy"*. International Affairs, October 1963, p. 501.
60. *The Times*, 13 December 1985.
61. Eliot Goodman, *The Fate of the Atlantic Community* (New York: Praeger 1975), p. 69.

Chapter 4: Between the Acts: Some Current Trends

1. Klaus Knorr *"The Strained Alliance"* in Knorr, (ed) *NATO and American Security* (New Jersey: Princeton University Press 1959) p. 3.
2. *The Financial Times*, 11 October 1986.
3. *The Times*, 10 October 1983.
4. *Interview with Egon Bahr* (FBIS II April 1984).
5. Schmidt's speech before the SPD Party conference at Cologne, 19 November 1983 in *Politik No. 18, November 1983 p. 5*.
6. *The Independent*, 13 November 1986.
7. *The Sunday Times*, 23 February 1986.
8. *The Guardian* 4 April 1983.
9. *The Spectator*, 15 November 1986.
10. Henry Kissinger *"The Years of Upheaval"* (Boston: Little and Brown 1982), p. 282.
11. Noam Chomsky *"Turning the Tide: US Intervention in Central America and the Struggle for Peace"* (Pluto 1986) p. 128.
12. *The Times*, 3 October 1986.
13. ibid.
14. Ben Lowe *"Peace through Non-alignment: the case against British membership of NATO"* (Verso 1986) p. 76.
15. *The Times*, 7 January 1987.
16. Anthony Crossland, *"The Future of Socialism"* (London: Jonathan Cape 1956) p. 106.
17. Westland represented everything that has gone wrong with British defence technology in recent years. The company was consistently unable to provide a product at the right price. The Lynx helicopter was good but its rotar head alone cost as much as the entire US Huey helicopter.
18. *The Spectator*, 15 February 1986.
19. *The Guardian* 12 February 1986.
20. Kim Holmes, *"The Greens, the Social Democrats and the Defence Consensus in West Germany"*, Atlantic Quarterly, 2:4, Winter 1984, p. 37.
21. Henry Kissinger, *"Britain and the United States: reflections on a partnership"*, International Affairs, 58:4, Autumn 1983, p. 587.
22. *The Observer*, 19 October 1986.
23. *The Guardian*, 30 May 1986.
24. The emigration of Jews fell from 51,000 in 1979 to 1,000 in 1985. Some 380,000 "refuseniks" still remain.
25. Sabin, *"The Third World War Scare"*, op. cit., p. 93.
26. E. P. Thompson, *"Protest and Survive"* (London: Penguin 1980) p. 4.
27. *The Economist*, 27 February 1982.
28. Peter Lager, *Transatlantic Discord and NATO's Crisis of Cohesion* (IFPA: 1986) p. 30.
29. Walter F. Hahn *"West German Ostpolitik: the grand design of Egon Bahr"*, Orbis Winter, 1973, pp. 859–80.
30. *Politik*, op. cit., p. 29.
31. Interview with BPA, 21 October 1983 (Nachrichtenabt Ref. 2/R3).
32. *The Guardian*, 15 October 1986.
33. ibid. See also Nikolaj Petersen *"The Scanlux Experiment Towards a Transnational*

Social Democratic Security Perspective", Co-operation and Conflict, 21:2, March 1985, pp. 1–22.
34. David Gress *"Peace and Survival: West Germany, the Peace Movement and European Security"* (Stanford: Hoover Institute 1985), p. 109.
35. Manfred Ritamin, *"Strategic Defence and West Germany's Social Democrats"*, Strategic Review, 14:2, Spring 1986, p. 303.
36. Martin Emch *"Is the West Over-estimating the Warsaw Pact's Strength?"* International Defence Review February 1985, p. 819.
37. William Kaufman, *"Non-nuclear Deterrence"* in John Steinbruner/Leon Sigal, (eds) *Alliance Security: NATO and the First Use Question* (Washington D.C.: Brookings 1983) p. 58.
38. Matthew Evangelista *"Threats Misperceived"* International Security, 7:3, Winter 1982, p. 36.
39. See for example Andrew Cockburn, *"The Threat: Inside the Soviet Military Machine"* (New York: Random House 1985).
40. Cited Heinz Pagelz *"Perfect Symmetry"* (London: Michael Joseph 1985) p. 36.
41. Louis MacKay/David Fernbach *"Non-nuclear Defence"*, op. cit., p. 115.
42. Nils Orvik, *"The Decline of Neutrality"* (London: Frank Cass 1971)
43. Michael Oakshott *"On Human Conduct"* (1973) p. 45, Cited G. M. Dillon, *"Dependence and Deterrence: success and civility in the Anglo-American special relationship 1962–82"* (London: Gower 1983).
44. Nils Orvik, (ed) *"Semi-alignments and Western Security"* (London: Croom Helm 1986) p. 189.

Chapter 5: Inadmissable Evidence: Party Preferences

1. *The Times*, 7 October 1986.
2. "horizon stretching" was one of Michael Heseltine's stock phrases.
3. I am grateful to Philip Windsor for this analogy.
4. Peter Southwood, *The UK Defence Industry Peace Research Report No. 8 September 1985* (Bradford School of Peace Studies).
5. *The Times*, 16 September 1981.
6. *Omega Report on Defence Policy* (London: Adam Smith Institute 1983) pp. 17–18.
7. Michael Chichester, *"Britain and NATO: The case for revision"*, The World Today November 1982, p. 415.
8. Speed *"Sea Change"*, op. cit., p. 158.
9. John Wilkinson/Michael Chichester, *"The Uncertain Ally: British Defence Policy 1960–90"* (Gower 1982) p. 229.
10. *The Times*, 23 April 1982.
11. Harold Macmillan, *"Tides of Fortune"* (Macmillan 1969) p. 483.
12. *The Daily Telegraph*, 26 February 1982.
13. David Carlton, *"A Parting of the Ways:" Britain and NATO Occasional Paper No. 2* (1982) (Institute for European and Strategic Studies) p. 9.
14. Peter Tatchell, *"Democratic Defence: a non-nuclear alternative"* (London: Heretic 1985).
15. *The Guardian*, 9 November 1986.
16. *"Who decides"? Study of British nuclear weapon making* (Oxford Research Group 1986).
17. ibid.
18. Ron Smith/Dan Smith *"The Economics of Militarism"* (London: Pluto 1983) p. 107.
19. *The Guardian*, 10 October 1986.
20. *"Nuclear Arms, Defence Spending and Jobs"* (Independent Labour Party Paper 1984).
21. The Politics of British Science, op. cit., p. 101.
22. *The Guardian*, 2 October 1986.
23. *The Times*, 6 October 1986.
24. *The Observer*, 5 October 1986.
25. J. E. Moore/R. Compton Hall, *"Submarine Warfare: Today and Tomorrow"* (London: Michael Joseph 1986) p. 271.

26. G. M. Seignious/J. P. Yates, *"Europe's Nuclear Superpowers"* Foreign Policy 55 (Summer 1984) p. 40.
27. *The Observer*, 19 October 1986.
28. *The Financial Times*, 11 October 1986.
29. *The Guardian*, 14 April 1986.
30. *The Financial Times*, 7 March 1985.
31. *The Guardian*, 9 December 1985.
32. *The Guardian*, 17 October 1986.
33. *The Financial Times*, 30 September 1986.
34. *The Guardian*, 7 October 1986.
35. David Steel, for example, believed that having once led the way in negotiating a Comprehensive Test Ban Treaty (1963), the United Kingdom could do so again. Had Mrs Thatcher opposed SDI from the outset, Britain might have tipped the balance against it (*The Daily Telegraph*, 16 October 1986).
36. *The Observer*, 5 October 1986.
37. Gordon Lee/Jim Meacham *"A Survey of the RAF – In and Out of the Clouds"* The Economist 17 December, 1977.
38. Brown, *"The Future of Air Power"* op. cit., p. 20.
39. Ibid, p. 24.
40. Tatchell *"Democratic Defence"*, op. cit., p. 188.
41. Denis Healey, *"Labour's Three Lines of Defence"*, Fabian Lecture 1986.
42. Richard Simpkin, *"Race to the Swift: Thoughts on Twenty First Century Warfare"* (London: Brasseys 1985) pp. 118–31.
43. *The Times*, 7 July 1982.
44. Tatchell *"Democratic Defence"*, op. cit., p. 189.
45. Steve Scofield, *"Employment Security: Alternatives to Trident"*, Peace Research Report No. 10 (August 1986) (University of Bradford).
46. *The Times*, 5 October 1986.
47. *The Financial Times*, 9 August 1982.
48. Gavin Kennedy, *"Defence Economics"* (Duckworth: 1983) pp. 181–2.
49. Pollard *"The Wasting of the British Economy"*, op. cit., p. 16.
50. Tatchell *"Democratic Defence"*, op. cit., p. 29.
51. *ADIU Report July-August 1986.*
52. Barbara Castle *"The Castle Diaries 1974–6"* (London: Weidenfeld and Nicolson 1980) p. 333.
53. *The Guardian*, 17 January 1987.
54. *The Guardian*, 16 March 1983.
55. *The Times*, 8 October 1986.
56. *The Guardian*, 17 January 1987.
57. *The Guardian*, 18 September 1984.
58. *The Times*, 20 September 1984.

Chapter 5: The Audit of War: Defence Budgeting (1988/95 Reviews)

1. *The Sunday Times*, 19 December 1982.
2. *Armed Forces*, April 1986.
3. *The Observer*, 19 August 1984. Since the first Polaris put to sea, Britain has caught up with the United States Navy in sonar design and will be providing Trident with its own sonar system.
4. *The Guardian*, 28 November 1985.
5. Chalmers *"Can the RN Retain "about 50" Frigates?"*, op. cit., pp. 4–6.
6. Janes Fighting Ships 1986–7 (Janes Publishing Co. 1986) p. 4.
7. *The Naval Review*, 70:2, April 1982.
8. Moore/Compton-Hall, *"Submarine Warfare"*, op. cit., p. 271.
9. *The Daily Telegraph*, 15 September 1986.
10. *The Times*, 13 May 1986.
11. Keith Hartley, *"Can the United Kingdom Afford a Rapid Deployment Force?"* RUSI Journal, March 1982, p. 20.

12. *The Times*, 6 November 1986.
13. *The Daily Telegraph*, 20 January 1984.
14. Hugh Beach, *"British Defence Policy in the South Atlantic"*, South Atlantic Occasional Papers No. 2, May 1986, p. 8.
15. Greenwood, *"Managing the Defence Programme"*, op. cit., p. 36.
16. *The Financial Times*, 20 March 1984.
17. *The Financial Times*, 24 July 1985.
18. Thus the 1956 Defence White Paper: *"The burden of defence cannot be allowed to rise to a level which would endanger our economic future. This burden does not consist only in the effect of high defence expenditure on the general level of taxation, important though that is. Defence production falls in the main upon the metal and metal using industries, which supply about half our exports and are of great importance in the re-equipment of British industry."*
19. *The Financial Times*, 4 May 1983.
20. Speed, *"Sea Change"*, op. cit., p. 65.
21. Greenwood, *"The Trident Programe"*, op. cit., p. 41.
22. *The Financial Times*, 9 September 1985.
23. R. Owen, *"Can the Cost of a High Technology Navy be Controlled and Still Fulfill its Roles?"* Naval Review, 71:4, October 1983.
24. Moore *"Submarine Warfare"*, op. cit., p. 287.
25. *House of Commons, Select Committee on Defence* (1985) p xiii.
26. *"The Church and the Bomb"* (London: Hodder and Stoughton 1982).
27. *Hill Norton "Return to a National Strategy"*, op. cit., p. 132.
28. Kennedy, *"Defence Economics", op. cit., p. 44.*
29. *Hansard*, 22 October 1984, p. 473.
30. Malcolm Chalmers, *"Paying for Defence: Military spending and Britain's decline"* (Pluto 1985) p. 156.
31. Peter Foot, *"The RN: Out of Area, Out of Mind?"* in Geoffrey Till *"The Future of British Seapower"* (Macmillan 1984) p. 132.
32. *The Times*, 20 May 1981.
33. *The Sunday Times*, 20 June 1982.
34. Ken Booth, *"Strategy and Conscription"* in Baylis, (ed) *"Alternative Defence Policies"*, op. cit., pp. 155–86. See also Chichester/Wilkinson *Uncertain ally* op. cit., p. 179.
35. *Flight International*, 9 September 1978.

Chapter 7: Towards a Conclusion: The Death of the Past

1. Correlli Barnett, *"The Collapse of British Power"* (Allan Sutton 1984); Fred Northedge, *"Descent from Power"* (Routledge and Kegan Paul 1973); Lawrence Martin, *"British Defence Policy: the long recessional"* Adelphi 61 (IISS: 1969).
2. Cited Chalmers, *Paying for Defence*, op. cit., p. 40.
3. Dan Smith, *"Defence of the Realm"*, op. cit., p. 122.
4. Julian Lieder *"Military Thought of a Medium Power: 1960's and afterwards"*, Research Report No. 8 (Swedish Institute of International Affairs 1983) p. 363.
5. Kennedy *"Strategy and Diplomacy"*, op. cit., p. 218.
6. Christopher Coker, *"A Nation in Retreat: Britain's defence commitment"* (Brasseys: 1986) p. 12.
7. Sir John Hackett, *The Profession of Arms* (1983) p. 162.

Index